The Diplomat's Dictionary

SECOND EDITION

D1041875

The Diplomat's Dictionary

Second Edition

Chas. W. Freeman, Jr.

UNITED STATES INSTITUTE OF PEACE PRESS
Washington, D.C.

The views expressed in this book are those of the author's alone. They do not necessarily reflect views of the United States Institute of Peace.

United States Institute of Peace
1200 17th Street NW, Suite 200
Washington, DC 20036-3011
www.usip.org

First edition 1994, published by the National Defense University Press.
Revised edition 1997, published by the United States Institute of Peace Press.
Second edition 2010, published by the United States Institute of Peace Press.

To request permission to photocopy or reprint materials for course use, contact the Copyright Clearance Center at www.copyright.com. For print, electronic media, and all other subsidiary rights, e-mail permissions@usip.org.

Printed in the United States of America.

The paper used in this publication meets the minimum requirements of American National Standards for Information Science—Permanence of Paper for Printed Library Materials, ANSI Z39.48-1984.

Library of Congress Cataloging-in-Publication Data
Freeman, Charles W.
 The diplomat's dictionary / Chas. W. Freeman, Jr.—2nd ed.
    p. cm.
 Includes bibliographical references and index.
 ISBN 978-1-60127-050-4 (pbk. : alk. paper)
 1. Diplomacy—Quotations, maxims, etc. 2. Diplomacy—Dictionaries. 3. Diplomatics—Quotations. I. Title.
JZ1163.F74 2010
327.203—dc22
                        2009041292

 Contents

Foreword

The books we keep close at hand are the ones from which we draw inspiration, and, if you are in my business of journalism, from which we occasionally borrow ideas and aphorisms. For a decade, *The Diplomat's Dictionary* has had that special place at my writing desk, so that I can turn to its pages when I am stuck for a concept or a definition, or am just in need of a jolt of acidulous wisdom from the mind of Chas Freeman.

This compilation mirrors Freeman's own eclectic and wide-ranging interests. He has gathered quotations over the millennia from Chinese mandarins, Arab kings, French philosophes, and even a few American journalists. The dictionary distills the compiler's barbed and ironic sense of humor. Who but Freeman could find in the writings of Konrad Adenauer this definition of appeasement: "An infallible method of conciliating a tiger is to allow oneself to be swallowed?" Who else would offer this definition of foolproof: "Nothing is foolproof to a sufficiently talented fool?"

The first requirement for a lexicographer is that he should not be afraid of words and ideas. And Freeman is that rare State Department officer who made a reputation not simply as a diplomat, but as a free-thinker and iconoclast. He joined the Foreign Service in 1965 after studies at Yale and Harvard Law School, and was assigned to the China desk. Such was his facility with languages that he served as President Nixon's interpreter during his 1972 visit to the People's Republic of China. Later he learned Arabic, and served as U.S. ambassador to Saudi Arabia during the first Gulf War.

The Diplomat's Dictionary can be read as a practitioner's guide. Freeman has gathered quotations from the statesmen he has studied over a lifetime of reading and from those with whom he has worked during his career. Here you will find Kissinger and Talleyrand, Sun Tzu and Mao Tse Tung, Demosthenes and Disraeli. Freeman is especially useful on the subject of negotiation—devoting nearly twenty pages to that subject in the original edition. And prospective emissaries abroad should consult the ten pages he devotes to ambassadors and their duties and foibles.

This new edition displays Freeman's customary erudition and also some dark new bits of humor that could have found their way into Ambrose Bierce's satirical work, *The Devil's Dictionary*. In this new edition, compiled in the shadow of Iraq and Afghanistan, Freeman wisely devotes space to war and related problems of strategy. He offers this rueful and apposite definition of disillusionment: "To be disillusioned, you must first allow yourself to develop illusions." And as a wry capstone for his endeavor he defines diplomats thusly in the new edition: "A diplomat is someone who, when he is run out of town, can make it look like he is leading a parade." Freeman, we can say, is the consummate diplomat.

The Diplomat's Dictionary can be read for pleasure, as well as practical advice, for these pages sparkle with intelligence and wit. I am certain of one thing: If this book comes into more general use among our diplomatic corps, and students learn their Freeman, then the State Department's briefings and statements will be much more worth our reading and listening.

—*David Ignatius*

David Ignatius is a syndicated columnist for The Washington Post *and the author of seven novels.*

 Preface

I dedicate *The Diplomat's Dictionary* to my friend, the late Custodian of the Two Holy Mosques, Fahd bin Abdulaziz Al-Saud.

Without King Fahd's entirely inadvertent assistance this book of diplomatic lore would never have been compiled. I put together most of the initial draft in the anterooms of his palaces in Riyadh and Jeddah. There, as the American ambassador to the Kingdom of Saudi Arabia from 1989 through 1992 (a busy three years that included a war to liberate Kuwait and defend Saudi Arabia from Iraq), I found myself spending many hours on many occasions, sipping the king's tea and waiting for him to receive me. His uniquely carefree approach to his schedule provided time I otherwise would not have had to read, meditate, and begin to record observations on the practice of diplomacy. I am grateful to him for this.

I began to compile these thoughts for use as footnotes in a book on the doctrine of statecraft and the practice of diplomacy that I eventually wrote called *Arts of Power: Statecraft and Diplomacy*. To my surprise, the compilation grew into a book in its own right.

Like its companion volume, *The Diplomat's Dictionary* was originally directed at practitioners with the purpose of stimulating thought about how best to solve practical problems of statecraft. Much to my pleasure, the book—doubling as a dictionary of quips and quotations—has become popular among students, teachers, journalists, and generalists as well. I hope this revision adds to its utility as both resource and reference.

I have added quite a few definitions and maxims to those in previous editions and made a correction or two. As before, unattributed entries are either commonplaces or personal observations of varying degrees of originality. If an individual source must be cited for these, feel free to attribute them to me.

—*Chas W. Freeman, Jr.*
Ambassador (United States Foreign Service, Retired)
December 2009, Washington

Abruptness: "Never do anything abrupt. It never pays."
—ALEXANDER KIRK, QUOTED BY GEORGE F. KENNAN

Absence: "The absent are always wrong."
—FRENCH PROVERB

Absence: If you're not at the table, you're on the menu.

Academics: Diplomats are charged with persuading enemies that they have no reason to attack; soldiers with deterring and fending off such attacks when they nonetheless occur. Academics and liberal philosophers take on the burden of explaining—after the fact— how the lapses of diplomats and soldiers came to justify the enemy's assault.

Accession: The procedure by which a state becomes a party to an agreement already in force between other states.

Accords: International agreements with a status below that of treaties.

Accreditation: The act of sending an envoy (normally an ambassador) with letters of authorization or credence (credentials) attesting to his status from the head of his state to the head of state of another government.

Ad referendum: A procedure in negotiations by which an agreement reached by a negotiator on a text or a point in dispute is made subject to the final, formal approval of his government, to which he has undertaken to forward the matter with a favorable recommendation.

Adjudication: The process by which a court settles cases and controversies by a decision to which the disputants are legally bound.

Adjustment: "Diplomacy is interested in achieving and making do with the adjustments that can be obtained by bargaining and compromise without resort to force or the disruption of international society. Adjustment is a valuable concept: related on the one hand to what is just, and on the other to the concept of balance, aiming at solutions which are not absolute but shifting, relying on persuasion, and like all diplomacy accommodating international society to the winds of change. These adjustments by persuasion are sometimes aptly called the brokerage of the system. Brokerage of this kind is more conducive to generally accepted norms of justice than the ever-present alternative of a resort to force."
—ADAM WATSON, 1983

Adjustment, ripe moments: "Conflict resolution is made possible by a 'ripe moment,' defined in terms of escalation that can best be understood in the context of policy alternatives."   —I. WILLIAM ZARTMAN, 1985

Adversaries: "An intimate knowledge of the psychological processes of your diplomatic adversary is invaluable, especially if he is more powerful than you."
—CHARLES W. THAYER, 1959

Adversaries, mutual dependence of: "If there is any possibility of avoiding a mutually damaging war, of conducting warfare in a way that minimizes damage, or of coercing an adversary by threatening war rather than waging it, the possibility of mutual accommodation is as important and dramatic as the element of conflict. Concepts like deterrence, limited war, and disarmament, as well as negotiation, are concerned with the common interest and mutual dependence that can exist between participants in a conflict."
—THOMAS C. SCHELLING, 1960

Adversaries, domestic difficulties of: An adversary's domestic difficulties are opportunities.

Advocacy, diplomatic: "The task of persuading another government to accept and perhaps actually help promote the policies which it is the ambassador's function to advocate still falls primarily on the ambassador himself and his senior diplomatic staff, even in these days of the communications revolution. The cordiality of his personal relations with key figures in the government (even, in countries where this is necessary, at the expense of cordial relations with opposition groups) and their confidence in him as a man of goodwill, make a great difference. An experienced ambassador will have learnt to cultivate such relations as best he can, so as to have a fund of confidence to draw on. Outside the government there are likely to be a large number of influential people, in the legislature, in political parties, in key economic or business positions, in the news media, perhaps in religious life, who influence decisions and public opinion. Ideally the ambassador must cultivate and influence all these people as well."   —ADAM WATSON, 1982

Advocacy, policy: "Most people do not mind being surpassed in good fortune, character, or temperament, but no one, especially not a sovereign, likes to be surpassed in intelligence. For this is the king of attributes, and any crime against it is lèse-majesté. Sovereigns want to be so in what is most important. Princes like to be helped, but not surpassed. When you counsel someone, you should appear to be reminding him of something he had forgotten, not of the light he was unable to see. It is the stars who teach us this subtlety. They are brilliant sons, but they never dare to outshine the sun."
—BALTASAR GRACIÁN

Advocacy, policy: "Ideas do not sell themselves. Authors of memoranda who are not willing to fight for them are more likely to find their words turn into ex post facto alibis than guides to action."   —HENRY A. KISSINGER, 1994

Agent-General: (Obs.) The chief representative to London of a self-governing dominion of the British Empire.

Agents, diplomatic: A general term denoting the persons who carry on the political relations of the states they represent with the government of the country where they are appointed to reside.

Agents, diplomatic: "It is perfectly idle to believe that we can get along without diplomatic representatives. We cannot rely on direct messages. We need the man in personal contact with other men in transacting business of government."
—CHARLES EVANS HUGHES

Agents, selection of diplomatic: "It is generally better to deal by the mediation of a third than by a man's self. In choice of instruments, it is better to choose men of a plainer sort, that are like to do that that is committed to them, and to report back again faithfully the success, than those that are cunning to contrive out of other men's business somewhat to grace themselves, and will help the matter in report for satisfaction's sake. Use also such persons as affect the business wherein they are employed; for that quickeneth much; and such as are fit for the matter; as bold men for expostulation, fair-spoken men for persuasion, crafty men for inquiry and observation, forward and absurd men for business that does not well bear out itself. Use also such as have been lucky, and prevailed before in things wherein you have employed them; for that breeds confidence, and they will strive to maintain their prescription."
—FRANCIS BACON

Agents, utility of diplomatic: "Why have a dog and bark yourself?"
—PROVERB

Aggression: "We cannot and will not condone aggression no matter who the attacker, no matter who the victim."
—JOHN FOSTER DULLES, 1956

Aggression: "There is no nation on earth so dangerous as a nation fully armed, and bankrupt at home."
—HENRY CABOT LODGE, 1916

Aggression: "Aggressors usually disguise their aggressions as self-defense."
—E.V. TARLE, 1955

Agréation: See *Agrément*.

Agreement in principle: "Don't ask me to agree in principle; that just means we haven't agreed yet."
—GEORGE C. MARSHALL

Agreements: "The only treaties that ought to count are those which would effect a settlement between ulterior motives."
—PAUL VALÉRY, 1931

Agreements, basis for durable: "There is no durable treaty which is not founded on reciprocal advantage, and indeed a treaty which does not satisfy this condition is no treaty at all, and is apt to contain the seeds of its own dissolution. Thus the great secret of negotiation is to bring out prominently the common advantage to both parties of any proposal, and so to link these advantages that they may appear equally balanced to both parties."   —FRANÇOIS DE CALLIÈRES, 1716

Agreements, duration of: "Treaties are like roses and young girls. They last while they last."   —CHARLES DE GAULLE, 1963

Agreements, duration of: "Treaties are observed as long as they are in harmony with interests."   —NAPOLEON

Agreements, enforcement of: "Covenants without swords are just words."
                                                                                    —ATTRIBUTED TO THOMAS HOBBES

Agreements, types of: There are several types of agreements frequently concluded between states. The most simple simply extend or renew preexisting agreements. Others terminate an abnormal situation by settling disputes, establishing cease-fires or more permanent forms of peace, or establishing diplomatic relations as the culmination of a process of rapprochement. Still others benefit one side at the expense of the other by changing territorial boundaries, financial obligations, or the share of political or economic influence in third areas. Finally, there are agreements that institute new frameworks for international relations, such as programs of economic cooperation and tariff reductions, which benefit all parties nearly equally.

Agreements, unbalanced, unwise: An agreement based on one-sided advantage does not promote amicable relationships but rather sows the seeds of future dissension and conflict. Inclusion of an unfair, unreasonable, or unbalanced provision in an agreement is a hollow victory. It only leads to trouble later. It follows that, when the other side has mistakenly accepted a proposal that the negotiator who put it forward comes upon reflection to consider as unjust, he should correct it rather than leave it unchanged. To allow the other side to make concessions that will inevitably foster discontent, ill will, and disputatious behavior threatens to vitiate both the agreement and the reputations of those who negotiated it.

Agrément: Approval by the head of state of the receiving state for the appointment of a named individual as the ambassador by another state, sought in confidence by the head of state of the sending state prior to the formal nomination or appointment of such an ambassador.

Ahimsa: The doctrine (in Jainism, Buddhism, and Hinduism) of the avoidance of harm, adopted by Mohandas Gandhi both as a principle and as a means of nonviolent struggle against foreign oppression. See also *Nonviolence*.

Aid, foreign: Annual subsidies and subventions are a time-honored means of assuring the loyalty of client states. Time, however, devalues their utility. They may come to be viewed as a matter of entitlement; their withdrawal would be greeted with bitterness by their foreign recipients and domestic partisans alike. The dependence they symbolize also invites resentment. On the whole, regular allotments of aid are therefore less effective at cementing relationships with foreign states than occasional gifts at moments of special need or to recognize and reciprocate notably helpful acts by those on whom they are conferred.

Aid, foreign: Foreign aid is the process by which the generous poor people of a rich country give money to the miserly rich people of a poor country.

Aid, foreign: "The Prince who contributes to the advancement of another power ruins his own. A Prince ought never to take the side of a neighboring state more powerful than himself, because even if he is victorious he is at the mercy of his neighbor."

—Niccolò Machiavelli

Aid, foreign: "Rich states have given subsidies and other forms of economic aid to allies and clients for political and strategic reasons since the earliest recorded history. Such aid is usually given as rent for bases and material facilities, or to induce support for the foreign policy of the donor power, but sometimes also for the more general reason that the donor considers that the economic well-being of an indigent ally will strengthen both parties in their pursuit of common objectives. The advantages of such political subsidies to the donor are normally short-lived: it is not possible to buy allegiance internationally, only to rent it short-term."

—Adam Watson, 1983

Aid, foreign, dangers of dependence on: "Each nation must work out its own salvation and, if it cannot stand on its own feet, it cannot stand at all. No amount of aid will permanently bolster up a people that abandons itself—on the contrary, foreign help, too much and too long, will weaken the fibres of the assisted nation, and will make its end as a free nation all the more certain and rapid."

—Sisley Huddleston, 1954

Aide-mémoire: Written summary or outline of important items of a proposed agreement or diplomatic communication, often prepared to record the gist of a discussion and thereby reduce misunderstanding.

Alcohol: "Drinking is a voluntary madness."

—Seneca

Alcohol, use of: A diplomat "should drink in such a manner as not to lose control of his own faculties while endeavoring to loosen the self-control of others."

—Françoise de Callières, 1716

Alignment: A national policy of political identification or military cooperation (short of alliance) with one great power or bloc against another.

Alliance: A relatively stable coalition of two or more states sharing common national security interests that has been formalized in a treaty or treaties. An alliance may be defensive (committed to upholding the status quo) or offensive (directed at changing the status quo). See also *Coalition* and *Entente.*

Alliance, basis of: "The only sure basis of an alliance [between equals] is for each party to be equally afraid of the other."   —THUCYDIDES

Alliance, purpose of: "The purpose of an alliance is to produce an obligation more predictable and precise than an analysis of national interest."   —HENRY A. KISSINGER, 1994

Alliances: "In international politics, [an alliance is] the union of two thieves who have their hands so deeply inserted in each other's pockets that they cannot separately plunder a third."   —AMBROSE BIERCE

Alliances: "Only weakness calls for conciliation and alliances."   —ARTHASASTRA OF KAUTILYA

Alliances: "When a man has committed himself to one side, he must take care to reinsure by negotiating with the other."   —POPE LEO X

Alliances: "An alliance is like a chain. It is not made stronger by adding weak links to it."   —WALTER LIPPMANN

Alliances: "A wise prince sees to it that never, in order to attack someone, does he become the ally of a prince more powerful than himself, except when necessity forces him."   —NICCOLÒ MACHIAVELLI, 1513

Alliances: "Alliances are held together by fear, not by love."   —HAROLD MACMILLAN, 1959, QUOTED BY RICHARD M. NIXON

Alliances: "Alliances, . . . [like] all fraternizations, if they do not have a strictly determinate aim, . . . disintegrate."   —METTERNICH, 1814

Alliances: "Alliances seldom assume their completed shape in the early stages of a conflict; there is generally an original nucleus of resistance around which the Coalition gradually forms. This process of development in its turn creates two causes of dissension. In the first place, the original partners, who stood alone when the danger was at its height, feel that it is they who merit priority of consideration: the later partners— whose assistance, though delayed, may have been decisive—feel that it was owing to their intervention that victory was won. In the second place, whereas the adjustment of war-aims as between the original partners may, owing to the presence of an immediate common danger, have proved comparatively simple, the arrival of new partners is bound to introduce fresh claims and further complications. And since the late arrivals usually

are less exhausted and more righteous than the original combatants, they are apt to press their claims with greater vigor than those whose war-weariness has become acute."
—HAROLD NICOLSON, 1946

Alliances: "Love for the same thing never makes allies. It's always hate for the same thing."
—HOWARD SPRING, 1938

Alliances: "Alliances, if they are to endure, require care, respect, and shared advantages."
—TALLEYRAND

Alliances, birth and death of: Alliances are born in mutual admiration; they expire in mutual contempt.

Alliances, buttressing: "In order to counteract the eroding pressures of constantly changing interests—the pressures of a highly mobile balance of power—all sorts of devices have been used to give alliances greater reliability. These devices have ranged from garrisons of the stronger states on the territory of the weaker through dynastic marriages between ruling families to solemn oaths, ideological declarations and cultural exchanges."
—ADAM WATSON, 1983

Alliances, friends, enemies: A friend, however weak, is better than a strong enemy.

Alliances, leadership of: Few tasks are as thankless as the leadership of alliances. If policy advocacy is too forceful, allies complain about disregard for their views; if too deferential, about indecision and lack of direction. If initiative is too prompt, allies grumble about the absence of consultation; if too slow, about lack of leadership.

Alliances, leadership of: "Nations that aspire to lead alliances or coalitions need a sensitive ear, connections with their partners on all levels, including the level of public opinion, and a willingness to adjust their policies to sustain the cohesion of the partnership."
—ROBERT J. O'NEILL

Alliances, sentimental: "For Heaven's sake no sentimental alliances in which the consciousness of having performed a good deed furnishes the sole reward for our sacrifice!"
—OTTO VON BISMARCK

Alliances, treaties: "Treaties of alliance, especially those with military clauses and therefore concerned with the use of force, are not by nature permanent. They are designed to deal with a specific situation; as and when that situation changes, so will the interests of the different signatories. But a state must know what other states it can count on, for how long and over what issues, both in negotiation and if necessary in war. More especially, its own military arrangements will partly depend on those of its allies. Therefore treaties of alliance are usually very specific about how long they are to remain valid and just what military obligations each party to the contract assumes."   —ADAM WATSON, 1983

Alliances, weakness of: "Alliances, if they are seriously meant, imply a framing of policies not solely in accordance with national needs, aspirations, and interests, but also in harmony with the needs, aspirations and interests of the associates. Sometimes national needs will be incompatible with the national needs of others, aspirations in opposition, ways of thought vastly different. That is the inescapable snag of alliances; it is their weakness when opposed to a homogeneous foe, and no amount of plastering labels of 'Unity' on disparate elements will make them one."
—SISLEY HUDDLESTON, 1954

Allies: "In war it is not always possible to have everything go exactly as one likes. In working with allies it sometimes happens that they develop opinions of their own."
—WINSTON CHURCHILL, 1950

Allies: "There is only one thing worse than fighting with allies—and that is fighting without allies."
—WINSTON CHURCHILL

Allies, defined by enemies: "Any nation that starts up with a determination to oppose a power which, whether professing insidious peace or declaring open war, is the common enemy of all nations, whatever may be the existing political relations of that nation with [our country], becomes instantly our essential ally."
—GEORGE CANNING, 1808

Allies, dependent: A dependent ally is a resentful ally.

Allies, distant: "Allies are preferable, other things being equal, in proportion to their distance."
—MARTIN WIGHT

Allies, weak: "Although in international affairs weak allies can be useful, they should not be in a position to commit the strong to a course of action."   —ELLIS BRIGGS, 1968

Allies, weak: "Never allow a weak ally to make decisions for you. Strong nations that [violate this rule] lose their freedom of action by identifying their interests completely with those of the weak ally. Secure in the support of its powerful friend, the weak ally can choose the objectives and methods of its foreign policy to suit itself. The powerful nation then finds that it must support interests not its own and that it is unable to compromise on issues that are vital not to itself, but only to its ally."   —HANS MORGENTHAU

Ally: A member of an alliance. See also *Alliance.*

Alternat: The practice of listing each state's own name ahead of the name of other signatories in the official copy of an international agreement that it retains for itself.

Ambassador: A diplomatic agent of the highest rank, accredited to a foreign sovereign or international organization as the resident representative of his own government, usually bearing the title "Ambassador Extraordinary and Plenipotentiary," and assisted in his work by an embassy. See also *Mission, Chief of*.

Ambassador, defined: "An ambassador is an honest man sent to lie [speak falsely; remain] abroad for the good of his country." —HENRY WOTTON

Ambassador, effective: "To have the perfect ambassador you must first have the perfect prince." —TASSO TORQUATO, 1582

Ambassador-at-large: An envoy without portfolio, but often specialized as to subject matter, who is not accredited to any government or international organization but who is used as a troubleshooter by his government.

Ambassadors: "Do you know why everybody wants to be an ambassador? It's because when an ambassador walks down the corridor of his embassy, everybody kisses his ass." —PHILIP HABIB

Ambassadors: "How should you govern any kingdom / That know not how to use ambassadors?" —WILLIAM SHAKESPEARE, KING HENRY VI

Ambassadors: "An Ambassador is one official the state cannot do without." —ABRAM DE WICQUEFORT, 1682

Ambassadors, accountability of: An ambassador is responsible "for his reports . . . for his advice . . . for the instructions received [by him from his government] . . . for the use of his time, and . . . for his integrity or lack of it in acquitting all his responsibilities. . . . His reports enable [his government] to examine the situation; if they are truthful, [his government] will decide directly, otherwise the opposite will happen." —DEMOSTHENES (384–322 B.C.)

Ambassadors, activities of: "There are a dozen kinds of activities, such as American marriages which they always want the ambassador to attend; getting them out of jail when they are jugged; looking after the American insane, helping Americans move the bones of their ancestors; interpreting the income tax law; receiving medals for Americans; hearing American fiddlers, pianists, players, sitting for American sculptors and photographers, writing letters of introduction, getting tickets to the House gallery; getting tickets to the art galleries, the House of Lords; people who are going to have a fair here; lunch for returning and outgoing diplomats, people who present books, women who wish to go to court." —WALTER HINES PAGE, DESCRIBING THE DEPRESSING REALITY OF WHAT HE WAS DOING AS AMERICAN AMBASSADOR TO LONDON, 1913

Ambassadors, age of: "[An] envoy should be neither so old as to be inactive through illhealth or the number of his years, nor so young as to prove immature or inconsiderate." —J.J. JUSSERAND

Ambassadors, amateur: In republics, which do not confer titles of nobility, the title of ambassador comes closest to such an honor. Many who should justly be recognized for notable achievement in fields unrelated to diplomacy therefore seek ambassadorships. As they are without experience to prepare them for the multiple duties of the office, such men are only seldom able to discharge it with full dignity. The appointment of such men to embassies therefore risks damage both to their own previously distinguished reputations and to those of the states and governments they represent. It would often be kinder, both to them and to their nation, were a less onerous honor found for them.

Ambassadors, amateur: "Even in those cases where success has attended the efforts of an amateur diplomatist, the example must be regarded as an exception, for it is a commonplace of human experience that skilled work requires a skilled workman."
—François de Callières, 1716

Ambassadors, amateur: "As we would not put a ship into the hands of a commander ignorant of navigation, an army under the control of a general without military training so we should not put the foreign affairs of our government into the hands of men without knowledge of the various subjects which go to make up the diplomatic science."
—Herbert H.D. Pierce, 1897, quoted by Kenneth W. Thompson

Ambassadors, authority of: "If you are to stand up for your Government you must be able to stand up to your Government."　　　　　　　　　—Harold Caccia

Ambassadors, collectors of intelligence: "We must remember that the real object of foreign envoys is not only that they should convey messages from their governments, but, if we were to look deeply into their purpose, secret information like the exact position and condition of roads, paths, valleys, canals and tanks; whether or not they are fit for the passage of troops and whether fodder is available anywhere near them. They also seek to know something about the ruler of the country, the exact state of the army and its equipments; the feelings of the soldiers as well as of the common people; and all about the wealth of the subjects and the comparative populations of different districts. They try to penetrate into the working of the government of the country and to know whether the ministers are honest or dishonest and whether the generals are experienced or not."
—Nizam al-Mulk Tusi

Ambassadors, command responsibilities: "The Ambassador is to take charge overseas. This does not mean in a purely bureaucratic sense, but in an active, operational, interested, responsible fashion. He is expected to know about what is going on among the representatives of other agencies who are stationed in his country. He is expected to supervise, to encourage, to direct, to assist in any way he can."　　　—Dean Rusk, 1961

Ambassadors, contributions to policy: "The contributions of a good ambassador are not limited to the persuasive articulation and skillful execution of policy, good or bad. What he [or she] reports and how he reports it; the astuteness of his recommendations; his will-

ingness to take the initiative; the courage to disagree and explain why these and many other attributes can make a vital difference to the shaping of policy. How much depends on the good sense of his principals."
—ELLIOT L. RICHARDSON, 1983

Ambassadors, credibility of: The government to which ambassadors are accredited will see them as interpreters of thoughts that are not their own and executors of designs handed to them by higher authority. The credibility of ambassadors therefore depends less on their own merits than on the use they know how to make of the fear or confidence inspired by the government they represent.

Ambassadors, duties: "The duties of an envoy are: sending information to his king, ensuring maintenance of the terms of a treaty, upholding his king's honor, acquiring allies, instigating dissension among the friends of the enemy, conveying secret agents and troops, suborning the kinsmen of the enemy to his own king's side, acquiring clandestinely gems and other valuable material for his own king, ascertaining secret information and showing valor in liberating hostages."
—ARTHASASTRA OF KAUTILYA

Ambassadors, duty of: "The first duty of an ambassador is exactly the same as that of any other servant of government, that is, to do, say, advise and think whatever may best serve the preservation and aggrandizement of his own state."
—ERMOLAO BARBARO, C. 1490

Ambassadors, empathy for host nation of: A great ambassador develops empathy for the interests and views of the nation to which he is assigned, but remains the advocate only of those of his own government and nation. He courts good relations with those in authority but never forgets that his object in doing so is to persuade them to accept the views of his capital and that honest disagreement, tactfully presented, can be seen as a mark of friendly concern.

Ambassadors, functions of: "[The ambassador's principal function consists] in maintaining effective communication between two Princes, in delivering letters that his Master writes to the Prince at whose court he resides, in soliciting answers to them, in protecting his Master's subjects and conserving his interests."
—ABRAM DE WICQUEFORT

Ambassadors, honor of: "[An ambassador] must be a man of the strictest honor if the government to which he is accredited and his own government are to place explicit confidence in his statements."
—JULES CAMBON

Ambassadors, informants about their country: In ancient times, ambassadors were regarded by the sovereigns to whom they were accredited as a primary source of information about events in their homeland. In modern times, when information on events around the globe is speedily and readily available through the media, ambassadors must still strive to make themselves trusted interpreters of events. They may thereby hope to shape the understanding and guide the responses of their host government to happenings back home and also to lay a basis for an exchange of insights with their interlocutors that will improve the accuracy of their reporting and analysis to their own government.

Ambassadors, innkeepers: Ambassadors serve also as innkeepers for itinerant officials and legislators from their capitals.

Ambassadors, judgment in: "There is nothing more loathesome than a man lacking in common sense, but for an ambassador judgment is truly the controlling qualification: it is what puts everything in focus. With it, a negotiator will save himself from subtlety and quibbling and bring to bear on everything that sharp sense of reality which is too often lacking in the men of the Cabinet." —Jules Cambon, 1926

Ambassadors, knowledge of host country by: "The ambassador who wishes to understand the origin of affairs in the kingdom where he is to reside must spend his spare time in reading its histories or chronicles, must gain a knowledge of its laws, of the privileges of its provinces, the usages and customs of its inhabitants, the character of the natives, their temperament and inclination: and if he should desire to serve in his office with the goodwill of his own and a foreign people, he must try and accommodate himself to the character of the natives, though at cost of doing violence to his own; he must listen to them, talk with them and even flatter them, for flattery is the magnet which everywhere attracts goodwill. Anyone who listens to many people and consorts with them, sometimes meets one who cannot keep a secret and even habitually makes confidant of someone, in order to show that he is a man of importance, trusted and employed by the heads of his Government. Should he lack friends and the ability to discover the truth and to verify his suspicions, money can help him, for it is and always has been the master key to the most closely-locked archives." —Anonymous, La embajada española

Ambassadors, management responsibilities: Ambassadors are responsible for the overall conduct of relations with the nations to which they are assigned. In a large diplomatic mission, this requires giving guidance to and coordinating the work of representatives of many agencies other than the Foreign Ministry. This presents a special challenge, as the future of such agency representatives depends more on how their performance is evaluated by their parent agency back home than on the ambassador's view of it. Ambassadors need strong leadership skills to weld those under them into a team responsive to their will.

Ambassadors, ministers of foreign affairs: "In truth, the qualities which suit an ambassador are not those which a Foreign Minister should have. The latter somehow focuses the actions of his agents dispersed at all points of the globe, compares the intelligence he sends them, puts them in balance and sustains the harmony in the conduct of his country's foreign policy which assures it unity and gains it success—but he lives in his own country; he is not in direct contact with abroad. The ambassador, by contrast, has this direct contact. He follows the instructions of his government but at the same time keeps it informed, enlightens it, warns it, and sometimes must restrain it. Doubtless, the indepen-

dence of his judgment should not extend to indiscipline, but a supervisory minister who is irked by this has no more judgment than a man who covers his eyes to walk forward, and, on the other hand, an ambassador who dares be nothing more than a mailbox is a peril to his government."
—JULES CAMBON, 1925

Ambassadors, misleading reasonableness of: An ambassador who is successful at fitting himself fully into the life of the capital where he is assigned can unwittingly undermine its understanding of his own nation. The officials with whom he is in contact may come to imagine that his reasonableness and empathy for their perspective are typical of his countrymen, when nothing is further from the truth. They may therefore be misled into ignoring underlying adverse trends in relations with his country until it is too late to do much about them.

Ambassadors, never off duty: "An envoy must consider himself, even in his moments of rest, as consecrated forever to a special service, the obligations of which should be ever present to his mind, be the object of his studies, and serve as a rule of conduct in his conversations and actions."
—ANTOINE PECQUET, 1737

Ambassadors, obedience to instructions by: "It should be noted that unswerving obedience fits only with precise and peremptory commands. Ambassadors have somewhat freer duties the filling of which, in several respects, entirely depends on their own dispositions. They do not simply execute, but form also and direct by their own advice the will of their masters."
—MICHEL DE MONTAIGNE

Ambassadors, peace and war dependent upon: "Peace and its opposite (that is, war) depend on the ambassadors, since it is they who create and undo alliances. The affairs that provoke war or peace between kings are in their power."
—THE LAWS OF MANU, THIRD CENTURY B.C.

Ambassadors, personality of: "Much depends on the personality and ability of ambassadors. They should be close to the top policy makers of their own countries if they are to present their nations' cases effectively, and if they are to supply their home governments with the information and advice necessary for policy decisions. They should possess a sure grasp of the political, economic and social forces at work in the country to which they are accredited."
—CHARLES ROETTER, 1963

Ambassadors, qualifications of: Distinguished credentials in other fields are not a self-evident qualification for appointment as ambassador. A genius for battlefield maneuver does not necessarily presage a talent for the peaceful conciliation of differences. The ability to make a profit from an idea or an enterprise cannot be taken to imply political acumen, tact, or cultural adaptability. The capacity to do brilliant academic research and deliver thoughtful lectures does not certify a facility for listening, interpreting the subtleties of foreign leaders, and reacting deftly to them on the spot. Political skills honed in parliamentary maneuver at home may not translate into adroit practice of the art of the possible abroad. The capacity to represent private interests effectively in the courts may not foretell a capacity to advocate both public and private interests persuasively to a foreign system of government and society.

Ambassadors, qualifications of: "An ambassador should be versed in all the sciences; he should understand hints, gestures and expressions of the face; he should be honest, skillful and of good family." —CODE OF MANU

Ambassadors, qualifications of: "An ambassador should be a trained theologian, should be well-versed in Aristotle and Plato, and should be able at a moment's notice to solve the most abstruse problems in correct dialectical form; he should also be expert in mathematics, architecture, music, physics and civil and canon law. He should speak and write Latin fluently and must also be proficient in Greek, Spanish, French, German and Turkish. While being a trained classical scholar, a historian, a geographer and an expert in military science, he must also have a cultured taste for poetry. And above all he must be of excellent family, rich and endowed with a fine physical presence." —OTTAVIANO MAGGI, 1596

Ambassadors, qualities of effective: To be effective, ambassadors must exemplify intelligence, trustworthiness, humaneness, foresight, courage, a sense of humor, and sternness. By doing so they may compensate, in part, for the not-infrequent lack of these qualities in the national leaders in whose names they act.

Ambassadors, reporting duties of: "Ambassadors are the eyes and ears of states." —FRANCESCO GUICCIARDINI, 1564

Ambassadors, selection of: The same men who would not put a man untried in private business at the head of a corporation can nevertheless think nothing of putting a man untried in diplomacy at the head of the nation's business in a foreign land. The same men who would demand youthful vigor from a corporate chief executive can be quick to put a man retired from business for actuarial decrepitude at the head of a physically and mentally demanding diplomatic mission. Yet the business of diplomacy lies in the heavily mined no-man's-land between peace and war; the business of corporations is in the flat gray zone between profit and loss. Businessmen risk men's money; diplomats risk men's lives.

Ambassadors, spies: Ambassadors are licensed spies; they should not forget that spies may also be unlicensed ambassadors.

Ambassadors, spies: "A sovereign should always regard an ambassador as a spy." —THE HITOPADESA, III, c. 500

Ambassadors, spies: "Ambassadors are, in the full meaning of the term, titled spies." —NAPOLEON

Ambassadors, use of: If you want someone to deliver your mail to a foreign government, get a postal clerk. If you want to communicate effectively, appoint an ambassador in whose professionalism and discretion you trust. Tell him what you want to accomplish and listen to his advice on how to persuade his hosts to agree to it. Don't tell him how to flatter and cajole them into doing what you want them to do. If he doesn't know how to do this, you shouldn't have appointed him; you need another ambassador. If he knows how to do it and normally does it well, but can't do it in a particular case, you probably need more realistic objectives and expectations—not a new ambassador—to deal with the issue.

Ambassadors, welfare of nations dependent on: "The welfare of nations is in the hands of ambassadors; their designs maintain calm or blow troubles. They arm or pacify nations."
　　　　　　　　　　　　—Lescalopier de Nourar, 1763, cited by J.J. Jusserand

Ambassadors, words as weapons: "Ambassadors have no battleships at their disposal, or heavy infantry, or fortresses; their weapons are words and opportunities. In important transactions opportunities are fleeting; once they are missed they cannot be recovered."
　　　　　　　　　　　　—Demosthenes

Ambiguity, creative: If two parties to a negotiation cannot agree, they may be able to set aside their disagreements, agreeing to disagree or agreeing not to challenge each other's positions on specific points. Such creative ambiguity is often the grease on which progress in relations between states turns.

Amiability: Diplomats must strive to build and maintain cordial personal relations with officials of the government to which they are accredited. Amiability on the surface, no matter how strained relations may be beneath it, keeps open channels of communication that can be vital to the resolution of issues between states when the time to resolve them is at hand.

Amity: "Amity itself can only be maintained by reciprocal respect, and true friends are punctilious equals."
　　　　　　　　　　　　—Herman Melville, 1866

Amity, cross-cultural: "There is a mutual bond of amity and brotherhood between man and man over all the world. Nor is it distance of place that makes enmity, but enmity makes distance. He therefore that keeps peace with me, near or remote, of whatever nation, is to me as far as all civil and human offices an Englishman and a neighbor. This is gospel."
　　　　　　　　　　　　—John Milton, 1649

Analysis, worst case: A mode of military reasoning that assesses requirements for force structure and draws up plans on the basis of what is known about the battlefield capabilities of potential foes, without regard to their policies or intentions or the logic of their national interests.

Analysts, statesmen: To do their jobs, analysts must be skeptics with flexible minds; to do theirs, statesmen must be optimists with firm convictions.

Anger: Never get angry except on purpose.

Anger: "A man who is naturally violent and easily carried away, is ill-fitted to the conduct of negotiations; it is almost impossible for him to be master of himself at those critical moments, and unforeseen occasions when the command of one's temper is of importance, especially at the acute moments of diplomatic controversy."
—François de Callières, 1716

Anger: "There are two things contrary to wise deliberation—precipitation and anger."
—Diodorus, the Athenian

Annexation: The formal incorporation of territory into a state, purporting to extinguish claims by other states or by its inhabitants to separate sovereignty.

Annihilation: When the result of conflict is certain to be the destruction of the enemy and suicide for oneself, war ceases to be a rational instrument of statecraft; it becomes an utterly immoral act of madness.

Antagonists, countering: Exchanging a fierce antagonist for a meek friend is a poor bargain.

Antagonists, instruction from: "He that wrestles with us strengthens our nerves and sharpens our skill. Our antagonist is our helper." —Edmund Burke, 1790

Appearance: "An ambassador should, as far as possible, be good looking; a man who is lame is received with laughter." —Etienne Dolcet, 1541, cited by J.J. Jusserand

Appeasement: A reduction of tension between two previously hostile states or groups of states by concessions on the part of one side to the other in the interest of assuaging the causes of disagreement and conflict between them.

Appeasement: "An infallible method of conciliating a tiger is to allow oneself to be swallowed." —Konrad Adenauer

Appeasement: "Yield to all and you will soon have nothing to yield." —Aesop

Appeasement: "A power which begins to yield is a finished power."
—Otto von Bismarck

Appeasement: "In international affairs appeasement stores up trouble, and appeasing the weak is worse than appeasing the strong, first because it is unnecessary, and second because the weak are thereby encouraged to go on misbehaving." —ELLIS BRIGGS, 1968

Appeasement: "An appeaser is one who feeds a crocodile hoping it will eat him last."
—WINSTON CHURCHILL, 1954

Appeasement: "In the language of diplomacy employed in the European balance-of-power system, appeasement referred to a policy of attempting to reduce tension between two states by the methodical removal of the principal causes of conflict between them. In this sense appeasement was regarded as a strategy for eliminating the potential for war in a conflict-ridden relationship between two states. Whereas the classic definition refers to the removal of all the principal causes of conflict in the relationship, partial appeasement is also possible, leaving some sources of conflict untouched."
—ALEXANDER L. GEORGE, 1993

Appeasement: "Establish the eternal truth that acquiescence under insult is not the way to escape war." —THOMAS JEFFERSON

Appeasement: "To show stubborn unyieldness to an opponent who possesses a real sense of grievance over specific issues may be as dangerous as to make concessions to an opponent whose ambitions are endless." —EVAN LUARD, 1967

Appeasement: "No prince should ever give up anything (wishing to do so honorably) unless he is able or believes himself able to hold it. For it is almost always better (matters having gone to the point that he cannot give it up in the above manner) to allow it to be taken from him by force, rather than by the apprehension of force. For if he yields it from fear, it is for the purpose of avoiding war, and he will rarely escape from that; for he to whom he has from cowardice conceded the one thing will not be satisfied, but will want to take other things from him, and his arrogance will increase as his esteem for the prince is lessened. And, on the other hand, the zeal of the prince's friends will be chilled on seeing him appear feeble or cowardly. But if, so soon as he discerns his adversary's intention, he prepares his forces, even though they be inferior, the enemy will begin to respect him, and the other neighboring princes will appreciate him the more; and seeing him armed for defense, those even will come to his aid who, seeing him give up himself, would never have assisted him." —NICCOLÒ MACHIAVELLI

Appeasement: "No man can tame a tiger into a kitten by stroking it. There can be no appeasement with ruthlessness. There can be no reasoning with an incendiary bomb."
—FRANKLIN DELANO ROOSEVELT, 1940

Appeasement, defined: "The reduction of tension between the two sides by the methodical removal of the principal causes of conflict and disagreement between them."
—ALEXANDER L. GEORGE, 1993

Appeasement, passive: "Passive appeasement is the practice of not explicitly agreeing to, but not opposing, the adversary's alteration of the status quo. Active appeasement, on the other hand, is a diplomatic agreement that acquiesces in a forthcoming alteration of the situation." —ALEXANDER L. GEORGE, 1993

Appointees, political: The purpose of appointing an ambassador or special envoy is often no more than to give someone who enjoys travel and craves prestige a chance to travel abroad at government expense and to write a book about the experience.

Appointees, political: "Political appointments are generally made for the good of the nominee, or the good of the dispenser of the patronage, or the good of the party in power. Professional appointments are made for the good of the country." —ELLIS BRIGGS, 1983

Appointees, political: "The word 'ambassador' would normally have a professional connotation but for the American tradition of political appointees. The bizarre notion that any citizen, especially if he is rich, is fit for the representation of his country abroad has taken some hard blows through empirical evidence. But it has not been discarded. Nor should the idea of diluting a rigid professionalism with manpower from less detached sectors of society be dismissed out of hand. [But] when the strongest nation in the world appoints a tycoon or wealthy hostess to head an embassy, the discredit and frustration is spread throughout the entire diplomatic corps in the country concerned." —ABBA EBAN, 1983

Appointees, political: "Ministers are considered as selected to enjoy the pleasures of foreign travel at the expense of the people; their places [are] sinecures; and their residence abroad [is] a continued scene of luxurious enjoyment. [But] there is scarcely an office of which the duties, properly performed, are more arduous, more responsible, and less fairly appreciated." —EDWARD LIVINGSTON, 1833

Appointees, political: "An ambassador is a man who had the most money and the fewest votes." —JOHN D. LODGE

Appointees, political: "Some persons are sent abroad because they are needed abroad, and some are sent because they are not wanted home." —WILLIAM HENRY SEWARD

Appointees, political, at the United Nations: "The ambassadorial appointments of many governments—and for some reason especially [those] to the United Nations in New York—can rate equally as dust-bin or pork-barrel, exile or accolade, political punishment or reward." —GEOFFREY JACKSON, 1981

Appointments, political: "Every time I make an appointment, I make five enemies and one ingrate." —ATTRIBUTED TO TALLEYRAND

Apprehension: "A just fear of an imminent danger, though there be no blow given, is a lawful cause of war."
—FRANCIS BACON, 1625

Apprenticeship in diplomacy: "Generally, the innate and indispensable diplomatic temperament develops by experience and study in the subordinate positions which mark the beginning of [the] career. It is in the course of his daily tasks that the young diplomat will acquire the essentials of his profession; an understanding of foreigners, which is increased by using their language; clear thinking, inculcated by practice in drafting in a lucid and comprehensive manner, in learning how to take in his stride tours of duty which give time for reflection, in turning over problems in his mind, consulting with colleagues and avoiding hasty commitments. Routine assignments should also teach him what he should do, and what he should avoid being constrained to do. An ambassador plays an important role as a teacher."
—JOHN R. WOOD AND JEANNE SERRES, 1970

Arbitral award: The decision of a tribunal engaged in arbitration of a dispute.

Arbitration: The process of adjudication of a dispute by a tribunal, a majority of whose members are appointed by the disputants, whose decision the disputants agree to accept as final and binding. Contrast *Conciliation*.

Arbitration: Arbitration should not be entered lightly. It can allow a third party to determine the destiny of your nation, perhaps at the expense of its vital interests. Arbitrate only if you manifestly have principle on your side but are so weak that you must call on others to enforce it.

Arbitration: "International arbitration may be defined as the substitution of many burning questions for a smoldering one."
—AMBROSE BIERCE

Arbitration, defense through resort to: "It is impossible to attack as a transgressor him who offers to lay his grievance before a tribunal of arbitration."
—KING OF SPARTA, QUOTED BY THUCYDIDES

Arbitration, preferable to war: "Fair arbitral awards, despite the normal dissatisfaction on both sides, are more likely to endure than solutions imposed by arms. Broadly speaking, a successful arbitration is to diplomacy what a military victory is to war. And a half-loaf is usually better than no bread or a shooting war. It is better to lose in the courts, especially when the issues are relatively minor, than in the foxholes."
—THOMAS A. BAILEY, 1968

Arguments: "Negotiation should never degenerate into an argument; it should always be kept on the level of a discussion."
—HAROLD NICOLSON, 1934

Armies: "If it is employed in the best possible way, the army can accomplish works and make the world peaceful. It is for this reason that rulers entrust generals with important mandates time and time again." —CHENG YI

Arms control: A process of cooperation among potential enemies directed at reducing the likelihood that their differences will erupt in war, or at diminishing the scope and violence of any conflict which may nonetheless occur, by adopting reciprocal measures to assure against surprise attack, to limit deployments, or to reduce armaments or the size and structure of armed forces. Arms control presupposes the continuing reality of a conflict of interests which it addresses only implicitly, through its possible contribution to an atmosphere of mutual confidence that may facilitate negotiated solutions of differences between enemies.

Arms control: "Arms control is not a substitute for defense. It is defense conducted by other means. Those means are diplomatic: the mutually agreeable rules of the road in the arms race—rules that will make the competition somewhat more predictable, that will set limits on the most dangerous kinds of weapons and help avert the sudden appearance of new weapons systems that might upset the balance. Arms control is a way of setting bounds to the twin threats of aggression and nuclear war—but not of ending them. Arms control does not involve trusting or relying on the goodwill of the other side. It is a matter of reaching accords that both sides deem to be in their mutual interest and of assuring each side's ability independently to verify the compliance of the other." —STROBE TALBOTT, 1984

Arms control, negotiations: "Arms-control negotiations are often misinterpreted as a form of conflict resolution, whereas they only affect a symptom of conflict, namely the derived military competition. On the other hand, it is possible to argue that the process of negotiations itself can have a calming effect." —EDWARD N. LUTTWAK, 1987

Arms, diplomacy without: "Diplomacy without arms is music without instruments." —FREDRICK THE GREAT

Arms sales: Arms sales are universally regarded as useful instruments of state policy. They reinforce political goodwill and habits of military cooperation, foster dependency on spare parts and upgrades, and assure interoperability of the purchasing nation's military with the forces of the vendor and its similarly equipped allies. By introducing economies of scale, they lower the cost of weapons procurement for the producing nation; at the same time, they secure its defense industrial base and generate additional domestic employment in sectors of its economy especially relevant to preparedness for war.

Arrests of citizens: "It is the duty of a Consular officer to go immediately to any [citizen] who from having been arrested or for any other difficulty in which he may find himself with the local Authorities, may request his aid; and such Consular officer is not performing his duties when he rests satisfied with the statements made to him by Authorities

who have arrested a [citizen] as to the grounds on which they have done so; and who neglects to go and hear from the accused himself what he may have to say on his own behalf. A [citizen] may be unjustly accused by the Officers of the Police. And a Consular officer would very imperfectly perform his duty by sending him the name of a lawyer to be employed, instead of enquiring into the case and giving such assistance as might appear expedient and proper."
—Palmerston, 1840

Assassination: Politically motivated homicide. See also *Terrorism*.

Assassination: "A single assassin can achieve, with weapons, fire or poison, more than a fully mobilized army."
—Arthasastra of Kautilya

Asylum, political: Sanctuary or protection from extradition granted to a foreign national temporarily resident in the territory of a state or, in the practice of some states, in an embassy, consulate, or other office enjoying diplomatic immunity abroad.

Attaché: A diplomatic title referring to officers in an embassy with a professional specialization—e.g., military, cultural, educational, or press liaison with officials and private persons in the host nation.

Attachés, military: "In every land and language, the term military attaché is only a synonym for spy."
—Pawel Monat

Attachés, military, duties of: "Today the service attaché has four functions. The first is information gathering and reporting (normally by fully overt methods). The second is advising the ambassador on military matters. The third may involve either helping sell or buy arms for his country. And the fourth is a wise representational and liaison one—from attending functions in full-dress uniform, to arranging exchanges of military personnel, to making sure that a visiting general gets the appropriate treatment."
—Eric Clark, 1973

Attachés, press: "The press officer who accompanies a foreign minister to a major capital abroad is likely to be more closely in touch with him than is a particular ambassador. What the diplomat accomplishes in the conference room may have to compete in importance with what a press officer reports about the proceedings."
—Kenneth W. Thompson, 1962

Attack, preemptive: Attitudes toward surprise attack to knock out an adversary of growing menace vary in proportion to geography and strength. Those whose geographical separation from enemies gives them time to assess events or to seek their own moment of maximum advantage for a military reaction to a threat tend to condemn preemption. Those whose geographical situation and relative weakness vis-à-vis an adversary or combination of enemies create a greater danger that they will be overwhelmed tend to resort more easily to preemptive attack.

Attack, preemptive: "I hold it lawful and Christian policy to prevent a mischief betimes, as to revenge it too late. Only you must resolve, and not delay or dally."

—Francis Drake

Attack, preemptive: "Self-defense sometimes dictates aggression. If one people takes advantage of peace to put itself in a position to destroy another, immediate attack on the first is the only means of preventing such destruction."

—Montesquieu

Attack, principles of: "(1) Do not attack unless attacked. Never attack others without provocation, but once attacked, do not fail to return the blow. (2) Do not fight decisive actions unless sure of victory. Never fight without certainty of success, unless failing to fight would likely present a worse outcome. (3) Know when to stop, when to counter, and when to bring the fight to a close. Do not be carried away with success."

—Mao Zedong

Attrition: The object of war is to achieve victory, not to test one's ability to accept more pain or suffer longer than the other side.

Authority: Legitimacy is the moral proof of authority.

Authority, defined: Authority is the capacity to inspire acceptance and hence obedience or acquiescence in decisions. It reflects deference to the supposed wisdom of the decision-maker, respect for the legitimacy of the decision-making process, and acknowledgment of the necessity, appropriateness, and timeliness of a decision being made.

B

Background: An agreed basis for a discussion between an official and a journalist that permits the journalist to quote or paraphrase what the official says and to attribute it to a source, such as "a senior foreign ministry official," without identifying the official by name or title.

Background, deep: An agreed basis for a discussion between an official and a journalist that permits the journalist to use the information provided by the official in writing a report but prohibits direct quotation of the information or its attribution to a source other than the journalist's own knowledge.

Bad, worse: "The difference between bad and worse is a lot bigger than the difference between good and better."
—AMERICAN PROVERB

Bag: See *Pouch, diplomatic.*

Balance of capabilities: A comparison of the relevant (political, economic, or military) capacities of each party to a dispute and their relative abilities to apply these elements of power to each other. Often misrendered as balance of power (q.v.). The balance of capabilities of the contending parties can decide the outcome if both are equally determined and well led.

Balance of fervor: A comparison of the relative importance of the interests at stake to the parties and the intensity of emotional commitment they attach to the issues in a confrontation. The balance of fervor measures the relative risks each side will take and the sacrifices it will make to cause its position to prevail. It explains why a smaller and weaker but more highly motivated party to a struggle can often achieve victory over a larger, stronger adversary that is less determined to win because it has less to lose.

Balance of power: A state of affairs among a community of nations such that no single nation or a few in combination may acquire or possess a degree of power that endangers the independence of any other. Also used, loosely, to refer to the distribution of power in a state system. See also *Power, balance of,* and *Power, distribution of.*

Balancer: A state that occupies the key swing position within an existing distribution of power, able to assure continuing equilibrium by joining with a defensive state or coalition to check the ambitions of another state or coalition whose accretion of power threatens otherwise to gain it a preponderance of power.

Bargaining: Bargaining is the process of concessions, conditional offers, threats, and inducements by which compromises and mutual accommodation are reached.

Bargaining: "A large part of diplomacy, as of all politics, is concerned with bargaining. Allies bargain to determine the extent and limits of their commitments to each other. Adversaries also bargain when elements of implied or explicit threat may be among the inducements used. All the economic discussions which bulk so large in the contemporary diplomatic dialogue involve bargaining. The essential feature of bargaining is that the other party does not know how far you will go, and it is therefore most effectively done in private discussion; though the final results of a bargain, or a package of limited conditional bargains, can of course be made public."   —ADAM WATSON, 1983

Bargaining: "The principle of give and take is the principle of diplomacy—give one and take ten."   —MARK TWAIN

Bargaining between states: "Governments represent states, not charities. If they are to give something up, they must know what they will receive in return."
          —BASHAR IBN HAFEZ AL-ASSAD

Bargaining position: "The bargaining position of a country depends on the options it is perceived to have."   —HENRY A. KISSINGER, 1994

Bargaining power: "Bargaining power is the capacity to generate intended negotiating outcomes."   —MICHAEL BLAKER, 1977

Battle: One may lose a battle, indeed one may lose every battle, and—with the right strategy—still win the war.

Battle: "[A battle is] a method of untying with the teeth a political knot that would not yield to the tongue."   —AMBROSE BIERCE

Battlefield results, diplomacy and: "Diplomacy has rarely been able to gain at the conference table what cannot be gained or held on the battlefield."
          —WALTER BEDELL SMITH, 1954

Belligerency: A legal state of armed conflict. Belligerents are direct participants in that conflict.

Benefits of peace or war: "When the benefits accruing to kings under a treaty, irrespective of their status as the weaker, equal, or stronger king, are fair to each one, peace by agreement shall be the preferred course; if the benefits are to be distributed unfairly, war is preferable."   —ARTHASASTRA OF KAUTILYA

Bilateral: Referring to interaction between one state and another, as opposed to dealings between more than two states (which are termed "multilateral").

Binational: Referring to organizations comprised of citizens or corporations from two states. Contrast *Multinational*.

Bloc: A group of states that usually acts in concert in international affairs.

Blockade: The use by a state or coalition of military force to prevent imports or exports from the territory of another state or coalition, a measure just short of war that leaves the actual initiation of hostilities to the decision of those being blockaded.

Bluffing: "Everything depends on what the adversary reads into one's intentions. A bluff that is believed is more effective than a sincere threat which is dismissed with incredulity."
                                                                    —ABBA EBAN, 1983

Bluffing: Avoid deadlines and ultimata unless you mean them. Otherwise, the other side may use them against you.

Blunders, bureaucratic: "In ninety-nine cases out of a hundred, when there is a quarrel between two states, it is generally occasioned by some blunder of a ministry."
                                                            —BENJAMIN DISRAELI, 1858

Blunders, diplomatic: "Our diplomats plunge us forever into misfortune; our generals always save us."   —OTTO VON BISMARCK, C. 1850

Borders, adjustment of: "History teaches that it is not conferences that change borders of states. The decisions of conferences can only reflect the new alignment of forces. And this is the result of victory or surrender at the end of a war, or of other circumstances."
                                                        —NIKITA S. KHRUSHCHEV, 1959

Bout de papier: See *Non-paper*.

Bribery: Timely bribery of a corruptible foreign government can serve to enlist its support or procure its neutrality in war, saving thousands of lives and preventing untold miseries. Given the alternatives, such bribery is among the best and most humane investments a state can make.

Bribery: "It is very true, that it is possible that a case may happen, that a man may serve his country by a bribe well-placed, or an intrigue of pleasure with a woman."
                                                                    —JOHN ADAMS

Bribery: "The Law of Nations is not concerned with bribery. It seems rather a question of morality."   —ERNEST SATOW

Brinkmanship: "The ability to get to the verge without getting into the war is the necessary art. If you cannot master it, you inevitably get into war. If you try to run away from it, if you are scared to go to the brink, you are lost." —JOHN FOSTER DULLES, 1956

Buffer: An independent state or geographical zone lying between two or more states in whose nonalignment or demilitarization they are mutually interested as a means of precluding the strategic threat that domination or military use of the zone by one or the other would pose.

Bureaucrats, caution of: "There are old bureaucrats and there are bold bureaucrats, but there are no old, bold bureaucrats."   —U.S. DEPARTMENT OF STATE SAYING

Bureaucrats, foreign ministry: Officials in foreign ministries have an advantage which few other bureaucrats have; when dealing with an especially awkward or apparently insoluble problem they can instruct their nation's ambassadors abroad to register concern about it, enabling themselves to claim to their superiors and to other interested parties at home that they have done something about the issue. If there are no results, they can impute blame to someone else for this deplorable outcome. If the issue is resolved, they will be in a position to claim credit for this.

Bureaucrats, statesmen: In times of crisis, statesmen go straight for the jugular; bureaucrats go directly for the capillaries.

Bureaucrat's credo: "(1) When in charge, ponder. (2) When in trouble, delegate. (3) When in doubt, mumble."   —JAMES H. BOREN

Business: An activity that provides goods or services in anticipation of profit.

Businesses and citizens, protection of: "An essential duty of an ambassador is the protection of his nationals and of the commerce and shipping of his country. The vigilance, as well as the inspiration, of a head of mission should be exercised to ensure not only that his fellow countrymen, ships flying the flag of his country, and their commercial relations are dealt with in accordance with treaties or agreements in force, but also that persons under his jurisdiction are not victims of discriminatory practices. He should seek to improve the status of his colony, increase commercial traffic and tighten the bonds of common intellectual and cultural interests: all essential elements in the development of good relations and peaceful exchange between the two countries. Objective consideration of business affairs, like moderation in language, is absolutely indispensable in these matters."   —JOHN R. WOOD AND JEAN SERRES, 1970

Calls: The process of self-introduction (or bidding farewell) to members of the host government and third country diplomatic colleagues in which a diplomatic officer, such as an ambassador, engages upon his commencing or preparing to terminate his official duties in a foreign locality.

Candid: When used to describe a meeting, generally indicates that there were sharp differences between the participants.

Candor: "Candor and probity are more likely to achieve success than subtlety and finesse." —Cardinal Richelieu

Candor: Guileless speech.

Candor, diplomatic: The technique of influencing others by appearing sincerely to share confidences with them while telling them only what one wants them to know.

Capabilities: Capacities to influence the decisions of other states through military, economic, political, or cultural actions. Capabilities vary in mass, relevance, impact, irresistibility, and sustainability (q.v.).

Capabilities and intentions: "Foreign policy must be planned on the basis of the other side's capabilities and not merely of its intentions." —Henry A. Kissinger, 1964

Capabilities and intentions: "A government needs to know what other governments could do to help or harm its state particularly in the military field, and also what non-military forms of aid or damage, for instance economic, they could bring to bear on its interests. It also needs to know what other governments seem likely to do. To be aware of what is possible and what the probabilities are, and to induce other governments to make favorable choices, is the object of foreign policy." —Adam Watson, 1983

Capitals: Great capitals foster great delusions; they lapse easily into political autism or disdain for the realities of the world at their periphery and beyond it.

Capitulation: An instrument of surrender or cession of rights, e.g., in connection with the cessation of hostilities or armistice.

Cartel: An international or transnational coalition formed to maximize profits or minimize losses among its members by regulating the production, price, sale, or purchase of specified goods or services.

Casus belli: An act or event that is cited as the justification for the commencement of hostilities.

Casus foederis: An act or event that invokes the clauses of a treaty of alliance.

Censorship: Censorship and lack of transparency foster greater distrust than disclosure because those from whom the truth is withheld infer that the purpose is to conceal menacing intent or improper behavior.

Ceremonies: "In statesmanship get the formalities right, never mind about the moralities."
—MARK TWAIN, 1897

Champagne: "No government could survive without champagne. Champagne in the throat of our diplomatic people is like oil in the wheels of an engine."
—JOSEPH DARGENT, 1955

Chancery: The office building in which an ambassador and his principal staff work. Also called the "chancellery." (Technically, the "embassy" is where the ambassador lives, not where he works. Thus the chancery is an "embassy office," as distinct from an "embassy residence.")

Chancery, Head of: The designation of an officer below the ambassador in a British embassy (usually the Political Counselor) charged with coordinating the substantive and administrative work of the embassy.

Change: The balance between societies shifts as compelling new ideas, political economies, and technologies arise, and new objects of competition emerge to stimulate conflict. War ruins some peoples; it invigorates others. Some peoples profit in peace; others rot in it. Nations wax and wane; states coalesce and cleave asunder.

Change, international: "Nations are changed by time: they flourish and decay; by turns command and obey."
—OVID

Change of government: "The three standard criteria for recognition are effective control of the instrumentalities of government, absence of resistance to the new regime, and professed intention to abide by international commitments."   —ELLIS BRIGGS, 1968

Character: "The best means of judging [men's character] is to ascertain whether they choose for their companions men of known respectability, good habits, and generally well reputed. For there is no better indication of a man's character than the company which he keeps; and therefore very properly a man who keeps respectable company acquires a good name, for it is impossible that there should not be some similitude of character and habits between him and his associates."   —NICCOLÒ MACHIAVELLI

Character, judging: "To understand the heart and mind of a person, look not at what he has already achieved, but what he aspires to." —KAHLIL GIBRAN

Chargé d'affaires: An officer in charge of an embassy who is not an ambassador, (as when, for example, the level of relations between two states has been lowered to below the ambassadorial level) and who is accredited to the minister of foreign affairs, rather than to the chief of state. In such circumstances, termed Chargé d'affaires ad hoc.

Chargé d'affaires, ad interim: The officer in charge of the business of an embassy during the temporary absence of the ambassador or in the interval between the departure of an outgoing ambassador and the arrival of his successor. Often abbreviated as Chargé d'affaires a.i.

Charity, absence of gratitude for: "He who confers a benefit on anyone loves him better than he is loved by him again." —MONTESQUIEU, REPEATING ARISTOTLE

Charity, effects of: "Generosity captivates the decent, but antagonizes the mean." —ARAB PROVERB

Charity, publicity about: "The giver of charity should not mention it; and the receiver should not forget it." —ARAB PROVERB

Charity, recipients of: "Beware of the evil from the recipient of your charity." —ARAB PROVERB

Charm: "Charm is a way of getting the answer yes without having asked any clear question." —ALBERT CAMUS

Charter: A document that states principles, procedures, and institutions by which to regulate decisions and conduct as well as relations between those who subscribe to it.

Choices, bad: When all choices are bad, the worst will not seem so dreadful.

Circumstance: "Circumstance is neutral; by itself it imprisons more frequently than it helps. A statesman who cannot shape events will soon be engulfed by them; he will be thrown on the defensive, wrestling with tactics instead of advancing his purpose." —HENRY A. KISSINGER

Citizens abroad: It is to their ambassador that his compatriots first turn in case of natural disaster, war, or civil strife. They imagine that ambassadors are pampered, indolent, overpaid, and able to command miracles of attentiveness to their distress from the host government. An ambassador who fails to show the proper degree of passion for the welfare and well-being of his countrymen will see them turn on him to the detriment of his standing both back home and among nationals of the host country, with whom his compatriots will inevitably share their unfavorable view of him. So the protection of the resident nationals of his country is not only a duty for an ambassador, it is a matter touching the essence of his standing as his nation's representative.

Citizens abroad, entertainment of: It is expected that an ambassador will entertain the more prominent among his countrymen and women at his residence from time to time. If he does so with obvious economy, they will accuse him of lacking elegance; if he does so with uncommon style, they will charge him with extravagance. It is therefore wise for an ambassador to serve the simplest fare of his homeland, and to do so abundantly, at occasions at which his compatriots are present in numbers.

Citizens abroad, relations with: "The better that a diplomat's relations are with his countrymen living abroad, the more surely will he discover how large are the reciprocal benefits to be gained by this, for it will often happen that unofficial persons receive information as it were by accident which may be of the utmost importance [and] unless good relations exist [the diplomat] may remain in ignorance of important facts."
—FRANÇOIS DE CALLIÈRES, 1716

Civil wars, intervention in: There are three rules for intervening in civil wars. First, do not. Second, if you do, pick a side. Third, if you do pick a side, make sure it wins.

Civility: "Be civil to all; sociable to many; familiar with few."   —BENJAMIN FRANKLIN, 1756

Classification: Classification of material to establish its level of secrecy is intended to determine the amount of effort that should go into its protection, not its importance.

Cleverness: If you are sufficiently clever you may be able to outwit even yourself.

Client state: A state dependent on the political patronage, economic largesse, or military protection of a more powerful or wealthier state.

Client states: See also *Favoritism among nations.*

Client states: "There is nothing so imperious as feebleness which feels itself supported by force."   —NAPOLEON

Clientitis: See *Localitis.*

Coalition: A partnership between two or more states sharing common national security interests. A relatively stable coalition that has been formalized in treaties is termed an Alliance. See also *Entente.*

Coalitions: Coalitions are created out of fear, not out of affection between states.

Coalitions: Many rush to the aid of the victor; the allies of the defeated melt away.

Coalitions: "The basis of any Alliance, or Coalition, is an agreement between two or more sovereign States to subordinate their separate interests to a single purpose. So soon, however, as ultimate victory seems assured, the consciousness of separate interests tends to overshadow the sense of common purpose. The citizens of the several victorious countries seek rewards for their own sacrifices and compensations for their own suffering; they are apt to interpret these rewards and compensations in terms, not of international, but of national requirements. And the jealousies, rivalries and suspicions which in any protracted war arise between partners to an Alliance generate poisons which war-wearied arteries are too inelastic to eliminate." —HAROLD NICOLSON, 1946

Coalitions, as enemy weakens: "As long as the enemy is more powerful than any single member of a coalition, the need for unity outweighs all considerations of individual gain. Then the powers of repose can insist on the definition of war aims which, as all conditions, represent limitations. But when the enemy has been so weakened that each ally has the power to achieve its aims alone, a coalition is at the mercy of its most determined member. Confronted with the complete collapse of one of the elements of the equilibrium, all other powers will tend to raise their claims in order to keep pace." —HENRY A. KISSINGER, 1964

Coalitions, command and control: Wars cannot be fought successfully by committee; a simpler structure of command and control is required for victory. Wars must be led single-mindedly; they need a single point of authority to lead the collective enterprise, but the jealousies of coalition members make this resolution difficult.

Coalitions, command and control: "If a great state is forced to act in a situation of great peril, it must at least secure for itself the position of supreme leadership." —METTERNICH, 1854

Coalitions, diplomacy of: Coalition diplomacy is inherently clumsy, reflecting inhibitions and complexities born of unequal power, divergent leadership styles, and differing emphases and interests among the members of the coalition.

Coalitions, dissolution of: An alliance or coalition breaks up for many reasons: because the factor that brought it into being has disappeared or significantly changed; because it no longer appears that it can accomplish its purpose and continuing association with it comes to be seen by one or more member states as posing a greater risk of harm than dissociation from it; because one or more members has switched sides; or because victory in war has accomplished its basic objectives.

Coalitions, making and breaking: "Never be ashamed of making alliances, and of being yourself the only party that draws advantage from them. Do not commit that stupid fault of not abandoning them whenever it is in your interest to do so."—FREDERICK THE GREAT

Coalitions, natural history of: "It is the essence of a coalition, by definition almost, that the differences between its members and the common enemy are greater than their . . . differences among each other. Since the appearance of harmony is one of its most effective weapons, a coalition can never admit that one of its members may represent a threat almost as great as the common enemy and perhaps an increasingly greater one as victories alter the relative position of the powers. Coalitions between status quo and acquisitive powers are always a difficult matter, therefore, and tend to be based on either misunderstanding or evasion. A misunderstanding, because such a coalition will tend to solve peripheral questions—those of concern to only some of its members and which do not affect the basic power relationship—relatively easily, by a mutual recognition of special claims. And an evasion because the longer the settlement of fundamental questions is delayed during a successful war, the stronger the position of the acquisitive power becomes both militarily and psychologically. The total defeat of the enemy removes, if nothing else, a weight in the balance [of power] and confronts the status quo power with the alternative of surrender or a war with an erstwhile ally whose relative position has improved with the enemy's defeat." —HENRY A. KISSINGER, 1964

Coalitions, objectives: The fewer the objectives a coalition attempts to pursue, the fewer the points of friction among its members and the more durable their cohesion.

Coalitions, victory: Coalitions habitually celebrate victory by dividing into their constituent parts.

Coercion: Coercive measures unaccompanied by dialogue and a willingness to negotiate are not coercive diplomacy. They are bullying; they do not induce cooperation but excite the resentful resistance that is due all thuggery.

Colleagues: "Of all the peculiarities of diplomatic life, what most strikes the general public is the amicable and often cordial relations which exist between the diplomatists of the different countries and which produce between them, if policy and patriotism do not oppose it, a sort of corporate spirit and sometimes comradeship. Those who are surprised at this do not know what it is to remain for long years abroad, isolated and far from home. The young men who enter into the profession could not live the whole of their life leaving each other and finding each other again in the various capitals of the world, experiencing sometimes the same adventures, and gaining, by the same steps, the grades of their career, without feeling pleasure at meeting each other again." —JULES CAMBON

Colleagues: "The term colleague, habitually used by one diplomatist in referring to another, is not a meaningless or empty form. Commanders of opposing armies or admirals of different national navies never call each other colleagues, although the military

and naval professions are more ancient and just as aristocratic and world-wide as the diplomatic. The idea of the 'collegiality' of the diplomatic profession must not be exaggerated, but it is real, has been recognized since the seventeenth century, and has always conduced to peace."
—R.B. Mowat, 1936

Colleagues, utility of: In every diplomatic corps there are envoys who are fat with information and there are those who, starved for intelligence because they are unable to obtain their own insights into the dynamics of decision making in the host country, prey on those better informed than themselves. A diplomat with his own ample sources of information is well advised to keep his distance from those of his colleagues who seek a parasitical relationship with him; these colleagues will, after all, be available to him whenever he needs them. Instead, he should cultivate those as well or better informed than himself and share as much information as he is able to share with them. By establishing a reputation for being worth consulting among those of his colleagues who are themselves well informed about local events, a diplomat can ensure that they rely on him to check information of which they are unsure. In this way, he will gain access to much of what they know shortly after they learn it and will be able to give his own government the benefit of this knowledge in a timely way.

Colleagues, utility of: "An Ambassador may very probably find that his colleagues of the diplomatic corps in the capital where he resides may be of value to him. Since the whole diplomatic body labors to the same end, namely to discover what is happening, there arises a certain freemasonry of diplomacy, by which one colleague informs another of coming events which a lucky chance has enabled him to discern."
—François de Callières, 1716

Command, leadership: Command is not leadership. The hierarchy of organization predisposes men to take orders but does not prompt them to strive for excellence or to exceed minimal expectations. For this, leadership is required. It presupposes relationships of mutual respect and loyalty between leader and follower. Strangers do not follow with enthusiasm. They must be roused, inspired, persuaded, cajoled, and, if necessary, coerced by their peers into superior performance.

Command presence: A talent for command is essential to ambassadors and heads of delegations, both of whom must bend a heterogeneous group to a common purpose and make its members function as a team.

Commerce builds community: "Political Connections between Governments are neither useful nor lasting, unless they are rooted in the Sentiments and Sympathies of Nations; and it is only by extensive Commercial Intercourse that a Community of Interests can be established between the People of different Countries."
—Palmerston, 1836

Commerce, contrasted with diplomacy: "Business, like the law, is conducted within a framework of a regulated system with self-enforcing powers. Business to a large extent is regulated by the law of contracts. Even international business deals generally provide for arbitration in the court of one or the other contracting party. Diplomacy has been defined as 'commerce in mutual benefit' or the harmonizing of interests. Only as long as mutual benefits accrue or harmony prevails is there any real assurance that the agreements will be fulfilled." —CHARLES THAYER, 1974

Commerce, diplomacy and: "From its beginnings, . . . diplomacy has been especially concerned with trade; . . . back to the earliest diplomatic records which still survive." —ADAM WATSON, 1983

Commerce, imperialism of: "Commerce is entitled to a complete and efficient protection of all its legal rights, but the moment it presumes to control a country, or to substitute its fluctuating expedients for the high principles of natural justice that ought to lie at the root of every political system, it should be frowned on, and rebuked." —J. FENIMORE COOPER, 1838

Commerce, peace: "The natural effect of commerce is to lead to peace." —MONTESQUIEU

Commerce, peace and friendship: "Equal and exact justice to all men, of whatever state or persuasion, religious or political; peace, commerce, and honest friendship with all nations—entangling alliances with none . . . these principles form the bright constellation which has gone before us, and guided our steps through an age of revolution and reformation. The wisdom of our sages and the blood of our heroes have been devoted to their attainment. They should be the creed of our political faith—the text of civil instruction—the touchstone by which to try the services of those we trust." —THOMAS JEFFERSON, 1801

Commerce, promotion of, by ambassadors: Ambassadors must be their nation's chief trade promotion officers in the countries to which they are accredited.

Commerce, promotion of, by ambassadors: It is an ambassador's duty to secure the general welfare of his homeland by advancing its commercial interests. He should strive to open doors to competition for contracts and investments by his country's businesses, but they, and he, must recognize that only they can actually conclude and implement such contracts. In the end, trade rightly goes to those who offer the most attractive product, the best price, the most advantageous financing, and the fastest, most reliable delivery of the goods or services at issue, not to those who invoke political preference.

Commerce, selfish spirit of: "The selfish spirit of commerce knows no country; and feels no passion or principle but that of gain." —THOMAS JEFFERSON, 1809

Commerce, source of war: "There was never a war at arms that was not merely the extension of a preceding war of commerce grown fiercer until the weapons of commerce seemed no longer sufficiently deadly." —HUGH S. JOHNSON, 1935

Commitments: "Treaties must be observed." *[Pacta sunt servanda.]* —Latin proverb

Commitments of negotiators: Fidelity to commitments is the badge by which the character of nations is recognized. A government must honor commitments made by its negotiators in the course of reaching agreement with another state if it is to preserve its reputation for just and reasonable conduct of its international relations and its ability to reach subsequent agreements with others.

Communication among diplomats: "Communication among diplomats is a two-way street: one cannot expect to obtain much information unless one is able and willing to convey information. The ambassador with whom everyone wants to talk is the one who is interesting to talk with." —Karl Gruber, 1983

Communication, strategic: The military version of public diplomacy, defined as the process of understanding and engaging key audiences to create, strengthen, or preserve conditions conducive to the attainment of military campaign objectives through focused programs, media products, themes, and messages coordinated with actions applying all elements of national power.

Communications, security of: "The peacemaker requires secure reporting channels that protect him as well as the parties. Foreign parties are less likely to divulge their thinking on life-and-death security issues if the details of sensitive trades are going to appear in legislative hearings or media reports. In a democracy, there is a natural urge for openness, including full disclosure of other people's business. While respecting that urge, the mediator soon learns that the 'right' to information is most often asserted by those with the strongest motivation to scuttle the negotiation." —Chester A. Crocker, 1992

Communiqué: An artfully written, agreed summary of the main points of a diplomatic dialogue conducted at senior levels between two or more governments.

Community: A group of individuals or nations united in their view that disputes among them should be resolved or adjusted through processes of peaceful change to which they have agreed, without interference by those outside their group.

Compact: A formal agreement between two or more parties.

Compellence: See *Diplomacy, coercive.*

Compellence: "Compellence" is the use of coercive measures, especially threats, in an explicit or implicit bargaining process directed at causing another to take a desired course of action or reverse a current one.

Compellence, deterrence: Compellence is more demanding than deterrence. It seeks changes in behavior or the accommodation of foreign demands that can often be costly in terms of prestige or political legitimacy. Deterrence asks only acquiescence in the status quo.

Compromise: "[A compromise is] such an adjustment of conflicting interests as gives each adversary the satisfaction of thinking he has got what he ought not to have, and is deprived of nothing except what was justly his due." —AMBROSE BIERCE

Compromise: "In diplomacy, as in politics in general, compromise is essential; the interests of the opposition cannot be ignored. Give and take is crucial. One must think in terms of fifty-fifty, not seventy-thirty." —ISHII ITARO

Concessions: In negotiation, the more concessions are made, the more are expected by those receiving them. Therefore, while minor concessions may be necessary to establish mutual confidence that agreement is possible and to demonstrate good faith, the best strategy is usually to withhold major concessions until the final stage of negotiation, when they can be used to secure an agreement.

Concessions: "The heart of diplomacy is to grant graciously what you no longer have the power to withhold." —EDMUND BURKE

Concessions: "If one side tries to win everything without concessions of its own, favorable results cannot be obtained, and trust will be lost." —INOUE KAORU, 1884

Concessions: "Good diplomacy succeeds in ceding only the minimum necessary; bad diplomacy will give up more than is necessary. But in any case, it is necessary to give something, The principal function of the diplomat is that of comprehending the possibilities for negotiations at a determined moment, and promptly notifying his government which moment is more opportune or less opportune for negotiations." —PIETRO QUARONI, 1954

Concessions, sham: "One common method of minimizing real concessions and taking advantage of situational pressures to reciprocate concessions is to incorporate sham conditions into a basic negotiating platform, elevate them to the level of other 'genuine' demands, and try to barter them off for some gain." —MICHAEL BLAKER, 1977

Conciliation: The quasi-judicial process by which a third party (or group of parties or international organization) attempts to broker a solution to a dispute by assisting the parties to it to define the facts of a dispute and to reach agreement on the trade-offs necessary to resolve it. Conciliation, unlike mediation, presupposes that the conciliator is impartial, has no direct interests of its own at stake in the dispute, and will not itself intervene to alter the calculus of the parties. Contrast also *Arbitration*.

Conciliation: See also *Prenegotiation.*

Conciliation: "First, all means to conciliate; failing that, all means to crush."

—Cardinal Richelieu

Conciliators, motivations of: Conciliators are usually motivated by the judgment that they have a greater interest in settlement of a dispute by compromise than in seeing either party to it win. If this is not the case, then mediation, with its active and direct engagement in the interests of the parties, rather than the more disinterested process of conciliation, is probably appropriate.

Concord: Harmony, mutual agreement, and the absence of contention between two or more parties. Contrast *Peace.*

Concordat: A treaty concluded with a foreign state by the Vatican to establish the rights of the indigenous Roman Catholic Church vis-à-vis that state.

Condescension: Condescension is neither an argument nor a seductive stance.

Conference: An international meeting.

Conference, diplomacy by: "The most important elements of diplomacy by conference are elasticity of procedure, small numbers, informality, mutual acquaintance and, if possible, personal friendship among the principals, a proper perspective between secrecy in deliberation and publicity in results, reliable secretaries and interpreters. The more delicate the subjects, the more essential are these conditions."   —Lord Hankey, 1946

Conference, diplomacy by: "Conference, as a method of diplomatic procedure and settlement, . . . is the regular resource of all Governments when they are seriously looking for the solution of international questions. Apart from the greater or lesser degree of difficulty of the question at issue, the success of a Conference depends upon three things. The first, of course, is the temper and views of the negotiating parties; if they are calm and accommodating and fair-minded, the Conference has obviously a reasonable prospect of success. Secondly, the preparations made beforehand with a view to the Conference have a vital effect on the final course and result. Thirdly, the attitude of the public during the Conference has a very great influence on the decisions of the Conference."

—R.B. Mowat, 1936

Conferences: Multilateral conference rooms are good places to ratify agreements, but poor places to reach them. Conferences engender speeches; small gatherings promote dialogue. The most effective diplomatic dialogue is conducted bilaterally, in informal settings, and in small groups. Nothing significant gets accomplished at a large international conference except in the corridors, lounges, restaurants, and hotel rooms.

Conferences: "Conferences at the top level are always courteous. Name-calling is left to the foreign ministers." —W. AVERELL HARRIMAN, 1955

Conferences: "Conferences only succeed when their results are arranged beforehand." —QUOTED BY A.L. KENNEDY, 1922

Conferences: "Open negotiations incline negotiators to consider their own prestige and to maintain the dignity, the interests and the arguments of their sovereigns with undue obstinacy and prevent them from giving way to the frequently superior arguments of the occasion." —LOUIS XIV, AS QUOTED BY HAROLD NICOLSON

Conferences, criteria for success of: "There are several conditions to be met before diplomacy by conference will succeed. In the first place, all the parties should desire a real and permanent settlement of the question or questions involved. In other words, before a conference is called, there must be a broad preliminary basic agreement. In the second place, there must be a genuine desire on the part of the parties concerned for such agreement. In the third place, the negotiation should be carried on in confidence, if possible, free from the attacks of pressure groups." —ROBERTO REGALA, 1959, CITING SIR DAVID KELLY, 1956

Conferences, defects of: "In diplomatic conferences conducted in public, statesmen have necessarily to declare their aims and to state the position and requirements of their country. Having thus taken up a definite stand before the eyes of the whole world, the statesmen are not able to depart from their declaration, but are bound to go on insisting upon it. Thus compromise and agreement would tend to become impossible." —AUSTEN CHAMBERLAIN

Conferences, diplomats at: "The first duty of a diplomat, after a Congress, is to take care of his liver." —TALLEYRAND

Conferences, war: "I have always said that a conference was held for one reason only, to give everybody a chance to get sore at everybody else. Sometimes it takes two or three conferences to scare up a war, but generally one will do it." —WILL ROGERS, 1933

Confidences: Keeping confidences is central to diplomacy. It is a mark of diplomatic professionalism never to confide anything except what one wants more widely known.

Congress: See *Conference.*

Conquest: "All territorial expansion, all seizures by force or by cunning are merely the cruel workings of political madness and abused power, the effect of which is to increase administrative expense and confusion and to diminish the comfort and security of the governed merely to indulge the whim or vanity of their governors." —TALLEYRAND

Consent: Consent is dignified acceptance; humiliating acquiescence does not convey it.

Consistency: "Vacillation and inconsistency are as incompatible with successful diplomacy as they are with the national dignity." —BENJAMIN HARRISON, 1888

Constancy: "In . . . cases which involve imminent peril there will be found somewhat more of stability in republics than in princes. For even if the republics were inspired by the same feelings and intentions as the princes, yet the fact of their being slower will make them take more time in forming resolution, and therefore they will less promptly break their faith." —NICCOLÒ MACHIAVELLI

Constitution: The national charter and supreme law of a state.

Constructive: When used to describe a meeting, indicates that both sides have achieved a better understanding of each other's views and objectives, having made an effort to reach agreement but failed to do so.

Consul: A consul is an official agent sent by a state to reside in a foreign territory to assist and see to the general protection of its nationals there. Consuls are of four ranks: consul general, consul, vice consul, and consular agent. They exercise their powers in a district defined in an exequatur issued by the appropriate authority of the receiving state. Consuls encourage the development of economic, commercial, cultural, and scientific relations and report on conditions in their district; issue passports and visas; act as notaries, civil registrars, and the temporary administrators of estates; transmit judicial and other official documents; assure nondiscriminatory treatment for their nationals in local judicial, police, and penal institutions and arrange their repatriation; control and assist their nation's vessels and aircraft and their crews; and see to it that treaties and agreements are respected by the local authorities.

Consul: "In American politics, a person who having failed to secure an office from the people is given one by the Administration on condition that he leave the country." —AMBROSE BIERCE, 1906

Consul general: The head of a consulate general or the chief of a large consular section in an embassy. The title ranks with that of counselor but consuls general are often much senior in personal rank to counselors of embassy.

Consul, honorary: A host-country national appointed by a foreign state to perform limited consular functions in a locality where the appointing state has no other consular representation. See also *Consular agent.*

Consular agent: An official doing consular work for a state in a locality where it does not maintain a regular consulate. This official is often, but not always, a national of his host state, and his work is usually part-time.

Consulate: An office established by one state in an important city of another state, usually outside its capital city (unless diplomatic relations have not been established), to support and protect its citizens traveling, residing, or doing business there, to promote bilateral trade, and to facilitate travel through the issuance of visas and passports. A consulate established in a country where there is an embassy is subordinate to the ambassador or chargé d'affaires. Consulates are headed by consuls.

Consulate general: A large consulate headed by a consul general. See *Consulate*. Also, the consular section of a large embassy.

Consuls: "Consuls are the Cinderellas of the diplomatic service."
—A CONSUL, QUOTED BY ERIC CLARK

Consuls: "The powers [of consular officers] are infinitely varied. They are in the position of exercising throughout the extent of their district the functions of judge, arbitrator, and conciliator for their compatriots; often, they are officers charged with vital statistics; they carry out the tasks of notaries, and sometimes those of shipping administrator; they survey and note health conditions. It is they who, through their regular reports, can give a true and complete idea of the state of commerce, of navigation and of the characteristic industry of the country in which they reside."   —TALLEYRAND

Contacts: "The chief task of a diplomat abroad is always . . . work on human flesh, that is to say, the correct treatment of strangers with the object of realizing tangible, factual successes. Keep in touch with colleagues and do not cower inside four walls like the werewolf. But at the same time, don't let your colleagues tell you any lies or exploit you. Pas trop de zèle is a golden rule when rightly understood."   —HEINRICH VON BÜLOW

Contacts: "Be very cautious in any country, or at any court, of such as, on your first arrival, appear the most eager to make your acquaintance and communicate their ideas to you. I have ever found their professions insincere, and their intelligence false. . . . They are either persons who are not considered or respected in their own country, or are put about you to entrap and circumvent you as newly arrived."   —LORD MALMESBURY, 1813

Contention: "Without sincerity and truthfulness, contention is merely intrigue and leads to misfortune."   —CHENG YI

Contentious situations: "There are four methods of dealing with these: conciliation, placating with gifts, sowing dissension, and the use of force. It is easier to employ a method earlier in this sequence than a later one. Placating with gifts is twice as hard as conciliation, sowing dissension three times as hard, and use of force four times."
—ARTHASASTRA OF KAUTILYA

Convention: A treaty, usually between more than two states, concerning matters of mutual interest.

Conversation: A diplomat must have a talent for making intimate talk unthreatening and easy.

Cooks: "Entertain handsomely. A good cook is often an excellent conciliator."
—FRANÇOIS DE CALLIÈRES, 1716

Coordination, policy: "One can always get an agreed paper by increasing the vagueness of its statements. The staff of any interdepartmental committee has a fatal weakness for this type of agreement by exhaustion."   —DEAN ACHESON

Cordial: When used to describe a meeting, generally indicates that the discussion was devoid of substance and yielded no concrete results.

Cordiality: "Cordiality as between nations can only rest on mutual self-respect."
—LORD ROSEBERY

Corps, consular: The community of consuls general, consuls, and vice consuls in a foreign city.

Corps, diplomatic: The community of foreign diplomats assembled in the capital of a state. The corps is headed by a Dean, who is usually the ambassador with the longest period of service as such in that capital.

Corps, diplomatic: "The diplomatic corps in each capital, that is the diplomatic missions taken together, acts as a multilateral network of diplomatic brokerage. . . . Ambassadors accredited to a capital often need to coordinate their actions and their reports with colleagues. These exchanges extend to most other diplomats in the capital, at various levels of seniority. There is a constant dialogue, and much mutual adjustment of the various embassies' assessments of the host government's policies and intentions. There can be no resident diplomat in an embassy abroad who has not had the experience of having his understanding of some aspect of the host government's policy corrected and amplified by a member of another embassy which happened to be better informed on that issue."
—ADAM WATSON, 1983

Counsel: "The first condition of a good counselor is that his ends, and interest, be not inconsistent with the ends and interest of him he counseleth."   —THOMAS HOBBES, 1651

Counselor (of Embassy): The title of a senior embassy official, usually charged with direction of an important function and embassy section, such as political, economic, commercial, or public affairs. Counselors rank with consuls general, below ministers and minister-counselors, and above first secretaries.

Coup d'état: The overthrow, usually by force, of an existing régime by elements within it.

Courage: Conspicuous courage by statesmen in war can lay a basis for transforming military defeat into political victory.

Courier, diplomatic: The diplomatically privileged escort of diplomatic pouches ("bags") between embassies and foreign ministries, whose passage may not be impeded by foreign states.

Courtesy: Courtesy keeps doors open; discourtesy locks them shut.

Courtesy: Courtesy seldom costs anything and the willingness to extend it in times of tension shows confident strength, firm self-control, and a judicious temperament.

Courtesy: "Courtesy means controlled elegance embodying feelings."
—HUAINANZI, AS TRANSLATED BY THOMAS CLEARY

Courtesy: "Courtesy, moderation, and self-restraint should mark international, no less than private, intercourse."
—THEODORE ROOSEVELT, 1904

Covenant: A morally binding agreement between two or more parties, committing them to do or to refrain from doing certain things.

Credentials: Letters given to an ambassador by his chief of state, addressed to the chief of state of his host country, to whom the ambassador delivers them when first received by him. The letters, which are termed "letters of credence," request the receiving chief of state to give "full credence" to what the ambassador will say on behalf of his government. An ambassador is not formally recognized as such by the host country until he has presented his credentials to its chief of state; he cannot act in his official capacity as ambassador outside his embassy until he has done so.

Credibility: Credibility like virginity, once breached, cannot be recovered.

Credibility: When policies begin to fail, those who crafted or supported them argue that national credibility would be irreparably harmed by their abandonment. But persistence in policies destined to fail produces not just failure but a reputation for failure.

Credibility: "Diplomacy is always equal. It's like good bookkeeping. He don't believe you and you don't believe him, so it always balances."
—WILL ROGERS, 1927

Crimes, war: Legal penalties for violation of the "laws" of war or crimes against civilian populations imposed by the victors on the defeated after a war. Threatening an adversary with trial for war crimes is usually counterproductive unless one is prepared to conquer and occupy the adversary's territory. Otherwise it simply gives the adversary an added reason to resist capitulation to one's demands, convincing the adversary that he has more to lose from meeting one's terms than from continued defiance.

Crises: "Never treat crises when they're cold, only when they're hot."

—HENRY A. KISSINGER

Crises: "International crises have their advantages. They frighten the weak but stir and inspire the strong."

—JAMES RESTON, 1967

Crises: "In critical situations, let women run things."

—TALLEYRAND

Crises, response of international organizations to: The usual response of international organizations to crises passes through predictable phases: they ignore the problem; they issue a statement of concern about it; they wring their hands while sitting on them; they declare that they remain seized of the matter; they adjourn.

Crises, talk: One time-honored way to deflate a crisis is to talk it to death. Lofty talk and platitudinous speeches are well-known antidotes for adrenaline.

Crisis, response: Better to do something adequate at once than something perfect when it's too late.

Criticism, of host country: "A native occasionally makes disparaging remarks about his own country. A diplomatist should think at least twice before he expresses agreement with them."

—ERNEST SATOW

Critics of diplomats and diplomacy: "The curious thing is that almost any critic of diplomacy or of diplomats would welcome a diplomatic appointment, if it were to take him to his favorite foreign locality, and providing he would not have to stay with it when the going got tough."

—RICHARD FYFE BOYCE, 1956

Cultural differences, in negotiation: Ideas often do not have the same meaning in different societies, especially where there is no obvious common cultural heritage. It can therefore be a fatal error to view an adversary's stance through the prism of one's own values. It is a delusion to base one's search for a peaceful resolution of differences on the self-centered premise that the other side feels secret guilt about its stance and can be embarrassed into concessions by public or private condemnation. Such an approach is more likely to infuriate than to conciliate.

Customs: "If one were to offer men to choose out of all the customs in the world such as seemed to them best, they would examine the whole number, and end by preferring their own; so convinced are they that their own usages far surpass those of others."

—HERODOTUS

Customs: "Never attempt to export [your country's] habits and manners, but to conform as far as possible to those of the country where you reside—to do this even in the most trivial things—to learn to speak their language, and never to sneer at what may strike you as singular and absurd. Nothing goes to conciliate so much, or to amalgamate you more cordially with its inhabitants, as this very easy sacrifice of your national prejudices to theirs." —Lord Malmesbury, 1813

Customs, consequences of ignorance of: "Ignorance of each other's ways and lives has been a common cause . . . of that suspicion and mistrust between peoples of the world through which their differences have all too often broken into war."
—United Nations Educational, Scientific and Cultural
Organization (UNESCO) Charter

D

Damage, battle: Battle damage is a measure of the pain that military operations are inflicting on an enemy, not a yardstick of success. Success in war is measured in the political effects of the pain it administers, not its intensity.

Damage, collateral: Injuries to noncombatants in military operations more often rouse a populace to active antagonism than cow it into submission. Injustice to civilians provides a motivation for enemy forces to fight on, not to surrender.

Deadlines: Don't set deadlines; they focus resistance. If you must set a deadline, make sure both that you can enforce it and that it is feasible and more likely than not to be met. If you set a deadline that passes, enforce it or forfeit credibility both at home and abroad.

Dean: The ambassador who represents the diplomatic corps to the host government on matters of a ceremonial or administrative matter touching the collective interests of the corps and its members. In most countries, the dean is the ambassador who has been at his post the longest. In some Catholic countries, however, the dean is always the papal nuncio. See also *Doyenne*.

Decadence: Decadence is the "point at which good intentions exceed the power to fulfill them."
                                                                    —Jacques Barzun

Deceit: "Although deceit is detestable in all other things, yet in the conduct of war it is laudable and honorable; and a commander who vanquishes an enemy by stratagem is equally praised with one who gains victory by force."   —Niccolò Machiavelli

Deceit: "The rulers of the state are the only ones who should have the privilege of lying, either at home or abroad; they may be allowed to lie for the good of the state."
                                                                    —Plato, c. 390 b.c.

Deceit: "The only real diplomacy ever performed by a diplomat is in deceiving their own people after their dumbness has got them into a war."   —Will Rogers, 1949

Deceit: "Whatever the qualifications of a modern diplomat, the art of deceit is certainly not one of them."
                                                                    —Charles W. Thayer

Deceit: "The frequent resort to deceit is self-defeating because a state which is careless about what credence is placed in the word of its diplomats on individual occasions will soon find that its word is not believed in any context. When that happens and its credibility is debased, a state finds it difficult to make agreements with any but fickle partners. There is no substitute for trust in diplomacy." —ADAM WATSON, 1983

Deceit, countering: "Modern students of international affairs . . . tend to identify peace, stability, and the quiescence of conflict with notions like trust, good faith, and mutual respect. To the extent that this point of view actually encourages trust and respect it is good. But where trust and good faith do not exist and cannot be made to by our acting as though they did, we may wish to solicit advice from the underworld, or from ancient despotisms, on how to make agreements work when trust and good faith are lacking and there is no legal recourse for breach of contract. The ancients exchanged hostages, drank wine from the same glass to demonstrate the absence of poison, met in public places to inhibit the massacre of one by the other, and even deliberately exchanged spies to facilitate transmittal of authentic information. It seems likely that a well-developed theory of strategy could throw light on the efficacy of some of these old devices, suggest the circumstances in which they apply, and discover modern equivalents that, though offensive to our taste, may be desperately needed in the regulation of conflict." —THOMAS C. SCHELLING, 1960

Deceit, the "Eleventh Commandment": "Thou shalt not be found out." —PALMERSTON

Deception: "I have found out the art of deceiving diplomatists. I speak the truth, and I am certain they will not believe me." —COUNT CAMILLO BENSO DI CAVOUR

Deception: "Deception is central to most of the techniques of statecraft." —JAMES EAYRS, 1965

Deception: "Force and deception govern international relations."—GYULA SZILASSY, 1928

Deception: "No enterprise is more likely to succeed than one concealed from the enemy until it is ripe for execution." —NICCOLÒ MACHIAVELLI

Deception, military: "Using force is a matter of deception. Therefore, if one has a certain capability, one should present oneself as having no such capability; if one is close to something, one should present oneself as being distant from that thing; if one is distant from something, one should present oneself as being close to that thing. If the other side's interest is at stake, induce it; if there is chaos on the other side, take it; if the other side is solid, be prepared; if the other side is strong, avoid it; if the other side is angry, provoke it; if the other side is humble, make it cocky; if the other side is well rested, tire it; if the other side is on good terms with someone, sow discord among them. Catch the other side unprepared, and take the other side by surprise. Such ways of winning militarily cannot be stated beforehand." —SUNZI

Deception, press reporting and: Open and apparently accurate reporting by journalists of preparations for war paradoxically places a premium on deceptive measures by responsible governments. When there is no censorship of the press, deception through diversionary measures is necessary to misdirect the attention of an observant enemy from the truth and to assure that war plans can be executed successfully, with minimal casualties.

Declaration: A statement of policy by a state or a statement by two or more states on a principle of international law as jointly understood by them.

Defeat: "In politics there is no place for pity."

—OTTO VON BISMARCK

Defeat: "There are always two parties to each treaty of peace, the victor and the vanquished. History has not yet witnessed a case where a defeated nation, or coalition of nations, rose from the signing of the treaty sealing its defeat with a feeling of friendship or gratitude to the victor, whose concessions are usually not large nor are they considered by the vanquished anything but the hardest terms of peace to which the victor can force him. The defeated nation naturally strives to obliterate moral and material losses and to avenge grievances sustained through the unsuccessful war and the treaty of peace dictated by the victor with only a semblance of negotiation on an equal footing."

—MICHAEL DEMIASHKEVICH, 1934

Defeat: "A nation defeated in war and . . . occupied by foreign troops has basically two choices. It can challenge the victor in the hope of making enforcement of the peace too painful; or it can cooperate with the victor while regaining strength for a later confrontation. Both strategies contain risks. After a military defeat, resistance invites a test of strength at the moment of maximum weakness; collaboration risks demoralization, because policies which appeal to the victor also tend to confuse the public opinion of the vanquished."

—HENRY A. KISSINGER, 1994

Defeat, diplomacy and: "Men begin with blows, and when a reverse comes upon them, then have recourse to words."

—ATHENIAN AMBASSADORS TO THE LACEDAEMONIANS, 433 B.C., QUOTED BY THUCYDIDES

Defeat, instruction from: Victory teaches those who gain it little. Even fools learn from defeat.

Defeat, strategic: Strategic defeat is the failure to achieve war aims, as much as loss on the battlefield, the discrediting of deterrent power, withdrawal under fire to more defensible positions, the forced surrender of territory, foreign occupation, or the annihilation of sovereignty. Withdrawal to more defensible positions is a tactical but not a strategic defeat. Sometimes it is necessary to accept a lesser defeat to avoid a greater one.

Defeatism: "The man who enters the conference room bowed by the conviction that he is likely to be beaten at the table is clearly a bad diplomat." —IVONE KIRKPATRICK, 1959

Defense, destruction: Military operations that invite the destruction of what they are intended to defend are self-defeating. One cannot save something by provoking others to destroy it.

Defense, retreat: It is not always true that the best defense is a good offense. Sometimes the best defense is retreat to a stronger and less vulnerable position.

Delay: "Time is the very material commodity which the Foreign Office is expected to provide in the same way as other departments provide other war materiel."
—Robert, 1st Baron Vansittart, 1936

Delay, in war: "In war, when adversaries are orderly in their movements and are at their sharpest, it is not yet time to fight with them; it is best to fortify your position and wait. Watch for their energy to wane after being on alert for a long time; then rise and strike them. You will not fail to win. The rule [from the Zuo Zhuan] is 'Delay until others wane.'"
—Liu Ji

Delay, incompetence as excuse for: Deliberate incompetence in communications or in carrying out a task may sometimes be the best means of gaining time. The best qualified to be credibly incompetent are educators and trainers, for the richest cookbook for such incompetence lies in the memorable errors of those they have trained.

Delay, utility of, in negotiations: Sometimes the best reason to negotiate is to temporize. Negotiation can preclude the imposition of a settlement by war. It can allow the situation to evolve in your favor. It can delay the outbreak of hostilities and give your own nation more time to prepare adequately to defend itself or to attack.

Demagoguery: Demagoguery needs an enemy and will always find one.

Demands, public: Don't make public demands of others unless you have reason to believe they will comply or are looking for an excuse to punish them for failing to do so.

Démarche: An official representation by a diplomat to host country officials, usually encompassing a request for action or decision on a matter of concern to the diplomat's government.

Démarches, level of: "Governments which attach importance to getting their messages to those in authority in other states as accurately and persuasively as possible have found by experience that the most effective way to do this is to instruct their own representative in a foreign capital to state and explain their views at or as close as possible to the effective level of decision-making in the other governments concerned. This does not always, or indeed usually, mean the top, even though the President or Chancellor or Prime Minister has the ultimate right of approval or rejection. For the effective decision is likely to be made lower down, by experts who understand the complexities of the subject, in the light of general guidelines laid down from the top. These effective decisions take the form of recommendations to the foreign minister, which he or the head of the government may reject but which he is unlikely to do if they conform to the government's lines of policy. A particular recommendation at the right level can thus often clinch the business. Unfavourable recommendations by experts in a ministry of foreign affairs, on the other hand, once fed in are much harder for a foreign ambassador to surmount at a higher level. Therefore well-run embassies make sure that they explain their government's views and wishes persuasively to the experts whose formulation of recommendations will go far to determine the decision their government makes."

—ADAM WATSON, 1983

Démarches, perils of embellishment: "If relations between states are close, they may establish mutual trust through daily interaction; but if relations are distant, mutual confidence can only be established by exchanges of messages. Messages must be conveyed by messengers [diplomats]. Their contents may be either pleasing to both sides or likely to engender anger between them. Faithfully conveying such messages is the most difficult task under the heavens, for if the words are such as to evoke a positive response on both sides, there will be the temptation to exaggerate them with flattery and, if they are unpleasant, there will be a tendency to make them even more biting. In either case, the truth will be lost. If truth is lost, mutual trust will also be lost. If mutual trust is lost, the messenger himself may be imperilled. Therefore, I say to you it is a wise rule: 'always to speak the truth and never to embellish it. In this way, you will avoid much harm to yourselves.'"

—ZHUANGZI

Demeanor: "One has to behave as friend or foe according to the circumstances."

—THUCYDIDES

Democracies, concessions by: Governments must be strong domestically to make concessions to foreigners and their interests. When nations are internally divided, governments are often too weak to compromise with foreign opponents, even when they judge it in the interest of their state to do so. Democratic systems of government presuppose the primacy of domestic interests and competition among them; thus, democracy entails a certain level of internal division on even the least controversial issues. Not surprisingly, therefore, democracies find it peculiarly difficult to accommodate foreign interests and thus to avoid the slide toward open conflict with foreign states.

Democracies, diplomacy in: "Ambassadors have no battleships at their disposal, or heavy infantry, or fortresses; their weapons are words and opportunities. In important transactions opportunities are fleeting; once they are missed they cannot be recovered. It is a greater offense to deprive a democracy of an opportunity than it would be thus to deprive an oligarchy or an autocracy. Under their systems, action can be taken instantly and on the word of command; but with us, first the Council has to be notified and adopt a provisional resolution, and then only when the heralds and the Ambassadors have sent in a note in writing. Then the Council has to convene the Assembly, but then only on a statutory date. Then the debater has to prove his case in face of an ignorant and often corrupt opposition; and even when this endless procedure has been completed, and a decision has been come to, even more time is wasted before the necessary financial resolution can be passed. Thus an ambassador who, in a constitution such as ours, acts in a dilatory manner and causes us to miss our opportunities, is not missing opportunities only, but robbing us of the control of events." —Demosthenes

Democracies, diplomacy in: "There is a propensity that induces democracies to obey impulse rather than prudence and to abandon a mature design for the gratification of momentary passion." —Alexis de Tocqueville

Democracies, unaggressive nature of: The thesis that democracies are inherently unaggressive will not withstand the scrutiny of history. In countries with a free parliament and a free press, legislators and journalists can arouse national passions and make it much more difficult for their government to place other interests ahead of ideological imperatives or to overlook insults to the national honor than is the case in autocratic systems of government. Passion is the most common, and at the same time the most tragic, cause of war; it is also a failing to which democracies are peculiarly susceptible.

Democracies, unaggressive nature of: "It is a profound and dangerous illusion to believe that war is always made in the Cabinets of statesmen, and that more and direct popular participation of the crowd in foreign policy will always be a guarantee of peace. Alas! crowds have their psychology, singular unforeseeable and dangerous, their fits of anger, their caprices, their anxieties, their summary and brutal enquiries."
—H. Hauser, 1929, quoted by R.B. Mowat, 1936

Democracies, war and peace: "There are two things that a democratic people will always find very difficult, to begin a war and to end it." —Alexis de Tocqueville, 1840

Deniability, plausible: Covert action that is not plausibly deniable incurs all of the political costs of overt action but few of its possible benefits.

Deportation: A legal procedure undertaken by a state to expel an undesired foreigner from its territory.

Desperation: If all choices are disastrous, the one that is worst for one's opponents is likely the best.

Detainee: A person held in custody for questioning, especially with regard to alleged political offenses.

Détente: An easing of acute tension between states that has carried with it the danger of war, without, however, settling most disagreements or removing the underlying conflicts of interest.

Détente: "A détente has no significance unless it represents facts." —JEAN MONNET

Deterrence: "Let them hate us as long as they fear us." —CALIGULA

Deterrence: "Deterrence consists essentially of an effort by one actor to persuade an opponent not to take action of some kind against his interests by convincing the opponent that the costs and risks of doing so will outweigh what he hopes to gain thereby. . . . The first step in formulating a deterrence policy is to weigh the interests of one's country that are engaged in the area which may be threatened by hostile action and to assess how important they are. The next step is to formulate and convey to the opponent a commitment to defend those interests. The deterring power backs its commitments by threats to respond if the opponent acts. Such threats must be both credible and sufficiently potent in the eyes of the opponent—that is, pose a level of costs and risks that he regards as of sufficient magnitude to overcome his motivation to challenge the defending power's position." —GORDON A. CRAIG AND ALEXANDER L. GEORGE, 1983

Deterrence: "When the aggressor judges a commitment to be lacking, the most rational strategy available to him for challenging the status quo is the fait accompli—the quick, decisive use of ample force to achieve the objective before the potential defender of the state subjected to attack can reconsider its policy and decide to intervene." —ALEXANDER L. GEORGE, 1993

Deterrence: "One sword keeps another in the sheath." —GEORGE HERBERT, 1651

Deterrence: "Mutual cowardice keeps us in peace." —SAMUEL JOHNSON, 1778

Deterrence: "The whole world stands in awe of the king ready to strike." —ARTHASASTRA OF KAUTILYA

Deterrence: "From the point of view of deterrence a seeming weakness will have the same consequence as an actual one. A gesture intended as a bluff but taken seriously is more useful as a deterrent than a bona fide threat interpreted as bluff. Deterrence requires a combination of power, the will to use it, and the assessment of these by the potential aggressor. Moreover, deterrence is a product of those factors and not a sum. If any one of them is zero, deterrence fails. Strength, no matter how overwhelming, is useless without the will to resort to it. Power combined with willingness will be ineffective if the aggressor does not believe in it or if the risks of war do not appear sufficiently unattractive to him." —HENRY A. KISSINGER, 1960

Deterrence: "Speak softly and carry a big stick; you will go far." —THEODORE ROOSEVELT, 1901

Deterrence: "To be prepared for war is one of the most effectual ways of preserving peace." —GEORGE WASHINGTON, 1790

Deterrence, defined: Deterrence is the use of the threat of violent retaliation to preclude others from the coercive use of violence or the threat of it.

Deterrence, defined: Deterrence is the forestalling of threats or adverse actions through the creation of a perception on the part of a potential opponent that such threats or actions will yield little or no net gain but may instead result in humiliation, loss, injury, maiming, or annihilation.

Deterrence, strategy of: "The strategy of deterrence requires communicating a threat so potent and credible in the opponent's judgment that he will conclude that the probable costs and risks of moving against the victim . . . clearly outweigh the expected benefits." —ALEXANDER L. GEORGE, 1993

Dialogue: Keep your friends close; keep your enemies even closer. —MAFIA ADAGE

Dialogue, diplomatic: Diplomatic dialogue is not a reward for good behavior by friendly countries but a tool for dealing with difficult ones.

Differences among friends: Small differences must not damage great friendships.

Dining, social bonding: "The man with whom I do not dine is a barbarian to me." —GRAFFITO PRESERVED ON A WALL IN ANCIENT POMPEII

Dinner parties: "Above all, do not fail to give good dinners, and to pay attention to the women." —NAPOLEON, ADVICE TO HIS AMBASSADOR TO LONDON, 1802

Diplomacy: "Men began . . . almost in the first infancy of the world to exercise this office, trying to make peace and coalitions for war." —GASPARO BRAGACCIA, 1626

Diplomacy: "Of survival it has been said that the bird is evolution's device for the perpetuation of the egg. Diplomacy too must sometimes appear to be the diplomat's invention for the perpetuation of his profession—hence the legendary diplomat riposting to the condescension of the generals that they would have no wars to fight were it not for him." —GEOFFREY JACKON, 1981

Diplomacy: "Diplomacy is the police in grand costume." —NAPOLEON, 1805

Diplomacy: "Diplomacy is the application of intelligence and tact to the conduct of official relations between governments of independent states." —ERNEST SATOW, 1917

Diplomacy, abuse of: "Diplomatic institutions . . . are designed for the business of adjustment. The abuse of diplomacy within its accustomed connections with power and interests is one thing: the damage is limited and usually reparable. But the misuse of diplomatic institutions as vehicles for propaganda and subversion, or for the championing of political righteousness and ideological warfare, is quite another, and can be more seriously damaging because it is more nearly an inversion than an abuse of diplomatic method and can inhibit real dialogue between certain states altogether."

—ADAM WATSON, 1983

Diplomacy, adjustment of quarrels: Diplomacy is the means by which states peacefully adjust their quarrels and quell their controversies.

Diplomacy, aim of, durable relations: "Diplomacy should aim, not at incidental or opportunist arrangements, but at creating solid and durable relations."

—HAROLD NICOLSON, CITING CARDINAL RICHELIEU

Diplomacy, alternative to force: "Diplomacy is the best thing which civilization has yet thought of for preventing force alone from governing the relations of states."

—ALBERT DE BROGLIE

Diplomacy, amateur: "Diplomacy is an ancient and much-maligned profession that commands about as much respect as the world's oldest. Indeed, both are being seriously undermined these days by ruinous competition from amateurs."   —MARSHALL GREEN

Diplomacy, bargaining: Diplomacy is tactfully intelligent bargaining based on interests and free from sentimentality.

Diplomacy, beginnings: "The beginnings of diplomacy occurred when the first human societies decided that it was better to hear a message than to eat the messenger."

—KEITH HAMILTON AND RICHARD T.B. LANGHORNE, 1995

Diplomacy, breakout: Breakout diplomacy bears the same resemblance to static, positional diplomacy as maneuver warfare does to the war of attrition. It punches through long established positions and lines of confrontation, bypasses fortified differences, and advances into previously unoccupied areas of agreement, leaving bypassed differences to be mopped up later or to wither away with time.

Diplomacy, coercive: "Coercive diplomacy (or compellence . . .) employs threats or limited force to persuade an opponent to call off or undo an encroachment—for example, to halt an invasion or give up territory which has been occupied. Coercive diplomacy . . . differs from deterrence, . . . which employs threats to dissuade an opponent from undertaking an action that he has not yet initiated. . . . It seeks to persuade the opponent to cease his aggression rather than bludgeon him into stopping. In contrast to the crude use of force to repel the opponent, coercive diplomacy emphasizes the use

of threats and the exemplary use of limited force to persuade him to back down. The strategy of coercive diplomacy calls for using just enough force to demonstrate resolution to protect one's interests and to emphasize the credibility of one's determination to use more force if necessary. . . . One gives the opponent an opportunity to stop or back off before employing force or escalating its use. . . . To this end, the employment of threats and of initially limited force is closely coordinated with appropriate communications to the opponent. All-important signaling, bargaining, and negotiating dimensions, therefore, are built into the strategy of coercive diplomacy."
—GORDON A. CRAIG AND ALEXANDER L. GEORGE, 1983

Diplomacy, coercive: "The general concept of coercive diplomacy becomes a strategy only when the policymaker . . . [decides]: (1) what to demand of the opponent; (2) whether—and how—to create in the adversary's mind a sense of urgency about complying with the demand; (3) how to create a threat of punishment for noncompliance that is sufficiently credible and potent in the adversary's mind to persuade him that compliance is more in his interest than facing the consequences; and (4) whether to couple the threatened punishment with positive inducements—a 'carrot'—to make it easier for the adversary to comply. It should go without saying that the more far-reaching the demand, the stronger the opponent's motivation to resist and the more difficult the task of coercive diplomacy."
—ALEXANDER L. GEORGE, 1993

Diplomacy, combat: Diplomacy is unarmed combat between states.

Diplomacy, communication: "To effect the communication between one's own government and other governments or individuals abroad and to do this with maximum accuracy, imagination, tact, and good sense."
—GEORGE F. KENNAN, 1961

Diplomacy, contrasted with law: "Diplomacy mediates not between right and wrong but between conflicting interests. It seeks to compromise not between legal equities but between national aspirations."
—CHARLES W. THAYER, 1959

Diplomacy, deceit: Diplomacy is "an honored mode of deceit."
—ANONYMOUS, LA EMBAJADA ESPAÑOLA

Diplomacy, deceit: Diplomacy is "to lie and deny."
—ATTRIBUTED TO TALLEYRAND

Diplomacy, defense and: "Diplomacy and defense are not substitutes for one another. Either alone would fail."
—JOHN F. KENNEDY, 1961

Diplomacy, defensive: "Diplomacy must be judged by what it prevents, not only by what it achieves."
—ABBA EBAN, 1983

Diplomacy, defined: Diplomacy is the pursuit of interests abroad by measures short of war.

Diplomacy, defined: "Diplomacy—the patriotic art of lying for one's country."
—AMBROSE BIERCE

Diplomacy, defined: "Diplomacy is to speak French, to speak nothing, and to speak falsehood."
—LUDWIG BOERNE

Diplomacy, defined: "Diplomacy . . . is skill or address in the conduct of international intercourse and negotiations."
—EDMUND BURKE, CITED BY SIR ERNEST SATOW

Diplomacy, defined: "Diplomacy is the art of saying 'Nice doggie' till you can find a rock."
—WYNN CATLIN

Diplomacy, defined: "Diplomacy [is] the peaceful conduct of relations amongst political entities, their principals and accredited agents."
—KEITH HAMILTON AND RICHARD T.B. LANGHORNE, 1995

Diplomacy, defined: "Diplomacy is the art of lubricating the wheels of international relations."
—SISLEY HUDDLESTON, 1954

Diplomacy, defined: "Diplomacy, the art of relating states to each other by agreement rather than by the exercise of force."
—HENRY A. KISSINGER

Diplomacy, defined: "Modern usage . . . generally employs the word ['diplomacy'] in two basic senses. First is the policy sense, as when one speaks of approving a nation's diplomacy, meaning the foreign policies which govern its relations with other nations. The second refers to the carrying out of foreign policy: that is the actual conduct of these relations. Professional diplomats . . . are those officials whom their governments have employed full time in support of their diplomatic efforts. The focus of professional diplomats is on policy execution, rather than on policy formation. They have, however, an important role in both."
—WILLIAM MACOMBER, 1975

Diplomacy, defined: "Diplomacy is the expression of national strength in terms of gentlemanly discourse."
—ROBERT McCLINTOCK, 1964

Diplomacy, defined: "If politics is the art of the possible, diplomacy is the art of taking the possible beyond its local dimensions."
—ROBERT J. MOORE, 1985

Diplomacy, defined: "Diplomacy is "the management of the relations between independent States by the process of negotiation."
—HAROLD NICOLSON

Diplomacy, defined: "Diplomacy is letting someone else have your way."
—LESTER B. PEARSON, 1965

Diplomacy, defined: "Diplomacy is the political process by which political entities (generally states) establish and maintain official relations, direct and indirect, with one another, in pursuing their respective goals, objectives, interests, and substantive and procedural policies in the international environment; as a political process it is dynamic, adaptive, and changing, and it constitutes a continuum; functionally it embraces both the making and implementation of foreign policy at all levels, centrally and in the field, and involves essentially, but is not restricted to the functions of representation, reporting, communicating, negotiating, and maneuvering, as well as caring for the interests of nationals abroad."   —ELMER PLISCHKE, 1972

Diplomacy, defined: "Diplomacy is the art of resolving international difficulties peacefully. It is also the technique which reigns over the development, in a harmonious manner, of international relations."   —JOHN R. WOOD AND JEAN SERRES, 1970

Diplomacy, defined: "All diplomacy is continuation of war by other means."
                                        —ZHOU ENLAI, 1954

Diplomacy, democratic: Diplomacy is the most difficult of the political arts. It requires empathy, which is especially hard for democracies, given their natural fixation on the views of their own citizen-voters and concomitant disdain for the views of foreigners, who, after all, can't and don't vote.

Diplomacy, domestic politics and: "Diplomacy must be handled outside domestic political conflict. Especially since it requires working with another side, diplomacy will fail if one presses his own extreme interests according to the dictates of domestic politics."
                                        —UGAKI KAZUSHIGE

Diplomacy, fairness in: "The best diplomacy is that which gets its own way, but leaves the other side reasonably satisfied. It is often good diplomacy to resist a score."
                                        —ANTHONY EDEN

Diplomacy, language: "Diplomacy is primarily words that prevent us from reaching for our swords."   —DRAZEN PEHAR

Diplomacy, logic of: "The ultima ratio . . . of all effective diplomacy . . . is war."
                                        —CARL J. FRIEDRICH, 1963

Diplomacy, management of nation's business: Diplomacy is the management of the business of the nation with foreign lands by measures short of war or the use of secret agents.

Diplomacy, mystery of: Diplomacy is "an obscure art, which hides itself in the folds of deceit, which fears to let itself be seen, and believes that it can exist only in the darkness of mystery."   —LE TRÔNE, 1777

Diplomacy, nasty things said nicely: "Diplomacy is to do and say the nastiest thing in the nicest way." —PROVERB

Diplomacy, necessity of: "If political entities could live apart from rivals and enemies and possessed no instincts of expansion, there would be no occasion for diplomatic policies. In that case political history would be mainly confined to constitutional development; but no state is thus isolated, and in this fact lies the necessity of international relations in which diplomacy becomes a creative agent." —DAVID J. HILL, 1906

Diplomacy, negotiation: Diplomacy is "the science or art of negotiation." —CHARLES DE MARTENS, 1866

Diplomacy, offensive: Diplomacy need not aim at fostering peace and friendship; it may be directed to fomenting feuds and rivalries between potential enemies of the state.

Diplomacy, open: "Open diplomacy is a contradiction in terms; if it is open, it is not diplomacy. The primary purpose of diplomacy is to achieve results by moderation, tact and compromise when possible. The ambassador can and should influence the course of events by his reports to his government and by his personal relations with the people with whom he is negotiating, but the broad lines of foreign policy should be settled by the governments." —DAVID KELLY, 1956

Diplomacy, parliamentary: "Parliamentary diplomacy is a type of multilateral negotiation which involves at least four factors. First, a continuing organization with interest and responsibilities which are broader than the specific items that happen to appear upon the agenda at any particular time—in other words more than a traditional international conference called to cover a specific agenda. Second, regular public debate exposed to the media of mass communication and in touch, therefore, with public opinions around the globe. Third, rules of procedure which govern the process of debate and which are themselves subject to tactical manipulation to advance or oppose a point of view. And lastly, formal conclusions, ordinarily expressed in resolution, which are reached by majority votes of some description, on a simple or two-thirds majority or based upon a financial contribution or economic stake—some with and some without a veto." —DEAN RUSK, 1955

Diplomacy, peace: "Diplomacy, the most honorable of professions, can bring the most blessed of gifts, the gift of peace." —RONALD W. REAGAN

Diplomacy, peaceable coercion: Diplomacy is peaceable coercion to promote the interests of the state and nation.

Diplomacy, personal: "When persons of supreme or high authority deal directly with one another, there is a tendency for their governments to take on a personal quality and to depend for their validity, to some extent, on the personal relationship that has been

established. This is sometimes fine as long as it lasts; but the agreement is then largely vitiated if one or the other of them falls from office. Agreements concluded through the regular diplomatic channels, time-consuming and cumbersome as they may be, and thus regarded as agreements between governments rather than between individuals, tend to be more carefully worked out, less personally conditioned, and more enduring."
—GEORGE F. KENNAN, 1977

Diplomacy, persuasion without violence: "Each state lives in relation to other States: when they live in peace, they must, cost what it may, communicate among themselves. Except when they use force, they try to convince each other. When they fight, they try to constrain each other. In this sense, diplomacy can be considered as the art of convincing without resort to force, and strategy the art of winning with the least possible cost."
—RAYMOND ARON, 1964

Diplomacy, pleasures of: "Diplomacy is a first-class stall seat at the theater of life."
—BERNARD VON BÜLOW

Diplomacy, plot and counterplot: "To know the intentions of one's neighbor, to defeat his hostile designs, to form alliances with his enemies, to steal away his friends, and to prevent his union with others, . . . [are] matters of the highest public interest. Less costly and hazardous than war, diplomacy . . . [can supersede] it with plot and counterplot."
—DAVID J. HILL, 1905

Diplomacy, popular view of: "Many have been in the habit of considering diplomacy an occult science as mysterious as alchemy and as dangerous to the morals as local politics."
—JOHN HAY, 1902

Diplomacy, power: "Diplomacy should be backed by power. But at the same time it should be flexible, always capable of adjustment."   —YAMAGATA ARITOMO, 1886

Diplomacy, practice of: "The practice of diplomacy is not in fact very different from the practice of sound business, in that it relies for its efficacy upon the establishment of confidence and credit. Experienced diplomats are traditionally suspicious of what is called 'brilliant diplomacy' or 'diplomatic triumphs,' since they are well aware that these feats of ingenuity are apt to leave resentment and suspicion behind."   —HAROLD NICOLSON, 1959

Diplomacy, practice of ways and means: "Diplomacy is the practice of ways and means. Those who ask of it grand designs or the transformation of society must forever be disappointed. The more profound changes take place outside the conference room. Yet the institutions of . . . diplomacy are sufficient to the day if the diplomat uses them wisely and well."   —KENNETH W. THOMPSON, 1962

Diplomacy, professional: Like war, diplomacy is too important a subject to be left to blundering amateurism. It marks the phase of policy prior to war; it makes and breaks military alliances; it ends war. There is much lore to it; it is a subtle calling. Diplomacy is too portentous to be entrusted to the politicians but it is too political to be left to the generals. Those who may be fatally affected by diplomacy's failures have every reason to demand that only its most skilled, professional practitioners represent their interests.

Diplomacy, public: Advocacy openly directed at foreign publics in support of negotiations or broad policy positions and couched in terms intended to enlist their backing for a particular position or outcome. Distinguish *Propaganda*.

Diplomacy, public: "Both information and cultural work are governed by foreign policy needs. Information is an integral part of embassy work. And much of the cultural work involves negotiating agreements over exchanges of people or events—a natural diplomatic job." —A DIPLOMAT, QUOTED BY ERIC CLARK

Diplomacy, purpose of: The purpose of diplomacy is not to outwit the opposing nation but to engage it in a web of common interests, thereby serving the interests of one's own nation.

Diplomacy, rape: Diplomacy is political rape convincingly disguised as seduction.

Diplomacy, revolutionary regimes and: "Diplomacy is one of the things which change least in the world, for it meets the great secular need of mankind, the need of peoples to make arrangements with each other, so that they can go about their several ways in peace. . . . It is therefore not surprising that revolutionary Governments, however drastically they break up the old régime of their country, either carry on the inherited diplomatic system or else return to it sooner or later." —R.B. MOWAT, 1936

Diplomacy, scope and subject matter of: "Diplomacy isn't anything in a compartment by itself. The stuff of diplomacy is in the entire fabric of our foreign relations with other countries, and it embraces every phase of national power and every phase of national dealing." —GEORGE F. KENNAN, 1947

Diplomacy, secret: "Secret diplomacy, if we use the words in their real meaning, [is] nothing more than the established method of unpublicized negotiation." —HUGH GIBSON, 1944

Diplomacy, shuttle: Continuous travel back and forth between negotiating parties by a mediator or conciliator.

Diplomacy, strategic software: Diplomacy provides the software of national security policy; the military provide the hardware. Neither computes without the other.

Diplomacy, subject matter of: "Peace and war, defence and aggression, commerce and its protection, and, subsidiary to these, systems of revenue and industry, are all mere elements in the calculations and programme of diplomatic action. Ships are built and manned, frontiers are fortified, and armies are formed and moved in obedience to its theory and practice." —DAVID J. HILL, 1906

Diplomacy, successful: "There are two parts to successful diplomacy: one is knowing one's own mind, and the other is letting the other people know it."
—ATTRIBUTED TO LORD CURZON

Diplomacy, sureness of footing: "In diplomacy, as in the dance, a good performance calls for sureness of footing." —ROBERT J. MOORE, 1985

Diplomacy, tactics: Diplomacy is the tactics of measures short of war.

Diplomacy, utility of: "Diplomacy sees to it that a nation does not perish heroically but maintains itself in a practical way." —ADOLF HITLER

Diplomacy, war: The notion that diplomacy is a substitute for military measures or the use of the military a substitute for diplomacy mistakes the relationship between the two. They are complementary elements of national power best applied simultaneously, with the degree of emphasis on each determined by grand strategy, rather than deployed sequentially through a policy of escalation.

Diplomacy, war: "It is better for aged diplomats to be bored than for young men to die."
—ATTRIBUTED TO WARREN AUSTIN

Diplomacy, with women: "Diplomacy lies in remembering to celebrate a woman's birthday while forgetting to note her age." —PROVERB

Diplomacy, women's, like eunuchs: "The diplomacy of women is very much like that of eunuchs; it is false and dangerous, ultimate good seldom comes of it. Women are good as counsellors but bad as actors. Perhaps no negotiation has ever been perfected since the creation of the world without their interference and advice, but they are best kept out of sight. Their judgment is shrewd and clear on any abstract question submitted to them; but their own conduct is always too much influenced by personal feelings to render their entire management of affairs either proper or expedient."
—GRENVILLE MURRAY, CITED BY SIR VICTOR WELLESLEY

Diplomatic life: "American diplomacy is easy on the brain, but hell on the feet."
—CHARLES G. DAWES
[HENRY PRATHER FLETCHER RETORTED: "IT DEPENDS ON WHICH YOU USE."]

Diplomatic life: "A diplomat's life is made up of three ingredients: protocol, Geritol, and alcohol." —ADLAI E. STEVENSON, JR.

Diplomatic mission, chief of: Within a foreign country, an ambassador must be the paramount authority for the coordination and implementation of his nation's policy.

Diplomatic mission, management of: An ambassador must be ever mindful that he is responsible for representing his whole state and nation, and his entire government, not just his foreign ministry, through which he receives his instructions. In large and important embassies, an ambassador directs a staff drawn from many civilian and military departments, not just the foreign ministry. In his management of relations between disparate elements of his diplomatic mission and in his direction of their work, he must be dedicated to getting the job done, and be seen to be impartial, regardless of the bureaucratic divisions of labor in his capital.

Diplomatic work, importance of: The work of diplomats affects the life of the nation. In ordinary times, it helps determine the sense of confidence, security, and well-being of the citizenry, their general welfare, the balance of trade and payments, whether employment opportunities are created or destroyed through exports and imports, and whether citizens traveling or residing abroad are treated with dignity or subjected to humiliations by foreign governments. In extraordinary times, diplomats manage the prelude to war, protect citizens from its consequences, and set the terms of the return to peace.

Diplomatists, business of: "The distinctive function of a diplomatist is to carry on political business by personal intercourse with foreign statesmen." —Lord Lyons, 1860

Diplomats: A diplomat is someone who always thinks twice before saying nothing.

Diplomats: A diplomat is someone who, when he is run out of town, can make it look like he is leading a parade.

Diplomats: "[A diplomat is] one who lessens tension and promotes understanding." —Anthony Eden

Diplomats: "Diplomats approach every problem with an open mouth." —Arthur Goldberg

Diplomats: "[A diplomat] can cut his neighbor's throat without having his neighbor notice it." —Trygve Lie

Diplomats: "A diplomat is a person who tries to solve complicated problems which would never have arisen if there had been no diplomats." —Roberto Regala, quoting an unidentified foreign minister

Diplomats: "A diplomat is a person who can tell you to go to hell in such a way that you actually look forward to the trip." —Caskie Stinnett, 1960

Diplomats, amateur: "A [diplomat] ought to have very quick parts, dexterity, cunning, wide knowledge, and, above all, discernment. And it is no wonder that men who engage in these pursuits for the sake of the title and the salary, without any idea of the duties involved, serve an apprenticeship most damaging to the affairs entrusted to them."
—François de Callières, 1716

Diplomats, anonymity of: "In general, diplomats, unlike soldiers, are not fussed over by historians, who barely mention their names; the secrecy of negotiations, so often disputed by their contemporaries, is largely forgiven in the silence of posterity."
—Jules Cambon, 1926

Diplomats, best: "The man who becomes intensely interested in what he finds at his diplomatic post, people or landscape, or even historical documents, is the best diplomat. He is a successful diplomat because the people appreciate his interest in them and trust him accordingly. After he has shown an enthusiasm for the local scene he is in a far better position to represent his own country effectively."   —E. Wilder Spaulding, 1961

Diplomats, best: "The best diplomat is he who, inspired solely by cold reason, asks himself only what he can obtain and how he will arrive at it."   —Gyula Szilassy, 1928

Diplomats, best and worst: "The worst kind of diplomatists are missionaries, fanatics and lawyers; the best kind are the reasonable and humane skeptics. Thus it is not religion which has been the main formative influence in diplomatic theory; it is common sense."
—Harold Nicolson, 1939

Diplomats, bureaucrats: "Given even ordinary ability and powers of observation, the man on the spot is likely to be much wiser than the bureaucrats of the Foreign Offices swayed very often by partisanship or public opinion at home."
—Maurice Francis Egan

Diplomats, caution of: "The training and life of a foreign service officer are not apt to produce men well fitted for the task [of innovating policy]. The bureaucratic routine through which foreign service officers must go produces capable men, knowledgeable about specific parts of the world, and excellent diplomatic operators. But it makes men cautious rather than imaginative."   —Dean Acheson

Diplomats, chameleons: Diplomats are a species of chameleon; they blend in most of the time but puff themselves up in a brilliant display when required.

Diplomats, chief purpose of: "It is, of course, true that our relations with any given country involve many factors other than the direct dealings between governments, and an effective and competent diplomat, whatever his rank, must be prepared and equipped to deal with these non-governmental aspects of his work. But [this] should not cause us to forget that the chief purpose of the diplomat is the transaction of business for his country with the government to which he is credited. The success or failure of a given diplomatic mission in any country will, in the last anaylsis, come down to the degree of success it has achieved with the government of that country. The settlement of disputes that inevitably arise between countries, as between individuals, the ability to influence without improper interference the course of the foreign country's action in a direction which would serve the overall objectives of our foreign policy—these are the real business of diplomacy, to which all other aspects are supporting and subsidiary."

—CHARLES E. BOHLEN, 1961

Diplomats, estrangement from compatriots: "Diplomacy calls for gifts that are as seemingly incongruous as cynicism and courtesy, sophistication and sincerity, and decisiveness and patience. The diplomat is the bearer of a view of the outside world which his fellow citizens cannot entirely follow or accept." —KENNETH W. THOMPSON, 1962

Diplomats, ethical responsibilities of: "A good ambassador must be a patriot—that goes without saying; but he must always bear in mind that every country is part of an international system and that the future of the world depends on at least a tolerably good functioning of that system." —HIDEO KITAHARA, 1983

Diplomats, exemplars of their nation: Diplomatists are symbols of their nation and icons of its people. Their intelligence, their professionalism, and their personal attributes project the image of their nation and are one basis by which the seriousness their nation attaches to relations with the country to which they are assigned is assessed.

Diplomats, function of: "The function of a diplomatic envoy, since the eighteenth century, has been a twofold one—to observe and report to his government all which may concern it and to affect the course of events, so far as he is able to do so, in favor of his own country." —DEAN ACHESON, 1961

Diplomats, function of: "Part of a diplomat's function [is] to establish and maintain relations of confidence with those in power in the country to which he is accredited. In totalitarian states he must be very careful to avoid the suspicion of flirting with the opposition since he will then be denounced as interfering in the internal affairs of the country. The party in power is the one which is most useful for the efficient conduct of business, whereas to establish contacts with those whom their party regards as enemies would (except in the most liberal countries) expose an envoy to suspicion."

—HAROLD NICOLSON, 1959

Diplomats, image of: "In their own mind's eye, diplomats are imperturbable, courteous, painstaking, capable of seeing all sides of a problem and firm or conciliatory, depending on the situation. In the view of many members of the general public, they are callous, cynical, standoffish, indolent, superficial, supercilious and vacillating."

—CHARLES ROETTER, 1963

Diplomats, insults: A diplomat is someone who never unintentionally insults another person.

Diplomats, journalists: "First rate diplomats and top notch journalists have at least one trait in common: they are effective reporters. And both the diplomat and the journalist should possess the essential qualities for reporting—keenness of observation, ruthlessness in separating the wheat from the chaff, and facility in expression. The journalist's audience is, of course, quite different from the diplomat's. The journalist writes with bold strokes of the pen for a broad, immediate audience. The diplomat writes for a small audience of experts who need to know all the if's and but's without regard to popular prejudices or personalities. The journalist expects the world to read what he writes; the diplomat often needs the assurance that the world will not read what he is reporting. For the diplomat should not confine himself, like the members of the fourth estate, to what will please his readers: whether they be officials or posterity."

—E. WILDER SPAULDING, 1961

Diplomats, listeners: "A diplomat must use his ears, not his mouth." —KOMURA JUTARO

Diplomats, negotiators, protectors of compatriots: Diplomats are their governments' negotiators with other governments, and they are the protectors of their compatriots abroad.

Diplomats, professional affinities of: "Professional diplomatists constitute a distinct society, which has its peculiar maxims, lights, manners, and desires, and maintains, in the midst of the disagreements or positive conflicts of the states it represents, a tranquil and permanent unity."

—F. GUIZOT, 1859

Diplomats, purpose of: "[The object of the diplomat is] to bring about a harmonized union between his master and the sovereign to whom he is sent. He must labor to remove misunderstandings, to prevent subjects of dispute from arising, and generally to maintain in that foreign country the honor and interests of his prince. This includes the protection and patronage of his subjects, assistance to their business enterprises, and the promotion of good relations between them and the subjects of the foreign prince to whose court he is accredited."

—FRANÇOIS DE CALLIÈRES, 1716

Diplomats, qualifications of: "The essential qualifications of a good diplomat are common sense, good manners, understanding of foreign mentalities, and precision of expression."

—DAVID KELLY, 1956

Diplomats, qualities of: "The good diplomatist must have an observant mind, a gift of application which rejects being diverted by pleasures or frivolous amusements, a sound judgment which takes the measure of things as they are, and which goes straight to the goal by the shortest and most natural paths without wandering into meaningless refinements and subtleties.

"The good negotiator must have the gift of penetration such as will enable him to discern the thoughts of men and to deduce from the least movement of their features which passions are stirring within.

"The diplomatist must be quick, resourceful, a good listener, courteous and agreeable. He should not seek to gain a reputation as a wit, nor should he be so disputatious as to divulge secret information in order to clinch an argument. Above all the good negotiator must possess enough self-control to resist the longing to speak before he has thought out what he intends to say. He must not fall into the mistake of supposing that an air of mystery, in which secrets are made out of nothing and the merest trifle exalted into an affair of state, is anything but the symptom of a small mind. He should pay attention to women, bur never lose his heart. He must be able to simulate dignity even if he does not possess it, but he must at the same time avoid all tasteless display. Courage is also an essential quality, since no timid man can hope to bring a confidential negotiation to success. The negotiator must possess the patience of a watch-maker and be devoid of personal prejudices. He must have a calm nature, be able to suffer fools gladly, and should not be given to drink, gambling, women, irritability, or any other wayward humors and fantasies. The negotiator, moreover, should study history and memoirs, be acquainted with foreign institutions and habits, and be able to tell where, in any foreign country, the real sovereignty lies. Everyone who enters the profession of diplomacy should know the German, Italian, and Spanish languages as well as the Latin, ignorance of which would be a disgrace and shame to any public man, since it is the common language of all Christian nations. He should have also some knowledge of literature, science, mathematics, and law. Finally, he should entertain handsomely. A good cook is often an excellent conciliator." —François de Callières, 1716

Diplomats, qualities of: "Sleepless tact, unmovable calmness, and a patience that no folly, no provocation, no blunders may shake." —Benjamin Franklin

Diplomats, qualities of: "In the exercise of the functions of the diplomat, the qualities which will be most useful are a sharp discernment, sound judgment, studied opinion, firm convictions, and a humble bearing." —Baron Silvercruys, 1956

Diplomats, qualities of successful: "The qualities for a successful diplomat . . . [are], in order of importance, (1) a good head for liquor and (2) a capacity for producing, orally and on paper, polite guff at a moment's notice." —Hume Wrong, 1927

Diplomats, qualities of the perfect: "The essential qualities of a diplomatist [are that]: He is conciliatory and firm; he eludes difficulties which cannot immediately be overcome only in order to obviate them in more favorable conditions; he is courteous and unhurried; he easily detects insincerity, not always discernible to those who are themselves sincere; he has a penetrating intellect and a subtle mind, combined with a keen sense of honour. He has an intuitive sense of fitness; and is adaptable. He is at home in any society and is equally effective in the chanceries of the old diplomacy or on the platforms of the new." —A.L. Kennedy, 1922

Diplomats, recruitment of: "[Apprentice diplomats] must have made serious studies, be of good morals, endowed with a well-tempered and flexible mind, but at the same time firm and penetrating; have an upright heart, full of noble and elevated sentiments."
—Marquis de Torcy, 1711, cited by J.J. Jusserand

Diplomats, role of: "While the final responsibility for all success or failure in diplomacy would seem to rest upon the King and his Ministers at home, it is nonetheless true that since these ministers can only act upon information from abroad, the influence which an enlightened diplomatist can exercise upon the actions and design of the home government is very large. Incapable men acting abroad will make nothing of even the most brilliant instructions; capable men by the accuracy and sagacity of their reports and suggestions can do much to improve the most mediocre instructions, and therefore the responsibility for diplomatic action is in reality shared in about equal degree between the home government and its servants abroad." —Robert McClintock, 1952

Diplomats, role of: "The priceless asset of the diplomat is that he is there. He is in the foreign country, on the spot. He is offered countless ways to come to a native's knowledge and understanding of it. It is he who knows where the true levers of power lie, as no fellow citizen can possibly hope to. His work, in Bismarck's words, 'consists of practical intercourse with men, of judging accurately what other people are likely to do in given circumstances, of appreciating accurately the views of others, of presenting accurately his own.' And being 'in practical intercourse with men' he is, as Demosthenes put it, 'in control of occasions': which in turn can influence, if not control, events. However swift modern communications, the competent diplomat, given proper latitude by his government on tactics and timing, can perform an indispensable role in the conduct of relations between governments." —Livingston Merchant, 1964

Diplomats, selection of: Aristotle counseled that "in the choice of a general, we should regard his skill rather than his virtue, for few have military skill, but many have virtue." Just so in the selection of ambassadors and other envoys: to do a skilled job, choose a skilled workman.

Diplomats, selection of: "Nations are judged by their representatives abroad. For this if for no other reasons governments should take special pains in selecting their envoys." —Charles W. Thayer, 1959

Diplomats, statesmen: "International politics has always been treated by diplomats as something of a game. Winners get to be called statesmen." —Richard J. Barnet

Diplomats, training of: "[Apprentice diplomats] must be made fully to understand that there is nothing more important for the good of the service and their own advancement than to secure for themselves a well-established reputation of being safe and trustworthy men, so that those who shall have to do with them may feel that they will not be betrayed

and that any secret revealed to them will be kept."
—Marquis de Torcy, 1711, cited by J.J. Jusserand

Diplomats, utility of: "Diplomats are useful only in fair weather. As soon as it rains they drown in every drop."
—Attributed to Charles de Gaulle

Diplomats, warriors: "What's the difference between the diplomat and the military man? The answer is . . . they both do nothing, but the military get up very early in the morning to do it with great discipline, while the diplomats do it late in the afternoon, in utter confusion."
—Vernon Walters

Diplomats, warriors and: In ancient times, military prowess was one of the principal qualifications of statesmen. Today, military and diplomatic officers are separated into distinct professions. But the capacity of a state at peace to resort successfully to war is what gives ultimate credibility to its diplomats; its capacity to end war through its enemies' endorsement of just concessions is what gives lasting meaning to the sacrifices of its warriors. War and diplomacy are different but intimately related aspects of national policy. Diplomats and warriors who recall this will therefore act as brothers in a potentially lethal common endeavor. They will understand that war is a means, costly in blood and treasure, to establish a peace on terms more favorable than those that prevailed before combat began; they will consider together when to fight and when to talk and when to press and when to stop.

Diplomats, warriors without weapons: Diplomats are warriors without weapons, pointmen for the armed men behind them. Diplomats and military commanders serve the same masters and the same causes; both are practitioners of the controlled application of the power of their own nations to others. Between them, diplomats and warriors regulate and traverse the course from protest to menace, from dialogue to mediation, from ultimata to the controlled application of force to other societies, from war to negotiated settlement and reconciliation.

Diplomats, wars: "Diplomats are just as essential to starting a war as Soldiers are for finishing it. You take Diplomacy out of war and the thing would fall flat in a week."
—Will Rogers, 1949

Diplomats, work of: Diplomats are envoys and messengers between sovereigns. They are the eyes and ears, the voice and hand of their government and nation in foreign lands.

Disagreements, resolving: To resolve disagreements, focus on active disputes with operational consequences. Leave the rest to be dealt with later or to fade away into practical insignificance.

Disarmament: The process of eliminating armaments or classes of armaments completely, usually on a reciprocal basis, in an effort to preclude their use in war. Contrast *Arms control.*

Disarmament, difficulty of: "The trouble with disarmament was [and still is] that the problem of war is tackled upside down and at the wrong end. Nations don't distrust each other because they are armed; they are armed because they distrust each other. And therefore to want disarmament before a minimum of common agreement on fundamentals is as absurd as to want people to go undressed in winter. Let the weather be warm, and they will undress readily enough without committees to tell them so."
—Salvador de Madariaga (as Chairman of the League of Nations Disarmament Commission)

Discourtesy: Discourtesy manifests arrogance, envy, belligerence, fear, and contempt. It buttresses hostility, resentment, distrust, anger, and obstinacy.

Discretion: "If I've regretted my silence once, I've regretted my words a thousand times."
—Arab proverb

Discretion: "Responsible diplomats will always be guarded in what they say to each other. They know that the constant application of discretion precludes neither cordial personal relations nor many mutually useful exchanges with competent colleagues. Rather than being put off when they encounter this quality in others, they take it as reassuring evidence that they are dealing with reliable and useful professionals. If this quality is not present, a wise diplomat will be warned off, and will take his dealings elsewhere."
—William Macomber, 1975

Discretion before valor: The easiest way to avoid hornet stings is not to intrude on the hornets' nest.

Dishonesty: "Diplomatists have no right to complain of mere lies; it is their fault, if, educated as they are, the lies deceive them."
—Henry Adams, 1907

Dishonesty: "A lie always leaves in its wake a drop of poison. The negotiator should recollect that he is likely for the rest of his life to be constantly engaged in diplomatic business and that it is essential for him to establish a reputation for straight and honest dealing."
—François de Callières, 1716

Dishonesty: "Dishonesty is only proof of the smallness of mind of him who resorts to it and shows that he is too meagerly equipped to gain his purposes by just and honorable means."
—François de Callières, 1716

Dishonesty: "A reputation for trickiness will follow a diplomat around the globe as tenaciously as the dossiers prepared by his diplomatic colleagues pursue him from post to post."
—Charles Thayer, 1959

Disillusionment: To be disillusioned, you must first allow yourself to develop illusions.

Dispatch: A written, as opposed to telegraphic, message from an embassy to its home office, or vice versa.

Displaced person: A person who has fled his or her homeland in search of sanctuary from war, unrest, famine, or other life-threatening conditions. Contrast *Refugee*.

Displaced person: Internally displaced persons are "persons or groups of persons who have been forced or obliged to flee or to leave their homes or places of habitual residence, in particular as a result of or in order to avoid the effects of armed conflict, situations of generalized violence, violations of human rights or natural or human-made disasters, and who have not crossed an internationally recognized state border."
—The Internal Displacement Monitoring Centre

Dissembling: "Blamable in a private man, it is excusable in public business, since it is impossible to manage government affairs well if one is unable to dissemble and feign. This ability is acknowledged as the true attribute of kings, and it has been observed long ago that one who does not know how to feign is inapt to reign."
—Juan Antonio de Vera y Çuniga, 1620, cited by J.J. Jusserand

Dissent: There is always a danger that the message will be mistaken for the messenger. Dissent is often taken for insult, as it implicitly condemns the judgment of those with whose policies it takes issue. The ultimate test of an ambassador's persuasiveness is to report and recommend honestly on the lapses and errors of his own country's policies without fatally offending those guilty of them.

Dissent: "There are strict limits, dictated by common sense and the realities of the situation, to how far an ambassador can go in opposing a position of his own government. If a compromise is not possible and once the final decision has been made, he must of course loyally and scrupulously implement it even if it goes against what he had recommended. But until the final decision is made an ambassador owes his government the frankest and most unvarnished advice." —François de Laboulaye and Jean Laloy, 1983

Diversity: See *Representivity*.

Divide and rule: A policy aimed at preserving paramountcy of influence through the deliberate perpetuation or aggravation of differences between smaller or weaker parties so that they cannot cooperate or coalesce in effective opposition to an imperial or hegemonic power.

Doctrine: Strategy and doctrine transform intelligence into effective action.

Doctrine, advantages of possessing: "Those who are possessed of a definite body of doctrine and of deeply rooted convictions based upon it will be in a much better position to deal with the shifts and surprises of daily affairs than those who are merely taking short

views, and indulging their natural impulses as they are evoked by what they read from
day to day."   —WINSTON CHURCHILL

Doctrine, rules: "Young men know the rules; older men have learned the exceptions to
these rules."   —CHINESE APHORISM

Domestic politics: "All diplomats suffer from what we might call the domestic-political
distractions of their official masters."   —GEORGE F. KENNAN

Domestic politics, foreign policy and: The conception that foreign policy can be a simple
extrapolation from domestic politics is an autistic delusion, but it is a common one, especially in nations imbued with an imperial sense of mission.

Domestic politics, foreign policy and: "History does not forgive our national mistakes
because they are explicable in terms of our domestic politics. . . . A nation which excuses
its own failures by the sacred untouchableness of its own habits can excuse itself into a
complete disaster."   —GEORGE F. KENNAN, 1953

Doyen: See *Dean*.

Doyenne: The wife of the dean of the diplomatic corps, charged with presenting at court
ladies who have no one else to do this for them (as would be the case, for example, if the
chief of the mission to which they belong is unmarried).

Drafting: "Never place an adjective before a noun, if it can be spared; it only weakens the
effect of a plain statement. Do not go out of your way to be witty."   —ERNEST SATOW

Drafts: Who does the drafting structures the agenda and shapes the outcome of negotiations. It is almost always advantageous to undertake to provide the first draft of a
potential agreement.

Duplicity: "Diplomacy is not a science of art and duplicity. If good faith is necessary
anywhere, it is in political transactions, for it alone can render them solid and enduring.
                                                                        —TALLYRAND

E

Eagerness: "Showing eagerness rarely speeds up negotiations. No experienced statesman settles just because his opponent feels a sense of urgency; he is far more likely to use such impatience to try to extract even better terms." —HENRY A. KISSINGER, 1994

Economic balance: "The desire of states to achieve an economic balance is basically the same as the desire to achieve a strategic balance, and the desire to regulate economic competition is the same as the desire to regulate war." —ADAM WATSON, 1983

Economic power: Economic power is a string one can pull but not push.

Economic reporting: See *Reporting, economic.*

Economic sanctions: See *Sanctions, economic.*

Economic section: The section of an embassy, usually headed by a counselor or first secretary, that is responsible for liaison with working levels of the receiving state's economic ministries (including its financial, foreign trade, and commercial agencies, as well as economic divisions of the foreign ministry, if any) on matters of mutual concern and for collecting, analyzing, and reporting information on foreign and domestic economic developments, trends, and trade and investment opportunities in the receiving state that are of interest to the sending state.

Economics: "Economics, national or international, . . . is not an end in itself, but a means of peace and a base on which may be developed a more satisfying life for peoples and individuals." —ADOLF A. BERLE, 1964

Eloquence: "Prudence and learning are of little avail, for an ambassador, without eloquence." —KONRAD BRAUN, 1548, CITED BY J.J. JUSSERAND

Embassies, locally hired staff of: Ambassadors come and go, as do their diplomatic subordinates. The locally hired staff of an embassy do not. They are the embassy's roots in the community and its essential continuity. Their morale, like their performance, is crucial to an ambassador's success and must not be neglected by him.

Embassies, need for: "We must be equipped for emergencies, and every now and then, even at the smallest and most remote courts, there is a critical need of a . . . representative to protect [our] citizens and [our] interests." —BENJAMIN HARRISON, 1889

Embassy: The residence of an ambassador. In loose, contemporary usage, also the office building of the ambassador and his senior staff. See also *Chancery.*

Emissary: A representative sent on an official or unofficial mission or errand. (Not a diplomatic title or status.)

Empathy: "Objectively analyzing and explaining other nations' goals and viewpoints is a basic duty of the diplomat, for information of this kind is essential to any sound process of foreign policy decision making. . . . This often makes trouble. It can be taken, and mistaken, by officials elsewhere in his government for an overly solicitous interest in the objectives and feelings of foreigners. The result is a suspicion within his own government that he is not to be fully trusted with the interests of his own countrymen—a taint which can plague him throughout his career." —William Macomber, 1975

Empathy: "The nature and purpose of diplomacy is accommodation and adjustment, and diplomacy is more effective the more diplomats and statesmen put themselves mentally in the place of their negotiating partners and understand the requirements and patterns of thought of those with whom they are dealing." —Adam Watson, 1983

Empathy, insight from: "What . . . makes a good diplomat, and thus a good ambassador, [is] the kind of empathy which comes from years spent in cross-cultural communication, Fingerspitzengefühl (the feeling one has in the tips of one's fingers) which is sometimes acquired by amateurs but is more frequently found among people who have had a great deal of experience. . . . A feel for what is about to happen may be derived from a lifetime of sniffing the political atmosphere of foreign countries. The crisis, which inevitably is the first diplomatic crisis to the newcomer, is reminiscent in many ways of crises experienced before by the professional—he knows what comes first and what not to worry about and is thus able to concentrate on what matters most. Inevitably, someone who has been through a dozen diplomatic crises behaves differently in one than someone who does not have that experience." —Martin F. Herz, 1983

Empathy, utility of: "Empathy involves the crucial ability to understand the other party's point of view, if only to counter it more effectively, and encompasses both the intellectual and the emotional of [the other party's] stand. The diplomat who has developed enough credibility with negotiators of the other party to be able to tell them how their position is striking his side and advise them on the changes necessary to move both parties toward an agreement stands in the advantageous position of 'mediator for his own side.'" —I. William Zartman and Maureen R. Berman, 1982

Empire, duration: Every empire claims to be eternal. None are.

Empire, hegemonic: "Hegemonic empires almost automatically enlist universal resistance, which is why all such claimants sooner or later exhaust themselves." —Henry A. Kissinger

Empires: "Great empires and little minds go ill together."

—EDMUND BURKE

Enemies, contact with: In diplomacy, as in war, one should never lose contact with the enemy.

Enemies, dealing with: The best way to deal with an enemy is to make a friend of him. The next best way is to persuade another to check or chasten him. Either is better than having to fight an enemy yourself.

Enemies, hating: "Never hate your enemies. It affects your judgment."—MARIO G. PUZO

Enemies, hatred of: "An enemy should be hated only so far as one may be hated who may one day be a friend."

—SOPHOCLES, C. 450 B.C.

Enemies, importance of choosing: Enemies should be made on purpose and not by inadvertence.

Enemies, instruction from: "Wise men learn much from their enemies."

—ARISTOPHANES, 414 B.C.

Enemies, learning from: "Observe your enemies, for they first find out your faults."

—ANTISTHENES

Enemies, making: The only reason to make an enemy is to make his enemies one's friends.

Enemies, neighbors as: "As your neighbor is your natural enemy, so the Power to your enemy's rear is your natural ally."

—MARTIN WIGHT

Enemies, respect for: Today's enemies may be tomorrow's allies. They should be treated with due respect and consideration.

Enemies, using: "Use your enemy's hand to catch a snake."

—PERSIAN, PROVERB

Enemies, utility of: Often it is necessary to make an enemy of one state in order to enlist the sympathy and support of another.

Enemies, weak: In diplomacy, as in war, it may be wise, when two of your enemies fall out, to support the weaker.

Enemies of enemies: "The enemy of my enemy is my friend; the friend of my enemy is my enemy."

—ARAB PROVERB

Enemy demands: If it is the national interest to do something, it does not make sense not to do it because it appears to coincide in whole or in part with a demand from one's enemies. To reject a course of action on these grounds concedes the power of decision to the enemy and denies it to oneself.

Enmity of nations: "I do not know the method of drawing up an indictment against a whole people."   —EDMUND BURKE, 1775

Enmity, poor basis for policy: "No quarrel ought ever to be converted into a policy."
                                                                —DAVID LLOYD GEORGE

Entente: Informal but often very close cooperation between two or more states to secure limited common objectives vis-à-vis other states or regions over a limited period of time. A feature of *Coalition*; contrast with *Alliance.*

Entente: "The two sides recognize a similarity of views and interests, but the understandings are limited to certain issues and the improvement in relations stops short of an alliance."   —ALEXANDER L. GEORGE, 1993

Entertainment: "An ambassador must be liberal and magnificent, but with judgment and design, and his magnificence should be reflected in his suite. His table should be served neatly, plentifully, and with taste. He should give frequent entertainments and parties to the chief personages of the Court and even to the Prince himself. A good table is the best and easiest way of keeping himself well informed. The natural effect of good eating and drinking is the inauguration of friendships and the creation of familiarity, and when people are a trifle warmed by wine they often disclose secrets of importance."
                                                        —FRANÇOIS DE CALLIÈRES, 1716

Entertainment: "Dining is the soul of diplomacy."   —PALMERSTON

Entertainment, purpose of: The purpose of parties at a diplomat's residence is not to amuse colleagues in the diplomatic corps. Still less is it to show off to them the breadth of the host's local contacts. The purpose of diplomatic entertainment is to cultivate relationships with influential members of the elite in the host country. If a party at a diplomatic residence does not succeed in this, however delightful it may have been for its participants, it should be reckoned a failure.

Entertainment, utility of: "More can be accomplished at one party than at twenty serious conversations."   —ABIGAIL ADAMS, 1784

Envoy: Originally, a diplomat of less than ambassadorial rank (but ranking above a minister); now used as a synonym for ambassador or special emissary between chiefs of state or government.

Envoys, efficacy of: "The best instrument at the disposal of a Government wishing to persuade another Government will always remain the spoken words of a decent man."
—JULES CAMBON, AS TRANSLATED BY HAROLD NICOLSON

Envoys, necessity of: "Ambassadors became a necessity among men at the moment, 'or shortly after,' when, Pandora's fateful box having been opened, evils were scattered throughout the world, and prospered, finding for their growth 'a fruitful well-tilled ground.'"
—FRANÇOIS DE LA MOTHE LE VAYER, 1579, CITED BY J.J. JUSSERAND

Envoys, special: "Why employ intelligent and highly paid ambassadors and then go and do their work for them? You don't buy a canary and sing yourself."
—ALEXANDER DOUGLAS-HOME, 1969

Equilibrium: A distribution of power among states such that the potential for resistance approximates the potential for aggression. See also, *Power, balance of.*

Escalation: Escalation is the progressive application of ever stronger means of pressure or higher levels of violence to coerce another to yield to one's will.

Escalation, grand strategy: Escalation is, in a sense, the opposite of grand strategy. It applies sequentially the elements of national power that grand strategy integrates and seeks to apply simultaneously in a coordinated fashion.

Espionage: Espionage is the sixth sense of the state.

Espionage: "Money opens the most secret cabinets of princes."
—HOTMAN DE VILLIERS, 1603, CITED BY J.J. JUSSERAND

Espionage, human foibles and: "If there were no knaves, honest men should hardly come by the truth of any enterprise against them."
—SIR FRANCIS WALSINGHAM

Espionage, imperative of: "How can any man say what he should do himself if he is ignorant what his adversary is about?"
—ANTOINE HENRI JOMINI, 1838

Espionage, importance of funding: "Well-chosen spies contribute more than any other agency to the success of great plans. . . . And as there is no expense better designed than that which is laid out upon a secret service, it would be inexcusable for a . . . State to neglect it."
—FRANÇOIS DE CALLIÈRES, 1716

Espionage, necessity of: "The necessity of procuring good Intelligence is apparent and need not be further urged. . . . Upon Secrecy, Success depends in most enterprises, . . . and for want of it, they are generally defeated, however well planned and promising a favourable issue."
—GEORGE WASHINGTON, 1777

Espionage, scruples about: Accurate insight into an adversary's plans is vital both to avoid war and to assure its efficient conduct by the nation if it cannot be avoided; to fail to give adequate attention to the collection of intelligence is to gamble both with the destiny of the nation and with the lives of its youth. Scruples about intelligence collection, though motivated by a humane concern about the propriety of the means by which information is obtained, may therefore, ultimately, produce suffering both for one's own people and for those of one's adversaries on a scale that is shockingly inhumane.

Espionage, vital importance of: "What enables an intelligent government and a wise military leadership to overcome others and achieve extraordinary accomplishments is foreknowledge.
   "Foreknowledge cannot be gotten from ghosts and spirits, cannot be had by analogy, and cannot be found out by calculation. It must be obtained from people who know the conditions of the enemy."
                                                                    —SUNZI

Esprit: Esprit is energy charged with enthusiasm.

Euphemism: Euphemism smoothes the path to agreement but lays a basis for subsequent misunderstanding, rancor, and recrimination.

Evasion: "Know the meaning of evasion. It is the prudent man's way of keeping out of trouble; with the gallantry of a witty remark he is able to extricate himself from the most intricate of labyrinths. He emerges gracefully from the bitterest encounter and with a smile."
                                                                    —BALTASAR GRACIÁN

Evasion: "If, as frequently happens, an indiscreet question which seems to require a distinct answer is put to you abruptly by an artful minister, parry it either by treating it as an indiscreet question or get rid of it by a grave and serious look; but on no account contradict the assertion flatly if it be true, or admit it as true if false."
                                                                    —LORD MALMESBURY

Ex gratia: A gesture of goodwill, usually in monetary form, which avoids the implication of legal obligation while precluding possible claims against the donor.

Exactions: Unrealistic demands for assistance, especially when oft-repeated, breed inattentiveness and indifference on the part of those to whom they are presented and undermine the relationship upon which they presume.

Excellency: A term of address commonly applied to ambassadors and ministers of government. (Ambassadors of the United States are properly addressed as "Mr./Mme. Ambassador" and members of the U.S. Cabinet as "Mr./Mme. Secretary" rather than as "Excellency.")

Exchange of notes: See *Notes, exchange of.*

Exequatur: A document issued to a consul by the state to which he is assigned authorizing him to carry out his consular duties in a designated district which may be all or part of the national territory of the receiving state.

Exiles: "It seems not amiss to speak . . . of the danger of trusting to the representations of men who have been expelled from their country, this being a matter that all those who govern states have to act upon almost daily. . . . We see . . . how vain the faith and promises of men are who are exiles from their own country. As to their faith, we have to bear in mind that, whenever they can return to their country by other means than your assistance, they will abandon you and look to the other means, regardless of their promises to you. And as to their vain hopes and promises, such is their extreme desire to return to their homes that they naturally believe many things that are not true, and add many others on purpose; so that, with what they really believe and what they say they believe, they will fill you with hopes to that degree that if you attempt to act upon them you will incur a fruitless expense, or engage in an undertaking that will involve you in ruin."
—Niccolò Machiavelli

Expertise: "In strange waters, sail in the wake of one who knows the ports."
—Norse proverb

Experts: "No lesson seems to be so deeply inculcated by the experience of life as that you should never trust experts. If you believe the doctors, nothing is wholesome. If you believe the theologians, nothing is innocent; if you believe the soldiers, nothing is safe. They all require to have their strong wine diluted by a very large admixture of insipid common sense."
—Lord Salisbury

Exterritorial: Referring to the exemption of diplomats, members of their families and suites, staffs, residences, and archives from the jurisdiction of the state in which they reside and to which they are accredited. Contrast *Extraterritorial.*

Extradition: The international legal process by which fugitives from justice in one state are forcibly returned to it from another.

Extraterritorial: Referring to the exercise of sovereign rights by one state in the territory of another; hence, a curtailment of the sovereignty of the state on whose territory such rights are exercised. Contrast *Exterritorial.*

Eye for an eye: "An eye for an eye leaves everyone blind."   —Mohandas Gandhi

Face: Face is dignity that arises from others conferring on one the respect one believes is due. It is the coincidence of reputation with honor: satisfaction born of an apparent coincidence between the attitudes and behavior others show toward one and the status and character one aspires to exemplify.

Faces, revealing nature of: "It is a point of cunning, to wait upon with whom you speak, with your eyes; as the Jesuits give it in precept: for there be many wise men that have secret hearts and transparent countenances."
—Francis Bacon

Fact-finding missions: Fact-finding missions are a standard diplomatic device when inaction is judged to be preferable to action. Such commissions take time to assemble, to organize their studies, to reach a consensus, and to write their reports. With luck, by the time they submit their conclusions to those who commissioned them, the problem will have taken a new form or gone away.

Facts: "Facts do not cease to exist because they are ignored."
—Aldous Huxley

Facts: "Of all public servants, the diplomatist and the general alone must, if they are to succeed, have a grasp of actual facts. Politicians, lawyers, administrators, financiers even, can pass their lives in a mist of fictions and go down to posterity as great men. But the general who fails to perceive the facts that surround him will inevitably pay the penalty in defeat. The facts with which the diplomatist has to deal are less specialized and immediate, more subtle, indeterminate, and diverse than those which confront the general; they are facts the perception of which requires an all-round intelligence; and thus, while it is possible for a great soldier to be a stupid man, a diplomatist who is stupid must be a failure."
—Lytton Strachey

Failure: There are some struggles that cannot be won, but there is no struggle that cannot be lost.

Failure, in negotiations: At times the collapse of negotiations without agreement is to be applauded rather than regretted. This is certainly the case where stalemate is tolerable and agreement could only have been reached through excessively disadvantageous concessions to the other side. It may also be the case where unilateral action or a resort to war can reasonably be expected to produce the adjustments negotiation could not, and at less long-term cost to the national interest.

Failure, intelligence: "There are only two possibilities: policy success and intelligence failure."
—Thomas Fingar

Failure, reinforcing: Never reinforce failure. Attempts to reinforce battlefield positions that cannot be held risk turning tactical reversals into strategic defeats. Efforts to save failing policies by doing more of the same risk turning setbacks into debacles.

Farewell parties, utility of: The etiquette of diplomacy requires that colleagues be seen off with warmth and consideration by members of the corps who have enjoyed especially close relations with them. Nevertheless, it is a wise rule for an ambassador to undertake this responsibility only for those of his colleagues whose prestige with the leaders and people of the host nation is higher than his own. In doing so, he may hope to ingratiate himself and his country with prominent natives of the country where he is stationed whom he could not otherwise attract to his table.

Faults, national: "Avoid the defects of your country. Water shares the good and bad qualities of the beds through which it runs; people share those of the region where they are born. Some owe more than others to their mother country or city, for they were born under favorable skies. No country, not even the most refined, has ever escaped some innate defect or other, and these weaknesses are seized on by neighboring countries as defense or consolation. It is a triumph to correct, or at least to dissimulate, such national faults. By doing so, you will be revered as unique among your people; for what is least expected is most valued." —Baltasar Gracián, 1647

Favoritism among nations: "A passionate attachment of one nation for another produces a variety of evils. Sympathy for the favorite nation, facilitating the illusion of an imaginary common interest in cases where no real common interest exists, and infusing into one the enmities of the other, betrays the former into a participation in the quarrels and wars of the latter, without adequate inducement or justification. It leads also to concessions to the favorite nation of privileges denied to others, which is apt doubly to injure the nation making the concessions by unnecessarily parting with what ought to have been retained, and by exciting jealousy, ill will, and a disposition to retaliate in the parties from whom equal privileges are withheld; and it gives to ambitious, corrupted or deluded citizens (who devote themselves to the favorite nation) facility to betray or sacrifice the interests of their own country without odium, sometimes even with popularity; gilding with the appearances of a virtuous sense of obligation, a commendable deference for public opinion, or a laudable zeal for public good, the base of foolish compliances of ambition, corruption, or infatuation.

"As avenues to foreign influence in innumerable ways, such attachments are particularly alarming to the truly enlightened and independent patriot. How many opportunities do they afford to tamper with domestic factions, to practise the arts of seduction, to mislead public opinion, to influence or awe the public councils! Such an attachment of a small or weak towards a great and powerful nation dooms the former to be the satellite of the latter.

"Against the insidious wiles of foreign influence (I conjure you to believe me, fellow citizens), the jealousy of a free people ought to be constantly awake, since history and experience prove that foreign influence is one of the most baneful foes of republican government. But that jealousy, to be useful, must be impartial, else it becomes the instrument of the very evil to be avoided, instead of a defense against it. Excessive partiality for one foreign nation and excessive dislike of another cause those whom they actuate to see danger only on one side, and serve to veil and even second the arts of influence on the other. Real patriots who may resist the intrigues of the favorite are liable to become suspected and odious, while its tools and dupes usurp the applause and confidence of the people to surrender their interests." —GEORGE WASHINGTON, 1796

Favors: "To receive a favor is to sell your liberty." *[Beneficium accipere, libertatem vendere.]*
—LATIN PROVERB

Favors: "There can be no greater error than to expect or calculate upon real favors from nation to nation." —GEORGE WASHINGTON, 1789

Fear: "No passion so effectually robs the mind of all its powers of acting and reasoning as fear." —EDMUND BURKE

Fear, politics of: "The whole aim of practical politics is to keep the populace alarmed (and hence clamorous to be led to safety) by menacing it with an endless series of hobgoblins, all of them imaginary." —H.L. MENCKEN

Fear-mongering: "In most communities it is illegal to cry "fire" in a crowded assembly. Should it not be considered serious international misconduct to manufacture a general war scare in an effort to achieve local political aims?" —DWIGHT D. EISENHOWER

Fervor: The measure of the importance assigned to the national interests at stake in a dispute and the extent to which they are charged with emotional intensity (imbued with a sense of moral rectitude) by national values. The balance of fervor (q.v.) between the parties to a dispute, in the absence of a capability and determination by one to annihilate the other, can determine which party will prevail in the contest of wills between them.

Final act: A formal summary statement at the conclusion of a conference (or congress).

Final offers: "Even in ordinary commercial transactions a 'final offer' is not inevitably the last proposal, and a fortiori the same is true in diplomacy." —TOGO SHIGENORI

Finance: "Finance, when coordinated with policy, becomes a weapon of diplomacy."
—VICTOR WELLESLEY, 1944

Flatterers: "He who knows how to flatter also knows how to slander." —NAPOLEON

Flattery: Diplomats must have no delusions of grandeur, but they should know how to induce them in others.

Flattery: "If you need something badly from even a dog, call him 'Sir.'" —Arab proverb

Flattery: "Kiss the hand that you cannot bite." —Arab proverb

Flattery: "Learn to compliment foreigners, their country, their language, their customs, without gushing and without running down your own or any other country. You will make new friends and not lose old ones." —Richard Fyfe Boyce, 1956

Flattery: "Flattery pleases very generally. In the first place, the flatterer may think what he says to be true; but, in the second place, whether he thinks so or not, he certainly thinks those whom he flatters of consequence enough to be flattered." —Samuel Johnson

Flattery: "Flattery is all right—if you don't inhale." —Adlai E. Stevenson, Jr.

Flattery, effects of: "Upon weaker minds the mere fact of being . . . a centre of public interest, the lavish hospitality of foreign Governments, the actual salutes of people dressed in foreign uniforms, have a most disintegrating effect. Affability, gratitude and general silliness result." —Harold Nicolson, 1946

Flattery, from enemies: "Praise from enemies is suspicious; it cannot flatter an honorable man unless it is given after the cessation of hostilities." —Napoleon

Flattery, influence through: "Praise other men whose deeds are like those of the person you are talking to; commend other actions which are based on the same policies as his. If there is someone else who is guilty of the same vice he is, be sure to gloss over it by showing that it really does no great harm; if there is someone else who has suffered the same failure he has, be sure to defend it by demonstrating that it is not a loss after all. If he prides himself on his physical prowess, do not antagonize him by mentioning the difficulties he has encountered in the past; if he considers himself an expert at making decisions, do not anger him by pointing out his past errors; if he pictures himself a sagacious planner, do not tax him with his failures. Make sure that there is nothing in your ideas as a whole that will vex your listener, and nothing about your words that will rub him the wrong way, and then you may exercise your powers of rhetoric to the fullest. This is the way to gain the confidence and intimacy of the person you are addressing and to make sure that you are able to say all you have to say without incurring his suspicion." —Han Feizi, as translated by Burton Watson

Flattery, mark of importance: "We love flattery, even though we are not deceived by it, because it shows that we are of importance enough to be courted." —Ralph Waldo Emerson, 1844

Flattery, objections to: "Those who object to flattery generally do so because they have never experienced it." —Vernon Walters

Flattery, tool of diplomacy: "Flattery is the magnet which everywhere attracts goodwill."
—Anonymous, La embajada española

Flattery, use in negotiations: By praising the experience and expertise of your opponent at the negotiating table and attributing to him knowledge he does not have, you may sometimes manipulate him into pretending that he is familiar with things he is not. Thus, by saying "you, of course, know" this or that document or precedent, you may be able to induce your opponent to accept your own interpretation of the point you are citing without challenge.

Flexibility: "Grant graciously what you cannot refuse safely, and conciliate those you cannot conquer."
—Charles Caleb Colton

Folly: "It may at times be the highest wisdom to simulate folly."—Niccolò Machiavelli

Foolproof: Nothing is foolproof to a sufficiently talented fool.

Forbearance: "Next to knowing when to seize an advantage, the most important thing in life is to know when to forego an advantage."
—Benjamin Disraeli

Force and diplomacy: "It is said that, force having abdicated, diplomacy must take over. But diplomacy may be handicapped in taking over precisely because force has abdicated. Diplomacy can provide a forum for the settlement of disputes which have become unprofitable for both sides. It can keep open channels for information. Most importantly, it can enable each side to convey its intentions to the other."   —Henry A. Kissinger, 1957

Force, language of: Those who describe others as understanding nothing but the language of force offer no insight; they reveal their own unwillingness to make the effort to consider how to deal effectively with the character, motivations, and concerns of real or potential adversaries by measures short of war.

Force, political results: "As professional soldiers are the first to recognize, successful military action can defeat enemy forces, topple regimes, seize and occupy territory, or deter immediate threats; but such action creates only brief moments of opportunity, not lasting political results. To exploit them, you need relationships, allies, expert knowledge of local and regional politics and cultures, security institutions, assistance and training resources, legitimacy and persuasive advocacy."   —Chester A. Crocker

Force, politically unguided use of: "Use of force unguided by political ends usually produces messy political results."
—Zbigniew Brzezinski, 1993

Force, resort to: It is stupid to seize by violence what diplomacy may persuade another he should give you.

Force, resort to: Sometimes resort to war can be necessary to create the conditions for a negotiated settlement of differences between states.

Force, resort to: "Let the sword decide after stratagem has failed."　　　—Arab proverb

Force, resort to: "It is the man who uses violence to spoil things, not the man who uses it to mend them, that is blameworthy."　　　—Niccolò Machiavelli

Force, resort to: "Weapons are inauspicious instruments, not the tools of the enlightened. When there is no choice but to use them, it is best to be calm and free from greed, and not celebrate victory."　　　—Sunzi

Force, show of: An attempt by a state to influence the behavior of another state or states through a demonstration of military capacity to act in furtherance or defense of its vital or strategic interests.

Force, strategy: Force unguided by strategy causes many more problems than it resolves.

Force, subjugation by: "The use of force alone is but temporary. It may subdue for a moment; but it does not remove the necessity of subduing again: and a nation is not governed, which is perpetually to be conquered."　　　—Edmund Burke, 1775

Force, subjugation by: "When one subdues men by force, they do not submit to him in their hearts. They submit because their strength is not adequate to resist."　　　—Mencius

Force, threat of use of: "Never draw the sword when a rattle of the scabbard will suffice."　　　—Thomas A. Bailey, 1968

Force, use of: "The use of force is . . . an end term in a series of ways in which states bring their power to bear on others so as to persuade them to alter their positions. Alliances are a means by which states add to their capacity to persuade others . . . . Only when a system of independent states is replaced by a single dominant power, or by an authority capable of enforcing compliance as a government does within a state, in other words only when the diplomatic dialogue between genuinely independent states ceases altogether is it reasonable to expect that states will not discuss and negotiate with each other about the use of force, or enter into contracts and alliances about it."　　　—Adam Watson, 1983

Foreign affairs: "This is the devilish thing about foreign affairs: they are foreign and will not always conform to our whim."　　　—James Reston, 1964

Foreign affairs, annoyance of: Foreign affairs often strike governments, especially those of large nations, as an annoyance which is to be evaded rather than addressed, but such annoyances are unavoidable and must, in the end, be addressed.

Foreign affairs, temptations of: "Each ruler says, 'By attending to foreign affairs I can perhaps become a king, and if not I will at least ensure security for myself'. . . . Neither power nor order, however, can be sought abroad—they are wholly a matter of internal government. . . . If the ruler does not apply the proper laws and procedures within his state, but stakes all on the wisdom of his foreign policy, his state will never become powerful and well ordered." —HAN FEIZI, AS TRANSLATED BY BURTON WATSON

Foreign policy: "There is nothing more dangerous than a foreign policy based on unreality." —ANTHONY EDEN, 1936

Foreign policy: "The Game of nations . . . differs from other games . . . in several important respects. First, each player has his own aims, different from those of the others, which constitute 'winning'; second, every player is forced by his own domestic circumstances to make moves in the Game which have nothing to do with winning and which, indeed, might impair chances of winning; third, in the Game of nations there are no winners, only losers. The objective of each player is not so much to win as to avoid loss.
  "The common objective of the players in the Game of nations is merely to keep the Game going. The alternative to the Game is war." —ZAKARIA MOHIEDDIN, 1962

Foreign policy: "There is a vital difference between foreign policy and diplomacy. Foreign policy is the strategy of diplomacy." —ROBERTO REGALA, 1959

Foreign policy, aims of: Diplomacy seeks to deter challenges to the nation's identity, interests, and beliefs, and to enhance its welfare, power, and influence.

Foreign policy, bureaucratic: Policies made by bureaucracies are the opposite of strategy. They are the vector of competing egos, institutions, and viewpoints—a compromise intended to appease contentious domestic interests rather than a serious attempt to grapple with the issues and interests of the foreign states to which they are purportedly directed. Such policies invite contempt from strong leaders; they often receive it.

Foreign policy, costs of: The conduct of foreign affairs is among the most costly activities of the state; the currency in which it is reckoned and paid is citizens' lives.

Foreign policy, defense of national interests in: "A wise Government in its home policy considers the reasonable wants of the people; in its foreign policy it is prepared to resist the unjust demands and the unreasonable views of foreign powers."—PALMERSTON, 1843

Foreign policy, diplomacy-free: Diplomacy-free foreign policy works no better than strategy-free warfare.

Foreign policy, diplomacy helps form: "States . . . use diplomatic channels not merely to communicate messages, but also to discuss, negotiate and assume mutual commit-

ments; and the experience of taking part in a continuous dialogue of this kind itself influences the discussion and molds the aims of the participants. Diplomacy makes states perpetually aware of the wishes and objections, the power to insist on them, of other states whose consent is necessary in order to reach agreement; and this awareness of the intentions and capabilities of other states provides the opportunities and sets the limits to every state's foreign relations, developing them from random thrusting and yielding to a systematic policy. The dialogue induces states to realize the necessity for compromise and restraint, and indeed the positive advantages of such conduct."
—Adam Watson, 1983

Foreign policy, diplomacy and war in: "While the most typical peaceful instrument of foreign policy is diplomacy, its most typical violent instrument is war."
—José Calvet de Maglhães

Foreign policy, domestic policy: What is a foreign policy issue for one nation is a domestic issue for another. It is essential for statesmen to remember this as they go about their business.

Foreign policy, domestic policy: "You can always survive a mistake in domestic affairs but you can get killed by one made in foreign policy."—Attributed to John F. Kennedy

Foreign policy, domestic support for: "The acid test of a policy is its ability to obtain domestic support. This has two aspects: the problem of legitimizing a policy within the government apparatus . . . and that of harmonizing it with the national experience."
—Henry A. Kissinger, 1964

Foreign policy, effectiveness in: "Effectiveness in foreign policy comes when power is harnessed to a strategic framework and translated into action by creative diplomacy."
—Chester A. Crocker, 1992

Foreign policy, innovation in: "The statesman is unlikely to make bureaucracy as he finds it into a cockpit for innovation, or to be able to make it over for that purpose. He is unlikely, too, to draw new ideas from outside help. Then where on earth are his ideas to come from? The answer is simple. They are to come from his own mind. He has to think them up himself. A statesman capable of innovation on his own is capable of statecraft on his own. A statesman incapable of statecraft should find himself another job."
—James Eayrs, 1967

Foreign policy, instruments of amoral: "Secret diplomacy, propaganda by mass media . . . [or] international conference, espionage, subversion, economic aid, the granting or withholding of foreign trade, guerrilla war, the threat of war, war with conventional forces and war with atomic weapons are all potential instruments of policy, to be used in accordance with the need of the moment, the chances and the cost of success."
—Hugh Seton-Watson, describing Soviet foreign policy, 1961

Foreign policy, measuring success in: "Success in the conduct of our foreign affairs is to be measured not in tally sheets, but by issues satisfactorily resolved, friendships consolidated, rivalries reduced or circumscribed."
—DEAN RUSK, 1955

Foreign policy, methodology of: "The methodology of foreign policy . . . is that we must be gardeners and not mechanics in our approach to world affairs. We must come to think of the development of international life as an organic and not a mechanical process. We must realize that we did not create the forces by which this process operates. We must learn to take those forces for what they are and to induce them to work with us and for us by influencing the environmental stimuli to which they are subjected, but to do this gently and patiently, with understanding and sympathy, not trying to force growth by mechanical means, not tearing the plants up by the roots when they fail to behave as we wish them to. The forces of nature will generally be on the side of him who understands them best and respects them most scrupulously."
—GEORGE F. KENNAN, 1954

Foreign policy, purpose: "The welfare of a state depends on an active foreign policy."
—ARTHASASTRA OF KAUTILYA

Foreign policy, negotiators and: "Success or failure of foreign policy is greatly influenced by the skill of negotiators, whose behavior can be more important for the course of history than is generally recognized. The skill of a negotiator, however, is determined not only by personal ability, but, more importantly, by the total political context, domestic and foreign, within which he operates."
—STEPHEN D. KERTESZ, 1959

Foreign policy, politicization of: "No administration can conduct a sound foreign policy when the future sits in judgment on the past and officials are held accountable as dupes, fools or traitors for anything that goes wrong."
—ADLAI E. STEVENSON, JR., 1954

Foreign policy, popular support for: "No foreign policy—no matter how ingenious—has any chance of success if it is born in the minds of a few and carried in the hearts of none."
—HENRY A. KISSINGER, 1973

Foreign policy, process by which formed: A camel is a horse designed by a committee. A platypus is a bird put together by bureaucrats. An elephant is a mouse built to military specifications. A shrimp is a fish conceived in the legislative process. More often than not, a foreign policy is a course of action devised by a committee of bureaucrats and military men under the oversight of a legislature. Not surprisingly, such a thing defies simple description.

Foreign policy, purpose of: "A political society does not live to conduct foreign policy; it . . . conducts foreign policy in order to live."
—GEORGE F. KENNAN, 1954

Foreign policy, purpose of: "The purpose of foreign policy is not to provide an outlet for our own sentiments of hope or indignation; it is to shape real events in a real world."
—JOHN F. KENNEDY, 1963

Foreign policy, sentiment and: "Foreign policy is not a matter of sentiment; its object is to shape events in conformity with the laws which govern national destiny. These laws exist and we cannot alter them. National interests never change; they are determined by nature, geography, and the character of a nation. History has a habit of repeating itself."
—JULES CAMBON

Foreign policy, strength and: "Foreign policy can be no more impressive and no more effective than the force, the power, the strength that supports it."—LAURIS NORSTAD, 1963

Foreign policy, strength and: "Diplomacy without strength behind it may be merely an aimless exercise."
—LESTER B. PEARSON, 1959

Foreign policy, toothless: "Toothless diplomacy is not . . . persuasive; diplomacy that eschews the use of force degrades into shameless appeasement."
—ZBIGNIEW BRZEZINSKI, 1993

Foreign relations: "Foreign relations are like human relations. They are endless. The solution of one problem usually leads to another." —JAMES RESTON, 1967

Foreign relations: "States receive so much benefit from uninterrupted foreign negotiations, if they are conducted with prudence, that it is unbelievable unless it is known from experience. . . . I dare say emphatically that it is absolutely necessary to the well-being of the state to negotiate ceaselessly, either openly or secretly, and in all places, even in those from which no present fruits are reaped and still more in those for which no future prospects as yet seem likely. . . . Some among these plantings produce their fruit more quickly than others. Indeed, there are those which are no sooner in the ground than they germinate and sprout forth, while others remain long dormant before producing any effect. He who negotiates continuously will finally find the right instant to attain his ends, and even if this does not come about, at least it can be said he has lost nothing while keeping abreast of events in the world, which is not of little consequence in the lives of states. . . . Important negotiations should never be stopped for a moment." —CARDINAL RICHELIEU

Foreign relations: "To most nations, foreign relations are a nuisance filled with anxieties and frustrations and few visible achievements." —KENNETH W. THOMPSON, 1962

Foreign Service, U.S.: "There are those who regard the Foreign Service as a kind of bird sanctuary for elegant young men, with the milk of Groton still wet upon their lips, arrayed in striped pants and spending most of their time handing sugar cookies to ladies of high society in Europe and Latin America. Conversely, there are those who regard diplomatists as an international gang of intriguers intent upon ensnaring the great white soul of the United States." —HAROLD NICOLSON, 1959

Foresight: Those who give no thought to distant opportunities may yet stumble into misfortunes nearer by.

Frank: When used to describe a meeting, suggests that the discussion was blunt and consisted of each side laying out its position in stark terms for the other.

Freedom: Freedom is self-fulfillment in the absence of control and humiliation by others.

Freedom, defense of: "How far can you go without destroying from within what you are trying to defend from without?"
—Dwight D. Eisenhower

Friendly: When used to describe a meeting, generally indicates that nothing much of substance transpired.

Friends: "Friendship is but seldom lasting but between equals, or where the superiority on one side is reduced by some equivalent advantage on the other. Benefits which cannot be repaid, and obligations which cannot be discharged, are not commonly found to increase affection; they excite gratitude indeed, and heighten veneration, but commonly take away that easy freedom and familiarity of intercourse without which, though there may be fidelity, and zeal, and admiration, there cannot be friendship."
—Samuel Johnson

Friends: "The friendships of nations, built on common interests, cannot survive the mutability of those interests."
—Agnes Repplier, 1924

Friends, choice of: "In choosing its friends and allies, a state should be governed not by sentimental attachments but by the respect the candidate commands because of his power."
—Attributed to Cardinal Richelieu

Friends, enemies: Friends come and go. Enemies accumulate.

Friends, enemies and: "Better a wise enemy than a foolish friend."   —Arab proverb

Friends, enemies and: "Treat your friend as if he will one day be your enemy, and your enemy as if he will one day be your friend."
—Laberius, c. 45 b.c.

Friends, help from: "He that is not with me is against me."   —Luke, c. 75

Friends, help from: "A friend who does not help you is the same as an enemy who does you no harm."
—`Abdullah bin `Abd Al-Aziz Al-Sa`ud

Friends, interests: "A state worthy of the name has no friends—only interests."
—Attributed to Charles de Gaulle

Friends, negotiations between: "Nothing is final between friends."
—William Jennings Bryan (as secretary of state, to the Japanese ambassador), 1913

Friends, negotiations between: Negotiation among friends may be less concerned with the conclusion of formal agreements than with the working out of concerted policies for coordinated action consistent with agreements and understandings of long standing.

Friends, negotiations between: Negotiations between friends proceed from common interests and shared ends; the objective is to find a means of carrying out a common course of action to realize these ends. It is a great mistake to approach such negotiations in an adversarial manner. This can only risk raising questions about the extent to which interests are truly held in common and erode the sense of partnership that is the greatest hope for success in both the negotiations and the relationship they are intended to advance.

Friends, support from: "The proper office of a friend is to side with you when you are in the wrong. Nearly anybody will side with you when you are in the right."
—MARK TWAIN

Friends, tending of: A first rule of foreign policy is to find out who your friends are and what their interests are, and then to help them along. If you don't, you must not be surprised if they ultimately decide to act without regard to your interests or fail to back you in times of need.

Friends, true: "A true friend, the one with whom a man may safely associate, will always stick closely to the right way, will worry secretly about his friend's welfare, will console him in misfortune, will offer him a helping hand when he needs it, will keep his secrets, and will always give him good advice." —BUDDHIST SCRIPTURE (SAMACITTA-SUTTA)

Friendship: "The only way to have a friend is to be one." —RALPH WALDO EMERSON

Friendship: "Friendships are tools to be used or abandoned according to circumstances."
—GERMAINE DE STAËL

Friendship, alliance: Friendship is not alliance and does not imply the defense commitments that an alliance entails.

Friendship between nations, basis of: "The circumstances of modes, language, and religion have much less influence in determining the friendship and enmity of nations than other more essential interests."
—JOHN ADAMS

Friendship between nations, invaluable: Over time, relations between nations can become so affable, honest, and reflexive that it becomes virtually unthinkable for one to act on an important matter without seeking and taking into account the views of the other. Such a relationship with a stronger state is the rarest and most valuable possession of a weaker; it must be cherished and nurtured, and never jeopardized by unilateral action.

Friendship, cross-cultural: "He who lives forty days among a people becomes one of them."
—ARAB PROVERB

Friendship, interests and: "Men may be linked in friendship. Nations are linked only by interests."
—ROLF HOCHHUTH, 1967

Friendship not a foreign policy objective: "Not for one moment do I think that the purpose of the State Department is to make friends. The purpose . . . is to look out for the interests of the United States. Whether we make friends, I do not care. I do not care in a lot of these cases [recipients of American aid] whether they are friends or not. We are doing these things because it will serve the interests of the United States."
—JOHN FOSTER DULLES

Friendship, rules of: "There should be mutual sympathy between friends, each supplying what the other lacks and trying to benefit the other, always using friendly and sincere words. One should keep his friend from falling into evil ways, should protect his property and wealth, and should help him in his troubles. If a friend has some misfortune, one should give him a helping hand, even supporting his family, if necessary. In this way, friendship will be maintained and friends will be increasingly happy together."
—BUDDHIST SCRIPTURE (SINGALOVADA-SUTTA)

Full powers: A delegation of authority, which can be shown to the government of another state, for a diplomat to consummate special business on behalf of his government with that state.

Future, predicting: "The best way to predict the future is to create it." —PETER DRUCKER

Gaffe, political: A politically embarrassing blunder, e.g., the inadvertent confirmation of a politically incorrect truth by a government spokesman or politician.

Generals, attrition: Few nations end wars of attrition with the same generals with whom they began them.

Generosity: See *Charity*.

Genius: Genius is seeing what is obvious before it becomes obvious to everybody else.

Geography: "Geography is destiny."

—CHINESE MILITARY APHORISM

Geography, politics: Geography is more permanent than politics.

Geopolitics: "Who rules East Europe commands the Heartland; who rules the Heartland commands the World-Island; who rules the World-Island commands the world."

—HALFORD MACKINDER, 1923

Geopolitics, defined: The strategic logic of interests derived from the relationships between national power and the domination of specific territories, bodies of water, airspaces, or extra-atmospheric orbital zones.

Geopolitics, influence on policy of: Whether a state is prone to act to forestall aggression or merely to oppose it once it has occurred depends in no small measure on its geopolitical circumstances. Powers that confront enemies directly, with no intervening space such as oceans or deserts to make their threat more distant and less immediate, generally are more active in efforts to forestall threats than are those that occupy a position of greater safety.

Gestures, cultural differences: Movements of the body regarded as innocent in one society are among the most offensive of gestures in another. One man's gauche and thoughtless burp is another's considered culinary compliment; one man's insult with the fingers or the feet is a meaningless movement or a gesture of affection for yet another.

Gestures, friendly: "Paranoid personalities tend to be very suspicious of friendly gestures."

—ALEXANDER L. GEORGE, 1993

Gifts: "If an envoy seeks by means of presents to secure the goodwill or friendship of those who can assist him in attaining his objects, but without either expressly or tacitly

asking from them anything wrong, this is not to be regarded as bribery."
—G.F. DE MARTENS

Gifts: "[An ambassador should refuse] to accept any gifts or presents, either from the prince to whom he is sent or from any of his people for any cause whatsoever, unless, having already taken leave, he is about to mount his horse."
—HOTMAN DE VILLIERS, 1603, CITED BY J.J. JUSSERAND

Glory, war: War grants soldiers the glory of compensating with their lives for the stupidity and negligence of politicians.

Good deeds: "No good deed goes unpunished."   —CLARE BOOTH LUCE

Good faith: "It is the task of the diplomat to make up for political misunderstanding, cultural ignorance, economic unequality in order to create the conditions of dignity, fairness, mutual understanding, sometimes even connivance, which are needed between people of different cultures, races or continents. International good faith requires permanent information and reflection on others and also a patient and constant effort to give a good impression of one's attitude, in order to be credible and to put others at ease. In a world in which a growing economic, technical and cultural integration has to be developed, responsible leaders and public opinion will no longer accept negligence, delusion, disloyalty, irresponsibility and incoherence in diplomacy. Of course, fair play is not silliness or lack of foresight; transparency (glasnost) and sincerity are neither levity nor imprudence; treaties do not exempt states from precautions, guarantees and adaptation. Herein lies the art of diplomacy."   —ALAIN PLANTEY, 1989

Good offices: An effort by a state, or by an international organization or other entity, not itself involved in a dispute, to stimulate the process of settlement in such a dispute between two or more other states. See also *Conciliation*.

Government: The individuals and institutions exercising political direction and control over a state or the political subdivision of a state.

Government, weak: "You can tell a weak government by its eagerness to resort to strong measures."   —BENJAMIN DISRAELI

Governments, foreign-installed: "Regimes planted by bayonets do not take root."
—RONALD W. REAGAN

Gratitude: "Gratitude is a word only fools use. You can find it in the dictionary, but not in the human heart."   —HONORÉ DE BALZAC

Gratitude: "To say that gratitude is never to enter into the motives of national conduct, is to revive a principle which has been buried for centuries with its kindred principles of the lawfulness of assassination, poison, perjury, etc."   —THOMAS JEFFERSON, 1789

Gratitude: "If you pick up a starving dog and make him prosperous, he will not bite you. This is the principal difference between a dog and a man."   —MARK TWAIN

Gratitude: "Nations are never so grateful as their benefactors expect."
                                                        —WELLINGTON, 1814

Gratitude: See also *Charity*.

Guarantee: A treaty obliging its signatory states to assure the maintenance of an agreed situation, if necessary by the use of force.

Guests, responsibilities of: "Please them as long as you are in their land; hail them while in their neighborhood you stand; and in their home, grant them the upper hand."
                                                        —ARAB PROVERB

Haste: Haste is the mother of pratfalls.

Hatred: "Men's hatreds generally spring from fear and envy." —Niccolò Machiavelli

Hatred: "The foremost art of kings is the power to endure hatred." —Seneca

Hatred, cure: The only cure for hatred is a brave act of love.

Head of Government: An individual who holds office as the highest leader of political administration in a nation but who is not its head of state, e.g., a prime minister.

Head of State: The individual who holds the highest constitutional office symbolizing state sovereignty, e.g., a king or president.

Healing: Wounds heal; humiliation festers.

Hedging: "Hedges guard against serious loss by limiting upside gain. For those who want to profit from the market, the better strategy is to hold a diversified portfolio that offers the possibility of substantial gain while reducing the risk of catastrophe. In international relations, strategic hedges limit rather than expand the realm of the possible. They undermine mutual confidence rather than building trust. Wise leaders seek instead to supplement military preparedness with the cultivation of as many good relationships as they can with other countries. They strive to sustain better relations with potential adversaries than such nations have with each other and to assure that an improved relationship with one does not result in worsened relations with another. They carefully nurture friendships that might come in handy if unexpected threats emerge. This is the essence of good diplomacy."
—J. Stapleton Roy

Hegemony: "A precarious preponderance of power on one side can always ensure peace for a time, but it cannot be relied upon to endure. If it should happen that that preponderance were in wrong hands we should have the wrong kind of peace—a peace enforced by tyranny and oppression—the peace of the grave. A lasting peace cannot depend upon a momentary preponderance of power possessed by one group of nations, but only upon the constant readjustment of policies having for their object community of interest."
—Victor Wellesley, 1944

Historians, statesmen: Historians must invent the past so that statesmen can use it to invent the future.

Historians, viewpoint of: "Until lions have their own historians, tales of the hunt will glorify the hunter!"   —AFRICAN APHORISM

History: "History is the foremost tool for political analysis."   —ADDA BOZEMAN, 1992

History: "The diplomatist should know the history of the great powers and of their relations with each other, as a competent physician would wish to know the life record of a delicate or dangerous patient, for the present is but the epitome and expression of the past. The future knows no other guide and it is from history that we are to gather the formulas of present action."   —DAVID J. HILL

History: "If people always understood, there would have been no history."
           —TALLEYRAND

History, diplomatic: "The narrative of brilliant campaigns and heroic military achievements may, at first glance, seem more attractive than the story of the reasons why battles have been fought; but, as after a storm the fallen trees in the forest, the fragments of wrecks upon the shore, and the general upheaval of nature, though more exciting, are of less abiding human interest than a knowledge of the atmospheric conditions out of which the tempest has been born, so the plans and purposes and policies of nations are intrinsically more important than the march of armies and the carnage of military conflicts. It is the psychological factor in moments of creative action that gives history its highest instructive value and its most lasting social utility."   —DAVID J. HILL, 1906

History, lessons from: It is not true that people do not learn from history. They just learn the wrong lessons.

History, prediction: "The longer you look back, the farther you can look forward."
           —WINSTON CHURCHILL

History, prediction: "Prudent men are wont to say—and this not rashly or without good ground—that he who would foresee what has to be should reflect on what has been, for everything that happens in the world at any time has a genuine resemblance to what happened in ancient times."   —NICCOLÒ MACHIAVELLI

History, statecraft: "In history, lie all the secrets of statecraft."   —WINSTON CHURCHILL

History, war: "Nothing in history is inevitable, including the probable. So long as war has not broken out, we still have the possibility of avoiding it. Those who think that there is little difference between a cold and a hot war are either knaves or fools."
           —REINHOLD NIEBUHR

History, worldview: Nations interpret the present by reference to their past. If that past includes traumatic events, their interpretation of the present will often diverge radically from objectively verifiable reality.

History, wrong side of: When history is going against you, it's time for a strategic retreat.

Homecoming for diplomats: ". . . if we do return, we find that the native air has lost its invigorating quality, and that life has shifted its reality to the spot where we have deemed ourselves only temporary residents. Thus, between two countries, we have none at all. . . . "
—Nathaniel Hawthorne

Honesty: "In addition to absolute honesty in relation to one's own government and to one's host's, the wise diplomat will be equally forthright toward his diplomatic colleagues. This does not mean that he will always tell them everything he knows but that he will never deliberately lie or mislead them. Temptations to do so are frequent in diplomatic life, where no two ambassadors represent identical interests."
—Charles W. Thayer, 1959

Honesty: "I hold the maxim no less applicable to public than to private life that honesty is always the best policy."
—George Washington

Honor: Considerations of honor, as much as of self-interest, fear, and domestic political calculation, determine national policy.

Honor: "A really great people, proud and high-spirited, would face all the disasters of war rather than purchase that base prosperity which is bought at the price of national honor."
—Theodore Roosevelt, 1907

Honor: "The policy of honor is also the policy of peace."   —Lord Salisbury, 1864

Honor, national: "National honor is national property of the highest value."
—James Monroe, 1817

Host government: See *Receiving state.*

Hostage: A person held for ransom or political effect.

Human rights: See *Ideology.*

Humility, in negotiations: Do not pretend to know what you do not. No one ever lost a point in a negotiation by asking for time to check it; many have conceded points they should not have because they were too proud to admit they needed to research them.

Humility, virtue of: "Never seem wiser or more learned than the people you are with."
—Lord Chesterfield, 1748

Humor: "Humor can create a pervasive sense of geniality which may help in solving difficult problems."   —Unidentified diplomat quoted by John St. G. Creaghe, 1965

Humor, sense of: "It's better to have a sense of humor than no sense at all."
—Attributed to Mark Twain

Hypocrisy: An ambassador is a man out to make the world safe for hypocrisy.

I

Idealism: A foreign policy of idealism risks defeating itself with its own weapons.

Ideas: "Bad strategy sinks good ideas."

—Anatoly Dobrynin, 1995

Ideas, false: "A false but clear and precise idea always has more power in the world than one which is true but complex."

—Alexis de Tocqueville

Ideas, guns: "Why should freedom of speech and freedom of the press be allowed? Why should a government which is doing what it believes is right allow itself to be criticized? It would not allow opposition by lethal weapons. Ideas are much more fatal things than guns."

—Vladimir Ilyich Lenin

Ideas, talk: When ideas fail, lofty talk will often do.

Ideas, words: "When ideas fail, words come in very handy."

—Johann Wolfgang von Goethe

Ideology: A mode of moral reasoning, consisting of myth, doctrine, and rhetorical style, that purports to explain cause and effect and that evaluates these with approval or disapproval.

Ideology: "It is the essence of a moral claim that it cannot be compromised, precisely because it justifies itself by considerations beyond expediency."

—Henry A. Kissinger, 1964

Ideology: "The belief that international politics should be the struggle not of interests but of principles accords awkwardly with diplomacy. It calls in question a fundamental premise of a states system, the independence of the member states and the right of each to decide for itself how to manage its domestic affairs. This difference of assumption goes with a difference in style. The dogmatic formulation of principles, especially in a political or religious crusade, is doctrinaire and inflexible, unlike the elasticity and preference for give and take of the diplomatic dialogue. The more a man is attached to dogmas, the less responsive he is to calls for agreement through compromise, believing that the fundamentals may be negotiated away if they are treated on a level with mundane balancing of interests familiar in negotiations between states."

—Adam Watson, 1983

Ideology in foreign policy: Ideological conviction implies the desire to export the system of government it justifies; it is inherently revolutionary and aggressive because it transforms relations between states from a difference of interests, which it is right to seek to conciliate, into a conflict between philosophies, in which to compromise is unrighteous.

It expands the arena of international struggle to include the internal policies and social structures of foreign states, explicitly challenging their legitimacy and implicitly inviting their overthrow. A foreign policy based on the impulse to propagate principles and ideas, no matter how noble and apparently benign, is therefore inherently more disruptive of international order and more likely to engender armed conflict than one based on tolerance of diverse systems of government and realistic accommodation of antagonists, morally flawed as they may be.

Ideology, intelligence: Ideology provides the mental filter through which intelligence is interpreted and translated into policy. It is therefore the proximate cause of most strategic misjudgments and surprises.

Ideology, perils of: "A mature and great power will make measured and limited use of its power. It will eschew the theory of a global and universal duty which not only commits it to unending wars of intervention but intoxicates its thinking with the illusion that it is a crusader for righteousness." —WALTER LIPPMANN

Ideology, terrorism: "Scratch any ideology and beneath it you will find a terrorist!" —ATTRIBUTED TO EDMUND BURKE

Ignorance, democracies: "A popular government without popular information, or the means of acquiring it, is but a prologue to a farce or a tragedy, or perhaps both. Knowledge will forever govern ignorance, and a people who mean to be their own governors must arm themselves with the power which knowledge gives." —JAMES MADISON

Ignorance, understanding: To act on the basis of ignorance is reckless; to understand and fail to act is irresponsible.

Illusion: "A little fact will sustain a lot of illusion." —ERIC AMBLER

Illusion: "Belief in his own magic is the downfall of the magician." —ITALIAN PROVERB

Illusion, dangerous: The most dangerous illusion is the belief that one has no illusions.

Image, changing: To change your image, do something that so fundamentally contradicts the common view of you that it surprises others into reconsideration of it.

Immunities: See *Privileges and immunities.*

Immunity, sovereign: The doctrine that a state and its instrumentalities may not be subjected to the judicial authority, administrative jurisdiction, or legal process of another state.

Impact: The extent to which the application of a capability is felt by an opponent. Impact is affected by distance, time, and experience. Nearness, both geographic and psychological, enhances the impact of actions by a state. Distance weakens capabilities; great distance weakens them greatly. With time and experience, what was once seen as intolerable may come to be suffered with equanimity. What was once seen as highly desirable may come to be taken for granted.

Impotence: Impotence is the root of rage; rage blossoms easily into passion for revenge; this bears fruit in zealotry.

Inanity: "To say nothing, especially when speaking, is half the art of diplomacy."
—Will Durant

Incidents: "Civil confusions often spring from trifles but decide great issues."
—Aristotle

Incidents: "International incidents should not govern foreign policy, but foreign policy, incidents."
—Napoleon

Independence: "The most important of all the interests of states, which are the real business of diplomacy, is independence, the very survival of the state. Where a powerful state threatens its neighbors, however great or small the ideological element in its motives may be, the threatened states will feel impelled to cooperate against the common danger, in spite of their own ideological differences."
—Adam Watson, 1983

Independence: "The price of a system comprised of a number of independences, a situation where no hegemonic power can lay down the law to the rest, is a world where no power is strong enough to enjoy absolute security: a world where insecurity is therefore endemic and in varying degrees universal, and not merely accidental or caused by the actions of evil, aggressive and disgruntled men. The mere coexistence of numbers of states does not hold out the promise, let alone the guarantee, of universal concord."
—Adam Watson, 1983

Indispensable men: "The graveyards are full of indispensable men."
—attributed to Charles de Gaulle

Inevitability: The belief that conflict is inevitable is often a major factor in making it so.

Influence: The persuasive effect of attractive leadership born of reciprocal commitment, admiration, desire for approbation, empathy, and loyalty or of coercive power that arouses fear of annihilation, chastisement, humiliation, and dishonor.

Influence: "Men are moved by feelings alone. Even actions that at first glance may appear to be farthest from what are commonly called emotional acts have some hidden

sentimental motive behind them. One man may appear to give in only to the strength of reason: his firm belief depends on a clearly perceived interest, on the interest of being convinced, and the interest itself is a sentiment that derives from the instinct for preservation. Another may faithfully follow the rules of justice: this love of justice is a sentiment mixed with the love of society and glory, and tempered by other parts of instinct. Thus, to make men act, to convince them, to persuade them is always a question of putting into motion an emotion that determines the will in the particular case. To know on which emotions to play in order to make a particular individual act, we must study his character and know the nature of his mind, his habits, and his passions."
—Fortune Barthélemy de Felice, 1778

Influence, ideas: It is not enough to be strong. To lead, one must have ideas worth following.

Influence, moral: "Moral influence is the most essential qualification of the diplomatist. He must be a man of the strictest honor if the government to which he is accredited and his own government are to place explicit confidence in his statements." —Jules Cambon

Influence, sphere of: A geopolitical zone within which the interests and influence of a major power are acknowledged by others to be paramount and worthy of deference.

Influence, virtues from which derived: "Influence is founded on seven specific diplomatic virtues, namely: truthfulness, precision, calm, good temper, patience, modesty, and loyalty."
—Harold Nicolson

Informality: "The more secure the social position of an individual is, the more casual and informal he is prepared to be."
—Adam Watson, 1982

Innovation, strategic: "No repetition of a winning move." —Chinese military maxim

Insincerity: "Insincerity is a grave defect in a public man, however harmless it may be in private life, for it betokens a lack of judgment which on occasion may prove disastrous."
—Jules Cambon

Insinuation: "One often meets men who are as difficult to convince as they are to arouse and who disdain all ideas other than their own. Neither a lack of intelligence nor a lack of sentiment is the cause of this difficulty: it is rather their attachment to their own thoughts, their vanity of never learning anything from anyone else, their suspicion of formal propositions, which renders men deaf to the voice of persuasion. With characters of this kind one must use insinuation, which is a roundabout way of suggesting ideas so that the hearer believes he has invented them himself. Since the little passions that block these minds' entrance to truth are very common and are found somewhere in every character, the art of insinuation is of more general usage than that of direct persuasion."
—Fortune Barthélemy de Felice, 1778

Inspectors: Itinerant inquisitors from the capital who investigate charges of misconduct by an embassy or consulate or visit to review its operations.

Instructions: Diplomatic instructions should concentrate on describing the desired results of a demarche, not the verbal choreography by which they are to be accomplished. At its most effective, diplomacy is an invisible dance to the alien music of a foreign capital, not a swagger conducted to the insistent rhythms of one's own.

Instructions: "As he is bound to know the interests of his master, the ambassador may and must make up his mind (without waiting for instructions) in accordance with events, and those are the occasions when the clever and true negotiator distinguishes himself from the common man and the ordinary minister of no parts."
—ROUSSEAU DE CHAMOY, 1697, CITED BY J.J. JUSSERAND

Instructions, ambassadorial role: "An ambassador is not a subaltern charged with executing instructions, he is a collaborator who must always, even at the risk of displeasing, explain himself freely on questions that are seen at [the capital] from only one viewpoint."
—PAUL CAMBON, 1911

Instructions, bureaucratic: An ambassador's instructions may represent a serious attempt to advance his government's interests or they may be no more than an effort by bureaucrats in his capital to avoid having themselves to register domestic political concerns about a disagreeable matter with his counterpart there. His government may in fact desire no more than to be able to announce that the matter is under active discussion, allowing it to fade from public attention. In carrying out such instructions, an ambassador should accept the implicit judgment of his capital that he is to act in a manner calculated to place his government's views on the record while avoiding damage to relations with his host nation.

Instructions, diplomatic: Well-formulated diplomatic instructions stress strategic objectives and leave a large arena for tactical adjustment to chance and local circumstances; nothing is sure in diplomatic intercourse, and those far from the scene of action are highly unlikely to be able to anticipate the state of play once engagement has occurred.

Instructions, flawed: An ambassador cannot exonerate himself from responsibility for failure by declaring that he was merely executing the instructions he received from his capital when he knew those instructions to be ill informed, flawed, or foolishly provocative to those they were intended to persuade. He should communicate his reasons for insisting on a change of instructions, and be prepared, finally, to resign his commission when consequences of carrying out his government's mandate would be ruinous to the interests of his nation.

Instructions, flawed: "An ambassador should possess sufficient authority with his home government to be able to persuade them from a course of action which, given the local circumstances, he knows will prove disastrous." —HAROLD NICOLSON, 1954

Instructions, initial: Initial bargaining instructions tend to be inflexible. They are usually the result of protracted domestic haggling and debate between agencies and individuals in the capital—the lowest common denominator of domestic interests rather than a considered judgment about what is feasible.

Insults: "Insults serve as arguments for those who are in the wrong."　　　—FÉNELON

Insults: "The use of insulting language towards an enemy arises generally from the insolence of victory, or from the false hope of victory, which latter misleads men as often in their actions as in their words; for when this false hope takes possession of the mind, it makes men go beyond the mark, and causes them to sacrifice a certain good for an uncertain better."　　　—NICCOLÒ MACHIAVELLI

Insurgency, defined: "An insurgency is an organized, protracted politico-military struggle designed to weaken government control and legitimacy while increasing insurgent control. Insurgencies normally seek to either overthrow the existing social order and reallocate power within the country, or to break away from state control and form an autonomous area."　　　—U.S. ARMY FIELD MANUAL

Insurrection: "Irregular warfare is far more intellectual than a bayonet charge."　　　—T.E. LAWRENCE

Insurrection: "Rebellion must have an unassailable base. It must have a friendly population, not actively friendly, but sympathetic to the point of not betraying rebel movements to the enemy. Rebellions can be made by 2 per cent active in a striking force, and 98 per cent passively sympathetic. Granted mobility, security, time and doctrine victory will rest with the insurgents, for the algebraical factors are in the end decisive, and against them perfections of means and spirit struggle quite in vain."　　　—T.E. LAWRENCE

Insurrection, defeating: To defeat an insurrection, one must frighten the people without enraging them; one must erode one's opponents' faith in their cause without driving them to desperate measures; and one must paint a clear picture of the future that can convince one's opponents and their adherents that accommodation will lead to an honorable and advantageous outcome.

Intellect, power of: "An archer letting off an arrow may or may not kill a single man, but a wise man using his intellect can kill—even reaching into the very womb."　　　—ARTHASASTRA OF KAUTILYA

Intellectuals, advocates: In the great whorehouse of politics, every policy, no matter how preposterous, will find some intellectual prepared to entertain it and willing, at the appropriate moment, to cry out its name with apparent passion.

Intelligence: Intelligence is the sensory apparatus of the state, without which it is blind, deaf, and numb.

Intelligence: "Intelligence is the Soul of all Publick business." —DANIEL DEFOE, 1704

Intelligence: "Forewarned, forearmed." —BENJAMIN FRANKLIN, 1736

Intelligence: "Great advantage is drawn from knowledge of your adversary, and when you know the measure of his intelligence and character you can use it to play on his weaknesses." —FREDERICK THE GREAT

Intelligence: "Information is power." —ATTRIBUTED TO ARTHUR SYLVESTER, 1962

Intelligence: "The true statesman does not despise any wisdom, howsoever lowly may be its origin." —MARK TWAIN, 1889

Intelligence: "It is essential to know the character of the enemy and of their principal officers—whether they be rash or cautious, enterprising or timid, whether they fight on principle or from chance." —VEGETIUS, 378

Intelligence, analysis: "It is not enough simply to collect information. Thoughtful analysis is vital to sound decisionmaking. The goal of intelligence analysts can be nothing short of the truth, even when that truth is unpleasant or unpopular." —RONALD W. REAGAN, 1981

Intelligence, analysis vs. operations: Analysis requires objectivity. Espionage demands deceit. The two presuppose fundamentally incompatible character traits in their practitioners. If they are carried out or managed by the same officials or organization, the analysis will be deceitfully subjective and the espionage will be ineptly naïve.

Intelligence officers, qualities of good: "The qualities of a good intelligence [and, equally, of a good diplomatic reporting] officer [are to]:
  Be perceptive about people
  Be able to work well with others under difficult conditions
  Learn to distinguish between fact and fiction
  Be able to distinguish between essentials and nonessentials
  Possess inquisitiveness
  Have a large amount of ingenuity
  Pay appropriate attention to detail
  Be able to express ideas clearly, briefly and, very important, interestingly
  Learn when to keep your mouth shut.
  "A good intelligence officer must have an understanding of other points of view, other ways of thinking and behaving, even if they are quite foreign to his own. Rigidity and

closed-mindedness are qualities that do not spell a good fortune in intelligence."
—ALLEN DULLES, ADVICE TO JUNIOR INTELLIGENCE OFFICERS, 1963

Intelligence, overt and covert collection: Most intelligence is collected openly, from the press or by diplomats. But in closed societies, the wall of secrecy can often only be breached by spies. It is there that they have there greatest utility.

Intelligence, policy: "The best intelligence is essential to the best policy."
—LYNDON B. JOHNSON, 1966

Intelligence, power of: "He who has the eye of knowledge, and is acquainted with the science of polity, can with little effort make use of his skills for intrigue, and can succeed by means of conciliation, and other strategic means and by spies and chemical appliances in overreaching even those kings who are possessed of enthusiasms and power."
—ARTHASASTRA OF KAUTILYA

Intelligence, predictions: "What we do at best (at worst we perform trivial tricks) when postulating the future, is to expand enormously the specious present."
—VLADIMIR NABOKOV

Intelligence, resistance of policymakers to: "A firmly established policy provides a framework and atmosphere that can subtly discourage intelligence from contradicting existing policy and reduce policy specialists' receptivity to information that calls policy into question."
—ALEXANDER L. GEORGE, 1993

Intelligence, views of foreign leaders: Among the most useful of all intelligence to a diplomat is reporting on how a foreign official views him and assesses his government, its motivations, policies, and actions. Knowing this, he can devise ways to correct misperceptions and misunderstandings and to cast his arguments in more persuasive form.

Intelligence reports, wartime: "Many intelligence reports in war are contradictory; even more are false, and most are uncertain."
—CARL MARIA VON CLAUSEWITZ

Interdependence: A condition in which the economies of two or more nations are so inextricably interwoven that conflict between them is inhibited by powerful domestic interests in both.

Interest, national: The relationship a state perceives to exist between its security, well-being, and power, and the security, well-being, and power of other states.

Interest, strategic: An interest, often geopolitical or economic in nature, that a state perceives as likely over time to determine its ability to defend or promote its vital interests.

Interest, vital: An interest that a state will defend or seek to further, if necessary, by military force, because it perceives it as bearing directly on its continued existence as an independent entity, its territorial integrity, or the lives of its people.

Interests: "Isolated states exist only as the abstractions of so-called philosophers. In the society of states each state has interests which connect it with the others. The great axioms of political science derive from the recognition of the true interests of all states; it is in general interests that the guarantee of existence is to be found, while particular interests—the cultivation of which is considered political wisdom by restless and short-sighted men—have only a secondary importance. History demonstrates the application of the principle of solidarity and equilibrium and of the united efforts of states against the supremacy of one power in order to force a return to the common law."

—METTERNICH, 1807

Interests: "It is a maxim, founded on the universal experience of mankind, that no nation is to be trusted farther than it is bound by its interest, and no prudent statesman or politician will venture to depart from it."

—GEORGE WASHINGTON, 1778

Interests, among allies: It is common for nations that are close allies to assert that their interests are identical. This is always hyperbole at best, and at worst delusion. The interests of two states may coincide for a time, or be parallel with regard to a particular subject matter or objective, but they are never identical. In the end, they will diverge and may even come into opposition.

Interests, as basis of agreements: Agreements between nations must rest on real interests and verifiable commitments, not trust. Trust is ephemeral; interests last. Intentions are important, and it is vital to understand them accurately. In the end, however, it is even more important to know how nations perceive their interests than to understand them objectively. A nation's view of its national interests determines whether its intentions are fantasies or plans of action.

Interests, as basis of foreign policy: "Self-interest is the mainspring of foreign policy. Sentiment changes but self-interest persists."

—THOMAS A. BAILEY, 1968

Interests, as basis of foreign policy: "Policies whose foundations are sunk, not in the firm rock of national interest, but in such ideologies as prejudice, unjustified fear, sentimental affections or hatreds, the spirit of reform and crusade, the sense of moral superiority, are built on quicksand."

—PAUL SCOTT MOWRER, 1924

Interests, diplomats and: "All diplomats are bound to place the interests of their own countries in the forefront of their consciousness."

—HAROLD NICOLSON

Interests, foreign: A great deal of diplomatic success rests on developing the credibility and empathy necessary to persuade foreign statesmen to discover compatible interests for their nation that they had overlooked or slighted and to assist them in pursuing these interests to mutual advantage.

Interests, harmonizing: "The secret of negotiation is to harmonize the real interests of the parties concerned."   —François de Callières, 1716

Interests, identification of: International society is held together not by law or authority but by common interests and by voluntary agreements and contracts. Identifying these interests and negotiating these agreements are the functions of diplomacy.

Interests, in democracies: "The foreign policy of a government chosen by the people obviously should be designed to serve their interests, and these become the national interest."   —Dean Rusk, 1964

Interests, moral duties and: "With nations as with individuals our interests soundly calculated will ever be found inseparable from our moral duties."
                                          —Thomas Jefferson, 1805

Interests, permanent: "It is a narrow policy to suppose that this country or that is to be marked out as the eternal ally or the perpetual enemy of [our country]. We have no eternal allies, and we have no perpetual enemies. Our interests are eternal and perpetual, and those interests it is our duty to follow. It is our duty not to pass too harsh a judgment upon others, because they do not exactly see things in the same light as we see; and it is our duty not lightly to engage this country in the frightful responsibilities of war."
                                          —Palmerston, 1848

Interests, policies and: When interests are not clearly defined and ranked, diplomacy is unsure. It is forced into self-wounding ambiguity and its impact on potential allies and adversaries alike is, at best, inconclusive. In such circumstances, policy invites challenge, deterrence may fail, and the risk of war by inadvertence rises. Leaving the identification of vital interests to the unpredictable actions of the adversaries who may challenge them is the highest form of policy futility.

Interests, policies and: "We must recognize that every nation determines its policies in terms of its own interests."   —John F. Kennedy, 1963

Interests, political: "Politics is the science of the vital interests of States in its widest meaning. The great axioms of political science proceed from the knowledge of the true political interests of all states; it is upon these general interests that rests the guarantee of their existence."   —Metternich

Interests, special: "Not even the King has the right to subordinate the interests of the state to his personal sympathies or antipathies." —OTTO VON BISMARCK

Interests section: A section within an embassy that represents a third state that has no diplomatic relations with the host state and government. In carrying out the business of such an otherwise unrepresented third state, an interests section is often staffed with its nationals, by approval of the host government.

Internal affairs, interference in: "The only safe principle is that of the Law of Nations— That no state has a right to endanger its neighbors by its internal Proceedings, and that if it does, provided they exercise a sound discretion, Their right of Interference is clear." —CASTLEREAGH, 1818

Internal affairs, interference in: "Obviously, no diplomat can long expect to remain at his post if he gives offense to his hosts, and the surest way to do so is to interfere in their politics." —CHARLES ROETTER, 1963

Internal affairs, intervention in: "A belief that it is possible for one country to modify the institutions of another country has some validity—at least, up to a point, and depending on the country." —ELLIS BRIGGS, 1968

Internal affairs, right of interference in: No state or group of states has the right to intervene in the domestic affairs of another nation unless the influence of these affairs reaches abroad to menace the security and liberties of others.

Internal affairs, sanctions as intervention in: "If one is going to interfere in the internal affairs of a country by economic sanctions, not only is one going to be unsuccessful, but also one is doing something basically wrong, if not indeed wicked. That is to say, one engages in an attempt to foment civil disturbance, uprisings, revolution, and violence." —DEAN ACHESON, 1969

International: Pertaining to two or more nations or their citizens. See also *Multinational* and *Transnational*.

International organizations: International organizations are often formed to give expression to a concept of regional or ideological unity that transcends the national interests of member states and their ruling elites. Such organizations are meant to harmonize the policies of their member states. To the extent they succeed in doing so, they pander to the lowest common denominator of their members' interests and paralyze initiative; they thereby become an embarrassing obstacle to problem solving. To the extent they fail to harmonize their members' policies, they come to be seen as impotent or irrelevant— diplomatic fog factories, filling the air with vapid rhetoric and sophistry that obfuscates rather than clarifies or facilitates solution of the questions before them. Such international organizations are obvious fora of choice for governments seeking formal refuge from efforts to address issues they would rather not see resolved.

International organizations, as police: "The paradox is that men of liberal mind, who would be offended by the idea that police are the most important factor in assuring social cohesion, do not hesitate to become fierce police enthusiasts when they discuss the international system. The zealots of world community and collective security might have spared themselves these anomalies if they had been less despairing about the wide field of cooperation that lies open to international organizations, once the fantasy of coercion is laid aside. If there is not much to be done by law and enforcement, there are still the alternatives of politics and adjustment. The tragedies of our age should not blind us to the achievements of noncoercive diplomacy. Indeed, unrealistic dreams about enforcement may have led statesmen and diplomats to underestimate the promise and dignity of their task as conciliators. Even in our unsatisfactory world clashes of national interest are usually settled without the threat or use of force. Most of them are resolved by routine processes of diplomacy and conference. If coercion is abandoned, only persuasion remains; and in a world of sovereign nation-states, each devoted to its particular national interest, there is no substitute for persuasion. In the final resort, the prevention of war, like the prevention of civil strife within society, does not depend on legal procedures or policy coercion, but on the art of adjustment." —ABBA EBAN, 1983

International organizations, effective use of: "The quiet use of the facilities of the United Nations, where all states are represented by professional diplomats, may be far more effective than rushing about in all directions." —ATTRIBUTED TO BRIAN URQUHART

International organizations, limitations of: Where patriotism is a virtue it is hard to espouse a brotherhood that laughs at boundaries.

International organizations, rhetoric at: "There is a theory that portrays debate as of intrinsic value in diplomacy: the more people talk to each other, the greater the chance that they will achieve mutual understanding. Most of us realize from personal experience that this is not necessarily true. If the style of rhetoric is self-laudatory denunciation of others and innocent of any element of compromise it is not unreasonable to conclude that debate can widen the gulf between nations and add to the difficulties of accommodation. The glib statement that it is better for nations to argue than to fight is superficial. The question is whether mere ventilation of grievances necessarily makes conciliation easier. Those of us who have worked in various fields of diplomacy cannot deny the assertion that 'the least inhibited language in the annals of diplomacy is recorded at the United Nations.' Diplomacy, traditionally associated with civility and courtliness, is turned on its head. Ventilation theorists allege that even these angry orations are beneficial since they are a substitute for physical violence. This is a nonsensical rationalization by those who cannot bear to hear a critical word about international organization. Descriptions of [other nations in derogatory terms] are an obstacle to conciliation, not a substitute for it.

In the restraint of its discourse, as in many other attributes, traditional diplomacy has a better record than multilateral debate."

—ABBA EBAN, 1983

Internuncio: The title carried by diplomatic officers of the Vatican equivalent to ministers.

Interpretation, simultaneous: "Simultaneous interpretation, so called, is actually consecutive by virtue of the necessary interpretive gap of two or three words or even a complete phrase. When done from one language into a closely related language of generally similar sentence structure the result is not only a brilliant performance but [one that is] quite acceptably faithful in sense and nuance. When, however, it is done into a language that belongs to a different family of languages and in which word and phrase order are radically different, the end product, no matter how brilliantly arrived at, is perforce nothing more than a loose running paraphrase which at best is awkward and which can be grotesque in structure and wrong in meaning. In such a case nuance loses any chance of survival."

—ROBERT B. EKVALL

Interpreters, briefing of: Interpreters should know the basis and logic of the case their side wishes to make before they are called upon to render it into the other side's language. They can play an invaluable role in shaping arguments in ways that the other side can most easily understand and accept.

Interpreters, knowledge required by: "A good interpreter must know almost as much about world affairs as the statesmen whose speeches he translates. Otherwise he will miss subtle but significant references to events in some distant part of the world or ignore nuances which may herald a change of attitude on the part of the government which the speaker represents. He must study the great international figures, because he will be translating them time and again. The more he can learn about their mannerisms, their turns of phrase, their cast of mind, the better he will do his job."

—AN UNIDENTIFIED INTERPRETER QUOTED BY CHARLES ROETTER, 1963

Interpreters, qualities of effective: "Complete linguistic competence alone does not make an interpreter. To be really successful, the interpreter must paradoxically combine in his character and personality two contradictions: he may not be stolid and at the same time he must grimly and successfully refuse to panic. Interpretation at its best is based on something very close to inspiration. And that flares its brightest when the nerves are taut and the sharp impact of the unexpected spurs mind and tongue to creative response. There is no time for studious reference such as is permitted the translator. A mere mechanical juggling with dictionary-derived equivalents may make some sense but not enough to be called interpretation and to echo faithfully all that is meant in the words that are said.

"At the same time, and in the very grip of nervous tension, the interpreter must not panic. He is caught in a torrent of words. Some make sense and some do not. His principal speaks too fast to permit the taking of adequate notes, changes his mind and figures of speech, doubles back out of sentences having no proper end, and links dangling phrase to dangling phrase with reckless abandon. Then he stops for breath and his interpreter must make it all equally clear or cloudy in another tongue. His refusal to panic must be constant and successful." —ROBERT B. EKVALL

Interpreters, statesmen and: The interpreter is the essential, "faithful echo" of the statesman. —ROBERT B. EKVALL

Interpreters, style of speech suited to: The statesman who wishes to assure the accuracy of interpretation and to hold the interest of a foreign interlocutor who does not speak his language is well advised to speak briefly in one or two sentences expressing a complete thought rather than at great and tangled length.

Interpreters, use of by negotiators: It is wise for a negotiator, even if he speaks the language of the other side well, to use an interpreter. This preserves the principle that he regards his own language as authoritative, assures that his statements reflect a full command of the nuances involved, maintains a record of discussion in his own language, reassures those on his own negotiating team who may not speak the foreign language as well as he, and gives him extra time to consider how best to conduct himself as discussion proceeds.

Intervention: Action by a state to control or direct the internal affairs of another, especially by military means.

Intervention, military: "Military action is a barbed hook; once it goes in, there is no quick release." —JAMES FALLOWS

Intolerable: In diplomacy, a situation described as "intolerable" is usually one that governments don't know what to do about and must therefore learn to live with.

Intrigue: "The king, with the eye of intelligence and science, is able to overreach enemies possessed of energy and might, by conciliation and other means and by secret practices." —ARTHASASTRA OF KAUTILYA

Invasion, withdrawal: It always takes less time to invade than to withdraw.

Invincibility: A reputation for invincibility is a significant deterrent to aggression by others. Such a reputation should not be lightly hazarded. Defeat on a minor battlefield risks attack on a greater one.

Invitations: "Never fish for invitations, especially for dinners. Dining out too often is a waste of time." —CARDINAL RICHELIEU

Irony: "Irony [is] always a mistake in diplomacy; for irony exposes an assumption of superiority on the part of the writer, and it cannot fail to offend the recipient. It is obviously a serious fault in a diplomatist, who is trying to persuade another party to agree with him, if he offends that party's personal feelings."
—R.B. Mowat, 1936

Irrational: To dismiss a foreign government, policy, or circumstance as "irrational" is to confess that one does not understand its motivations, causes, or calculus, has no idea how to deal with it short of the use of force, and has no intention of making the effort to discover how to do so.

Irresistibility: The extent to which a capability cannot be countered or offset, devalued through countermeasures, eliminated through reprisal, or frustrated by evasion.

Irritation: "It is but seldom that any one overt act produces hostilities between two nations; there exists, more commonly, a predisposition to take offense."
—Washington Irving

Irritation, concealment of: "Not only must the negotiator avoid displaying irritation when confronted by the stupidity, dishonesty, brutality, or conceit of those with whom it is his unpleasant duty to negotiate; but he must eschew all personal animosities, or personal predilections, all enthusiasms, prejudices, vanities, exaggerations, dramatizations, and moral indignations."
—Harold Nicolson, 1960

Isolation: Isolation of another country deprives one of influence, information, and insight and leaves one powerless to exploit political opportunities when they occur.

Isolation: Regimes at odds with the existing world or regional order often come perversely to depend on international isolation for their political survival. Thus, efforts to isolate them, though intended to cause their fall, inadvertently bolster their hold on power.

Jokes: Most jokes entertain through plays on words, double entendres, the clever alteration of clichés, anecdotes embellishing individual or group stereotypes, or surprise twists to apparently familiar stories. But clichés differ from language to language and words seldom have the same overlapping meanings or sounds. Different cultures single out different individuals and groups to exemplify exaggerated character traits and behavior. Tales familiar to one culture are often unknown or meaningless to the members of another. So it is a rare joke that translates effectively across a linguistic or cultural divide. That is why interpreters generally wince when speakers begin to tell one.

Jokes, confidences: To enjoy a joke is to share a confidence.

Jokes, friendship: Shared laughter is a step toward friendship.

Journalism: "Journalism is concerned with effect and with newsworthiness; it is written under the pressure of time, and based on much less information than is usually available even to secondary embassies; and newspapers normally only cover important or momentarily newsworthy countries, so that the general presentation is unbalanced and patchy. More broadly it may be stated that even in countries where press reporting is uninhibited, what governments say in public and what is gleaned and surmised by journalists are together no substitute for what governments are prepared to say to other governments in confidence." —ADAM WATSON, 1983

Judgment: "All too often diplomatists are so afraid of being accused of lack of judgement that they avoid expressing any judgement at all. In evading these responsibilities they are omitting to perform one of their most desirable duties." —HAROLD NICOLSON, 1939

Judgment, strategic: "There are roads one does not follow. There are armies one does not strike. There are cities one does not attack. There are grounds one does not contest. There are commands of the sovereign one does not accept." —SUNZI

Justice: Justice is vengeance imposed by a judge.

Justice: "America goes not abroad in search of monsters to destroy. She is the well-wisher to the freedom and independence of all. She is the champion and vindicator only of her own." —JOHN QUINCY ADAMS

Justice: "Justice is what we get when the decision is in our favor." —JOHN W. RAPER

Justice: "Justice without force is impotent; force without justice is tyranny. Justice without force is a myth because there are always bad men; force without justice stands convicted of itself." —PASCAL

Justice: "Into human affairs the question of justice only enters when there is equal power to enforce it, and the powerful exact what they can, and the weak grant what they must." —THUCYDIDES

Justice, charity: "Charity is no substitute for justice withheld." —ST. AUGUSTINE

Knowledge: "[An ambassador] must be an indefatigable reader, else he is sure to fail, as a soldier who should be indifferent to physical exercise."

—Bishop Germonius, 1627, cited by J.J. Jusserand

Knowledge of foreign nations: "The temper, qualities, and limitations of many a man can be divined on short acquaintance; those of a nation need a longer contact."

—J.J. Jusserand, 1924

Language: Language is more than our means of communication; it is the means by which we explain what we experience and the vehicle for our culture. To know another man's language is to know something of his soul.

Language: "All nations whatsoever have a right to treat with each other in a neutral language." —British government instruction of 1753

Language: "The man who speaks in a foreign tongue, not his own, is to a certain extent wearing a disguise. If one wants to discover his ideas de derrière la tête encourage him to use his own language." —Ernest Satow

Language: "A language is a dialect with an army and a navy." —Max Weinreich

Language, body: The body often speaks before the mouth and even when the mouth is silent.

Language and culture in diplomacy: Unlike academics and intelligence analysts, diplomats must apply their knowledge of foreign cultures and languages in their daily work. Diplomatic expertise with regard to a foreign culture and language is not an end in itself; it is a means to an end. The test of this expertise is the diplomat's capacity to understand the mental baggage and mindsets of foreign leaders sufficiently well to be able to anticipate how they will perceive certain circumstances and what they will do in response to specific statements or events. It is, moreover, the responsibility of the diplomat to advise his government on how to shape circumstances, statements, and events to produce the desired response from foreign leaders, and to take a hand in shaping these himself.

Language defines reality: "Each and every tongue is a distinct window into the world. Looking through it, the native speaker enters an emotional and spiritual space, a framework of memory, a promontory on tomorrow, which no other window in the great house of Babel quite matches. Thus every language mirrors and generates a possible world, an alternate reality." —George Steiner

Languages for diplomats: In every age and region there is a language that is the most common means of communication between educated men. A diplomat must speak that language; he should also speak the languages of the great powers whose interests bear most heavily on the state he is representing.

Large nations, strategic incoherence of: Empires and states of continental dimensions slip easily into self-absorption and solipsism; the ideological and other interests of domestic factions set their policy. With survival apparently assured, national interests are obscured in a fog of selfish preoccupations. Coherent strategy is a rarity in such states.

Law: "International law is that body of rules which the states in an international society agree at a given time to observe in their relations with each other, and in the main do observe, and which they thus recognize as having the status of laws. Since there is no supranational executive, these rules are unenforced, except by the power of other states acting individually or collectively. They depend for their executive effectiveness not on consent, as is sometimes claimed, but on their active observance by the member states, particularly the more influential ones. On what corresponds to the legislative side, the conventions and rules of international society are established, and continually elaborated and modified, by the member states, by means of negotiations between executives in multilateral dialogue. This body of international rules obviously differs from domestic law, which is enforceable by a sovereign executive and which can be enacted and modified by a sovereign legislature. Much of the mistaken thinking about the role of law in the relations between states comes from transposing ideas, derived from law inside a single state under the authority of a government, to the quite different context of a society of states which recognize no common government." —ADAM WATSON, 1983

Lawyers: "It is true that sometimes a lawyer diplomat has made a great success of negotiation, especially in countries where the final responsibility for public policy lay in public assemblies which could be moved by adroit speech, but in general, the training of a lawyer breeds habits and dispositions of mind which are not favorable to the practice of diplomacy. And though it be true that success in the law-courts depends largely upon a knowledge of human nature and an ability to exploit it—both of which are factors in diplomacy—it is nonetheless true that the occupation of the lawyer, which is to split hairs about nothing, is not a good preparation for the treatment of grave public affairs in the region of diplomacy. If this be true of the advocate or barrister, it is still more true of the magistrate and judge. The habit of mind engendered by presiding over a court of law, in which the judge himself is supreme, tends to exclude those faculties of suppleness and adaptability which are necessary in diplomacy, and the almost ludicrous assumption of dignity by a judge would certainly appear as arrogance in diplomatic circles." —FRANÇOIS DE CALLIÈRES, 1716

Lawyers, contrasted with diplomats: "The lawyer, like the diplomat, deals in debate and compromise. A knowledge of law is essential to the diplomat, an ability to negotiate is essential to the lawyer, and a knowledge of human nature is essential to both. But when the lawyer turns to international problems these similarities lead him to the false conclusion that diplomacy is a form of law. His whole training has accustomed him to presuppose a court where right is distinguished from wrong, legal from illegal, and where there are police and jails to enforce decisions. Moral as well as legal concepts govern his thinking. . . . He seeks to regulate affairs by hard and fast formulas within a completely ordered system. None of these concepts applies to international

affairs. Even international law, which covers only a tiny part of the field of diplomacy, has few sanctions."
—CHARLES W. THAYER, 1959

Leaders, incompetent enemy: When the enemy is poorly led, finish him off fast. Do not give him time to discover more competent leadership by the process of elimination.

Leaders, vulnerabilities of: "One who is courageous and treats death lightly can be destroyed by violence. One who is hasty and impatient can be destroyed by persistence. One who is greedy and loves profit can be bribed. One who is benevolent but unable to inflict suffering can be worn down. One who is wise but fearful can be distressed. One who is trustworthy and likes to trust others can be deceived. One who is scrupulous and incorruptible but does not love men can be insulted. One who is wise but indecisive can be suddenly attacked. One who is resolute and self-reliant can be confused by events. One who is fearful and likes to entrust responsibility to others can be tricked."
—JIANG TAI GONG'S SIX SECRET TEACHINGS (4TH CENTURY B.C.)

Leadership: "Only he is capable of exercising leadership over others who is capable of some real degree of mastery over himself."
—GEORGE F. KENNAN, 1954

Leadership, elements of: Leadership is based on strategic vision and focus on future outcomes, the ability to organize and motivate others so that they can be relied upon to deliver results, constant attention to identifying and encouraging the development of future leaders through delegation of responsibility to them, and the cultivation of a reputation for decisiveness, trustworthiness, integrity, and personal commitment to others that will inspire loyalty.

Leadership, essence of: "All of the great leaders have had one characteristic in common: it was the willingness to confront unequivocally the major anxiety of their people in their time. This, and not much else, is the essence of leadership."—JOHN KENNETH GALBRAITH

Leadership, surprise: One proof of leadership is the ability to turn the unexpected to the common advantage.

Leadership, team: To be a team leader, you must be a team player.

Leaks, motivations for: Leaks of information to the press are generally motivated by: (1) a naïve concern to show that, unlike others, one is truly in the know; (2) a vile aspiration to discredit those who harbor contrary views by insinuating that they are idiots, dupes, or traitors; (3) an undisciplined impulse to reopen and publicly prove a point rejected in policy debate within the councils of government; (4) logorrhea born of a severely challenged sense of self-importance and a corresponding compulsion for self-aggrandizement; and (5) a noble desire, worthy of the greatest educators, for revelation of the truth to the ignorant. There are undoubtedly other motivations, but of those mentioned, the last is surely the rarest.

Legal adviser: "The abominable no-man."   —ANTHONY EDEN

Legate: A member of the Roman Catholic clergy (usually a cardinal) appointed by the Pope as his personal agent to carry out a special religious or political mission in a foreign land. A "legate a latere" has diplomatic status; other classes of legate (e.g., "nati" or "missi") do not. (See also *Nuncio* and *Internuncio*.)

Legation: A second-class embassy, headed by a minister (rather than an ambassador) who carries the title of "envoy extraordinary and minister plenipotentiary."

Legislation: Attempts by legislatures to legislate the actual conduct of diplomacy in detail are almost always counterproductive. Legislation restricts diplomacy's freedom of maneuver and greatly reduces its suppleness, leading to large opportunity costs as efforts to amend or repeal laws to respond to new developments compete with other legislative priorities.

Legislation: Legislators may proclaim a policy, but they cannot implement it except by enacting into law punishments and prohibitions on trade and travel. That is why the first resort of lawmakers is to sanctions, embargoes, and other restrictive measures on intercourse with foreign states. But little is gained by name-calling, and laws directed at foreign sovereigns usually damage rather than advance prospects for peaceful resolution of international disputes. The inherent rigidity of statutes precludes essential flexibility in response to unexpected change. Amendment or repeal of a law requires new action by the legislature. Legislation thus makes all diplomacy ad referendum to the lowest common denominator of the special interests that enacted it. This is a powerful inhibitor of diplomatic efforts to achieve the very results those who sponsored the legislation intended. Moreover, such laws are rightly taken by foreign sovereigns as a hostile act. They invite a hostile response, which may well injure unrelated interests the legislators would, upon mature reflection, have wished to save from harm.

Legislatures: "As large clumsy bodies, parliaments cannot effectively exercise initiative and their participation upsets diplomacy."   —JOSEPH FRANKEL, 1963

Legislatures: "The fluctuating and . . . multitudinous composition of [a popularly elected legislature] forbid us to expect in it those qualities which are essential to . . . [the formation of treaties]. Accurate and comprehensive knowledge of foreign politics; a steady and systematic adherence to the same views; a nice and uniform sensibility to national character; decision, secrecy, and despatch, are incompatible with the genius of a body so variable and numerous."   —ALEXANDER HAMILTON, 1788

Legislatures, belligerent nationalism of: "Parliaments are usually more nationalistic and belligerent than executives, and people than parliaments, because they are less aware of the risks."   —QUINCY WRIGHT, 1955

Legislatures, intervention in diplomacy by: "Whatever [the] purpose, the effect of legislative intervention at the outset of delicate and uncertain international discussions is almost always bound to be unfortunate. By throwing the spotlight of public attention on negotiators at the preparatory stage of their work, legislators destroy freedom of maneuver and the prospects for a successful outcome of the negotiations. By forcing . . . diplomats to outline in advance both maximum and minimum positions, . . . [a legislature] makes of the forthcoming conference table a forum reiterating fixed positions, not an instrument for reconciling differences. Once positions are publicly announced and all possibilities laid bare before . . . the public, genuine negotiations based on responsible give and take and the skillful modification of positions to meet changes initiated by the other party become difficult, if not impossible. Worse still, rancorous debate and deep public division may compromise a negotiator's position even before he reaches the conference table." —Kenneth W. Thompson, 1962

Legislatures, war crises and: "A steadily pursued, traditional policy is not likely to produce wars because other Governments come to know this policy and to take it into their calculations; but policy dependent on a changing legislature is liable to breed fear and uncertainty abroad, and so to lead to war crises." —R.B. Mowat, 1936

Legitimacy: Legitimacy is a measure of the extent to which power over others derives from their consent to one's leadership rather than fear of punishment should they fail to submit to one's will.

Legitimacy: "Legitimacy is the elixir of political power." —Fareed Zakaria

Leverage: Strategic advantage conferred by the ability to punish.

Liberalism, bellicose nature of: "Liberalism is not a philosophy of innocence, and it should make tyrants quake, not smile." —Leon Wieseltier

Liberty: "Human nature is universally imbued with a desire for liberty, and a hatred for servitude." —Julius Caesar

Liberty: "Only a few prefer liberty—the majority seek nothing more than fair masters." —Sallust

Liberty, defined: "Liberty is the right to do whatever the laws permit." —Montesquieu

Lies: "If you are a habitual liar, you'd better have a good memory." —Arab proverb

Lies: "Lies I never tell, but the truth not to everyone." —Paolo Sarpi

Lies: "It is scarcely necessary to say that no occasion, no provocation, no anxiety to rebut an unjust accusation, no idea however tempting—of promoting the object you have in view—can need, much less justify, a falsehood. Success obtained by one is a precarious and baseless success. Detection would not only ruin your reputation forever, but deeply wound the honor of your court."   —TALLEYRAND, 1813

Lies, explanations: "A little inaccuracy sometimes saves tons of explanation."   —SAKI

Lies, rulers: It is the duty of rulers to remember always that men lie.

Linguists: Beware of men who can speak a dozen languages and are able to think in none.

Linkage: Linkage is an effort by one side in a negotiation to promote compromise and encourage greater flexibility by another through demonstrating that a broad rather than a narrow range of its interests is at stake—that is, that it stands to benefit or suffer in regard to matters beyond those to which it wishes to restrict the bargaining.

Listening: The most influential persons are those who listen most intently and ask the most pertinent questions.

Listening: "You have to listen to lead, and it's pretty hard to listen when you are screaming at each other."   —GERALD FORD

Listening: "The first and best advice . . . is to listen, not to talk—at least not more than is necessary to induce others to talk. . . . By endeavouring to follow this example, [I have] drawn from my opponents much information, and concealed from them my own views, much more than by the employment of spies or money."   —LORD MALMESBURY, 1813

Listening, diplomatic: The ability to listen agreeably without agreeing is a central art of diplomacy.

Listening, in negotiations: Do not allow yourself to assume that your opponent in a negotiation has said something he has not. In relations between states, an optimistic imagination is as sure a road to ruin as the failure to heed what has been said.

Listening, persuasion through: "One of the best ways to persuade others is with your ears—by listening."   —DEAN RUSK

Listening to what is not said: It is as important to listen for what your opponent at the negotiating table does not say as to what he says. Often the first signal of a shift in the other side's negotiating position will be its failure to reiterate an argument or demand it has previously stressed.

Localitis: "The problem [of 'localitis'] is that in addition to speaking for the interests of his own country, a diplomat's responsibility is to ensure that his own government understands the attitudes and concerns of the host government as they bear on the relations between the two states—and it often becomes a fine line, indeed, between explanation and advocacy. It is normal and commendable for a diplomat to develop an interest and sympathy for the nation where he has been assigned. The fatal flaw, however, is to forget that he is sent abroad to represent the interests of his own country to the host country, and not vice versa. It is a problem which comes especially to the fore when, as is sometimes the case, with . . . countries . . . inexperienced in foreign affairs, a diplomat stationed there feels that his host government's own diplomats are not adequately explaining the legitimate reasons impelling the host government to act and think as it does. In these circumstances, the tendency to focus on explaining host government views to his own, rather the other way around, becomes most acute."   —WILLIAM MACOMBER, 1975

Localitis: "A diplomatist must be on his guard against the notion that his own post is the centre of international politics, and against an exaggerated estimate of the part assigned to him in the general scheme. Those in whose hands is placed the supreme direction of foreign relations are alone able to decide what should be the main object of state policy, and to estimate the relative value of political friendships and alliances." —ERNEST SATOW

Logic: "Logic is of no use in diplomacy."   —LORD SALISBURY

Loyalty: "The basic quality for the diplomat is not intelligence but loyalty."
—C. NORTHCOTE PARKINSON, 1961

Loyalty: "Loyalty means . . . that a . . . diplomat must never do anything of a public or private character which would in any way undermine the leaders of the government he serves. But . . . if a . . . diplomat disagrees with a policy he has not only the right to speak up but the obligation to do so. In fact, he is being disloyal if he does not exercise that right. Loyalty, if it requires anything, requires the giving of one's best judgment at all times."
—WILLIAM MACOMBER, 1975

Magnanimity: "If great enmities are ever to be really settled, we think it will be, not by the system of revenge and military success, and by forcing an opponent to swear to a treaty to his disadvantage, but when the more fortunate combatant waives these his privileges, to be guided by gentler feelings, conquers his rival in generosity, and accords peace on more moderate conditions than he expected. From that moment, instead of the debt of revenge which violence must entail, his adversary owes a debt of generosity to be paid in kind, and is inclined by honor to stand to his agreement. And men oftener act in this way towards their greatest enemies than where the quarrel is of less importance; they are also by nature as glad to give way to those who first yield to them, as they are apt to be provoked by arrogance to risks condemned by their own judgment." —Lacedaemonian Ambassadors, quoted by Thucydides

Manners: "One learns manners from those who have none." —Persian proverb

Manners, defined: "Good manners is the art of making those people easy with whom we converse. Whoever makes the fewest persons uneasy is the best bred in the company." —Jonathan Swift, c. 1720

Market economies, freedom: "It is not easy to keep markets open and ideas constrained." —John Lewis Gaddis

Mass: The preponderance and concentration of a capability. Mass determines the capacity of a state to dominate an arena of contention. Military mass consists of a concentration of forces capable of overwhelming opposing forces. Economic mass is measured by the degree of monopoly or control over the supply or demand for specific goods and services. Political mass consists of dominant persuasiveness. Cultural mass is represented by intellectual preeminence.

Mediation: The process by which a third party (or group of parties), whose interests will be affected by the perpetuation of a dispute or by its particular outcome, fosters and participates in negotiations between the direct parties to a dispute, assisting them to recognize common interests and to compose a solution on the basis of these interests. Unlike the more disinterested process of conciliation, mediation may entail intervention by the mediator to alter both the situation and the calculus of the parties in a manner designed to reinforce stalemate, preclude unilateral action by one of the parties to impose a solution, and thereby promote the trade-offs necessary to achieve a settlement of differences between the parties. It is a process that makes especially heavy demands on the skill and tact of the mediator. See also *Conciliation.*

Mediation: "The only [mediated] deal that will work is one that is good for all the parties to it and tolerable to those who have the capacity to wreck it, i.e., a peace without losers. A formula that has the logic of fundamental national interests behind it is worth sticking with; patience will reward such a formula."　　　　　　　—CHAS. W. FREEMAN, 1989

Mediation, compromise: "Reinforcing the attractions of compromise may require using both carrots and sticks. Inducements may include economic and military aid, arms sales, supportive policy statements, and other instruments of diplomacy. . . . Negative inducements . . . frequently take the form of contingent withdrawal of benefits, or threats, but may also be framed as warnings, or authoritative indications of consequences outside the control of the parties [to a dispute]. . . . The reinforcement of conflict is often required to force recognition of . . . deadlock and . . . deadline. This may mean reinforcing a faltering party, . . . making the conciliator a distant balance-holder. By shifting weight from one party to the other in the conflict, a conciliator can reinforce deadlock and enforce deadline, particularly if it is able to reduce support for a client that is on top but not firm enough to be able to win."　　　　　　　—I. WILLIAM ZARTMAN, 1985

Mediation, creating formulae for settlement: "Creating a formula is an analytical art. . . . The formula must be logically consistent with the underlying power relationships in the conflict; otherwise, one or another side will simply refuse to take it seriously—'they will never get at the conference table what they cannot achieve on the ground.' The problem, of course, is that the peacemaker's analysis will likely differ from that of one or both parties. Still, it is no bad thing for a peacemaker to inform the various audiences of his considered judgment as to the basic shape of the deal. By doing so, he indicates what sort of outcome he is prepared to facilitate and why. He defines the agenda."
　　　　　　　—CHESTER A. CROCKER, 1992

Mediation, diplomacy of: "Any successful diplomacy is based on some form of power. In a mediatory triangle, effective leverage will more often than not be 'borrowed'. . . from third parties. . . . A peacemaker also exploits the leverage within the military situation itself."　　　　　　　—CHESTER A. CROCKER, 1992

Mediation, distinguished from negotiation: "Mediation is different from negotiation per se. It provides an opportunity to guide the parties to definitions of their national interests and toward outcomes compatible with the mediator's objectives, but in the end they—not the mediator—determine the results. . . . Recognition of the limits of the mediator's role and of his power to compel a result is his first virtue; forbearance from pointing out the petty and grand stupidities of the parties to the negotiation is his second."
　　　　　　　—CHAS. W. FREEMAN, 1989

Mediation, dynamics of: "The mediator's intervention has a structural influence on the negotiation. . . . It changes a [two-way relationship] into a [three-way one]. . . . The mediator introduces new values into the game. He has his own representations, goals, strategies and tactics. By intervening in the interaction, he increases the number of issues at stake.

A mediator involved in an international dispute has his own conception of what international order should be and what an acceptable attitude within a relationship should be."
—GUY-OLIVIER FAURE, 1989

Mediation, formulae for settlement: "When a peacemaker moves to lay down the conceptual framework for a settlement, this action tends to rule out and discredit the obvious alternatives. Ripening cannot take place until a consensus develops—not only about the need for a negotiated deal, but also for a specific kind of deal. If a number of approaches remain in play and appear to be equally viable and attractive, the conflict remains unripe. The peacemaker's move may cause the parties to collude tacitly against him, escaping behind the cover of each other's non-cooperation. If this keeps happening, he can prepare his moves with one side first, and claw his way toward agreement like a skipper tacking toward the wind. There may be times when a proposed framework of principles drives the parties toward another approach which has merit. The original initiative will still have served a useful purpose by shaking things up and injecting some movement into the picture. But the most important reason for taking the initiative is to block the parties' unilateral options and discredit their wishful thinking."   —CHESTER A. CROCKER, 1992

Mediation, joint: "Statesmen should adhere rigorously to an ad hoc approach, looking at each conflict on its merits. The peacemaker must be a tailor, not a haberdasher. When considering joint peacemaking endeavors . . . with . . . anyone else, we should apply common-sense criteria: what clout do they have with the protagonists? How 'relevant' are they to the conflict at hand, and how will their participation (or non-participation) be perceived? What do we get in return for accepting or creating a role for them, and what must we pay for it? What is the cost of excluding them?"   —CHESTER A. CROCKER, 1992

Mediation, knowledge of peacemakers: "Every conflict contains unique properties. It is the peacemaker's first obligation to study the particular factors of history, culture, and power that are found in all conflicts. The peacemaker is doomed to fail—no matter how powerful or credible or 'legitimate'—unless he can place himself (like a good historian) inside the minds of the parties while remaining coldly realistic about them."
—CHESTER A. CROCKER, 1992

Mediation, leverage from third parties: "The peacemaker examines the 'environment' of the conflict and the interests of other external players. Are there other third parties who crave an acknowledged role in resolving it? Great: make 'em pay. Being included and recognized is an important factor for governments that are insecure about their role and status. Is there a club somewhere which one or more of the parties is eager to join? Fine: link it to performance and co-opt the admissions committee. If the current facts are not good enough, create some new ones. Build leverage through investments in your own credibility."   —CHESTER A. CROCKER, 1992

Mediation, leverage in: "The richest source of leverage for the peacemaker may already be built into the existing situation. How badly are the parties hurting, and how can they be persuaded that a settlement is their best option? What is it that one or the other side really wants but cannot get on its own? Is one or more of the parties isolated and eager to gain external support for its positions? Can their standing and legitimacy be put in question if they fail to cooperate? What pressures are built into the military situation, and what can be done to strengthen or accelerate the necessary stalemate?"

—CHESTER A. CROCKER, 1992

Mediation, motivations of peacemakers: "Peacemakers typically intervene in conflicts precisely because their interests are affected, and they tend to act in support of a settlement compatible with those interests. By the same token, parties are more likely to respond to a peacemaker whose clout and prestige demand that he be taken seriously— even if that response is largely tactical and defensive. Bias (in the sense of having an interest in the issues and a preference about the outcome) is not an obstacle to success. But ignorance or prejudice will guarantee failure. . . . It will not be possible to design a 'fair' (win-win) formula without a feel for each party's way of thinking and priorities. This is why the peacemaker must, first, invest in knowledge; no one should know the brief better than he. Procedural even-handedness and fair play are important because they signal a readiness to listen, to learn, and to protect the parties' soft parts. They also protect the peacemaker from his own parochialism. There is little room for 'liking' or naively 'trusting.' If the various parties were not in some sense opposed to what he is doing, there would be no need for peacemaking!"

—CHESTER A. CROCKER, 1992

Mediation, perils of: "It is better to mediate between enemies than between friends, for one of the friends is sure to become an enemy and one of the enemies a friend."

—BIAS, c. 550 B.C.

Mediation, price of stability: Powers whose primary interest is in international stability will find themselves acting as arbitrators and mediators of the rivalries of other states, with all the penalties that attach to these roles.

Mediation, ripe moments: "The success of mediation is tied to the perception and creation of a ripe moment in the conflict—either when the parties are locked in a mutual, hurting stalemate marked by a recent or impending catastrophe; when unilateral solutions are blocked and joint solutions become conceivable; or when the 'ups' and 'downs' start to shift their relative power positions. Parties can come to perceive these moments themselves, to be sure, but they frequently need the help of a conciliator."

—I. WILLIAM ZARTMAN, 1985

Mediation, ripening a conflict: "Obviously, peacemaking is most fruitful when a conflict is becoming ripe for resolution. But . . . the absence of 'ripeness' does not tell us to walk away and do nothing, Rather, it helps us to identify obstacles and suggests ways of handling them and managing the problem until resolution becomes possible. Each conflict situation will contain its own ebbs and flows, and each peacemaker will have his own rhythm. To ripen a conflict that appears to be deadlocked, it may be desirable to shake the parties up by giving them something fresh to mull over."

—CHESTER A. CROCKER, 1992

Mediation, success in: "Success is only achieved when there is no clear diplomatic victory or defeat. The defeat of a country is a serious matter. It carries the seed of profound resentment, magnified by those collective pressures we call nationalism. This is especially true when 'triumph' is publicized. Each side must be led to perceive that certain concessions will produce a situation which is more endurable than the existing state of affairs. The mediator must find this common ground so that each government, if publicly challenged (as it usually is), can proclaim some kind of achievement."

—PARKER T. HART, 1990

Mediation of adjustments: "Conflict resolution plays on perceptions of an intolerable situation. Things 'can't go on like this.' Without this perception, the conciliator must persuade the parties that escalation to break out of deadlock is impossible. Indeed, the conciliator may be required to make it impossible, if necessary. Thus, deadlock cannot be seen merely as a temporary stalemate, to be easily resolved in one's favor by a little effort or even by a big offensive or a gamble or foreign assistance. Rather, each party must recognize its opponent's strength and its own inability to overcome it. For the conciliator, this means emphasizing the dangers of deadlock as each party comes to recognize the other's strength. Each party's unilateral policy option (the action that it can take alone without negotiation) must be seen as a more expensive and less likely way of achieving a possible, acceptable outcome than the policy of negotiation."

—I. WILLIAM ZARTMAN, 1985

Mediators, credibility of: Credibility for a negotiator comes from granting the other side's national interests and seriousness of purpose, if only for the sake of argument. Accusations of lack of sincerity are inherently frivolous. Only a fool trusts someone on the other side of the negotiating table to do anything other than what that party believes to be in its interests. For a mediator, all parties are on the other side of the negotiating table.

Mediators, power and leverage of: "The peacemaker needs power and leverage to be effective. Where does this come from? Sometimes, we fall into the trap of imagining that leverage in peacemaking is like leverage in a bilateral . . . negotiation. But the structure of peacemaking is fundamentally different because it is triangular. The mediator's direct, bilateral leverage with each of the parties is most unlikely to be the decisive factor. To be sure, there is a time and place for shifting weight from one side to another in order to strengthen or restore a stalemate. The threat of pain or the promise of reward may tip the balance among decisionmakers within a government at a particular moment. . . . However, ... gestures toward one side may drive the other into stupid behavior. Threats or sanctions toward a misbehaving party are likely to let the other side off the hook. A test of wills can develop between a reluctant party and an ardent mediator. The peacemaker who operates by doling out rewards rapidly becomes an object of manipulation. Threats and punishment can produce their own perverse effects: the mediator's objective is, presumably, to obtain forward movement by both sides on the settlement track, not to weaken or punish the parties." —CHESTER A. CROCKER, 1992

Mediators, requirement to respect parties: "The would-be peacemaker who cannot treat the parties and their concerns with respect should find another line of work. I am speaking about more than protocol and bedside manner. The list of desirable attributes for success in this field starts with a rigorous commitment to accomplishing something and shaping events, not posturing or finding ways to feel good. This strong orientation takes precedence over all other priorities, including domestic sentiment in the peacemaker's own country." —CHESTER A. CROCKER, 1992

Mediators, role of: "Warring parties cannot communicate and explore doing business without having a mechanism and an appropriate forum in which to do these things. The peacemaker seeks to become the indispensable channel by asserting political will, demonstrating technical competence and unrivaled grasp of the brief, consistently possessing state-of-the-art information, and performing reliably (from the parties' standpoint). He demonstrates how the bidding might proceed and what the structure of and agreement might look like. Will there be a shuttle or proximity talks? Would an international conference make sense? Who should participate and who are the parties to the ultimate agreement? . . . The parties will want to know that an acceptable mechanism for negotiation and an appropriate forum for registering agreement are available." —CHESTER A. CROCKER, 1992

Memory, attention: "The true art of memory is the art of attention." —SAMUEL JOHNSON

Messengers: "A nuncius is he who takes the place of a letter: and he is just like a magpie, and an organ, and the voice of the principal sending him, and he recites the words of the principal." —AZO

Messengers, messages: "When you don't trust the messenger, you don't trust the message, even if it's a good one." —SHIBLEY TELHAMI, 2004

Might: "Might is above right; right proceeds from might. . . . Right is in the hands of the strong. . . . Everything is pure that comes from the strong. . . . When thou findest thyself in a low state, try to lift thyself up, resorting to pious as well as to cruel actions. Before practicing morality wait until thou art strong. . . . If men think thee soft, they will despise thee." —THE MAHABHARATA

Might: "Where there is no might, right loses itself." —PORTUGUESE PROVERB

Might, right: "The strongest is never strong enough to always be the master, unless he transforms strength into right, and obedience into duty." —JEAN-JACQUES ROUSSEAU

Militarism: Militarism espouses the belief that what previous applications of force have failed to accomplish can be achieved by applying still more force.

Military attachés: See *Attachés, military.*

Military matters: "Military matters should be left to military men."

—JAMES MONROE, 1814

Military matters: "In military affairs only military men should be listened to."

—THEODORE ROOSEVELT, 1897

Military strategy, diplomacy and: "That the soldier is but the servant of the statesman, as war is but an instrument of diplomacy, no educated soldier will deny. Politics must always exercise an extreme influence on strategy; but it cannot be gainsaid that interference with the commanders in the field is fraught with the gravest danger."

—G.F.R. HENDERSON, 1898

Military strength, power: Military strength is an element in power but not synonymous with it. Nor is it a guarantee of survival. The Soviet Union fell without a blow and with its military strength intact.

Minister: The rank of diplomats just below that of ambassador; the chief of a legation. Also, the politically appointed head of a ministry of government.

Minister-Counselor: A senior diplomatic rank between minister and counselor, often denoting an ambassador's principal deputy in an embassy.

Minister for foreign affairs: The chief diplomatic officer of the state and its regular intermediary with foreign governments and their ambassadors resident in his capital.

Minister for foreign affairs, qualities of: "A sort of instinct, always prompting him, should prevent him from compromising himself in any discussion. He must have the faculty of appearing open, while remaining impenetrable; of masking reserve with the manner of careless abandon; of showing talent even in the choice of his amusements. His conversation should be simple, varied, unexpected, always natural and sometimes naïve; in a word, he should never cease for an instant during the twenty-four hours to be a Minister for Foreign Affairs. Yet all these qualities, rare as they are, might not suffice, if good faith did not give them the guarantee which they almost always require."

—TALLEYRAND, 1837

Ministers: "A minister who flies to a foreign capital to undertake negotiation is inevitably short of time, ill equipped in technical knowledge, subjected to great publicity and inclined to conclude some vague and meaningless agreement rather than to return empty-handed to his home.

"More misery has been caused to mankind by the hurried drafting of imprecise or meaningless documents than by all the alleged machinations of the cunning diplomatist. Thus I should, wherever feasible, leave it to the professional to do his job quietly and without fuss."   —HAROLD NICOLSON, 1953

Ministers, how to influence: "Ministers are but men and as such have their weaknesses, that is to say, their passions and interests, which the ambassador ought to know if he wishes to do honor to himself and his Master."   —ABRAM DE WICQUEFORT

Ministers, relationship to experts: "A minister, who is likely to be a somewhat transient occupant of his office, will be well-advised to listen to his country's experts both on the technical matters at issue and on the conduct of negotiations and what in any given circumstances can be achieved through diplomacy. An elected or politically nominated statesman is, in Henry Kissinger's apt phrase, not hired as a whiz kid on technical answers but to supply a sense of direction to the diplomatic dialogue conducted by the state he represents."   —ADAM WATSON, 1983

Ministry of foreign affairs: The department of government responsible for supervising the foreign relations of a state and conducting official contacts with foreigners on its behalf.

Mission: The permanent embassy or legation of a state resident in another state. The term is also used to denote a delegation sent from one country to another to conduct specific and finite diplomatic negotiations.

Mission, chief of: The senior diplomatic official at a diplomatic mission, usually bearing the title "Ambassador Extraordinary and Plenipotentiary."

Mission, deputy chief of: The designation of the senior-ranking officer below the ambassador in an embassy of the United States. The deputy chief of mission supervises the diplomatic and administrative staff of the embassy for the ambassador, serves as his alter ego, coordinates the work of mission elements outside the embassy for him, and assumes the ambassador's duties as chargé d'affaires ad interim in his absence.

Mistakes: It is better to learn from the mistakes of others than to learn by making the same mistakes oneself.

Mistakes by enemies: "Never interrupt your enemy when he is making a mistake."
                                                                                        —NAPOLEON

Moderation: "He who walks in the middle of the road gets hit from both sides."
                                        —GEORGE P. SHULTZ, QUOTED BY RICHARD M. NIXON

Modus vivendi: A temporary understanding pending the negotiation of more definitive arrangements for the resolution of disputes.

Money: Money is the solvent and softener of principles.

Morale, in diplomatic missions: A good ambassador molds the spirit of his subordinates not only through example but also through a shrewd understanding of the psychology of morale. He must seek to give those who work for him confidence in their cause and in their ability to make it prevail. He must keep them active in promoting the interests of their nation. The worst enemy of morale at an embassy is lack of well-directed activity.

Morality: "A diplomatic corps is certainly far from being a school of virtue!"
—GYULA SZILASSY, 1928

Morality: "Always do right. This will gratify some people and astonish the rest."
—MARK TWAIN

Morality in diplomacy: "To lie, mislead, betray, to attempt a sovereign prince's life, to foster revolt among his subjects, to steal from him or trouble his state, even in peace-time, and under cover of friendship and alliance, is directly against . . . the law of nature and of nations; it is to break that public faith without which human society and, in truth, the general order of the world would dissolve. And the ambassador who seconds his master's views in such a business doubly sins, because he both helps him in the undertaking and performing of a bad deed, and neglects to counsel him better, when he is bound to do so by his function which carries with it the quality of councillor of state for the duration of his mission." —HOTMAN DE VILLIERS, 1603, CITED BY J.J. JUSSERAND

Morality in foreign policy: "Where an important purpose of diplomacy is to further enduring good relations between states, the methods—the modes of conduct—by which relations between states are carried on must be designed to inspire trust and confidence. To achieve this result, the conduct of diplomacy should conform to the same moral and ethical principles which inspire trust and confidence when followed by and between individuals." —DEAN ACHESON, 1964

Morality in foreign policy: "A statesman cannot afford to be a moralist."
—ATTRIBUTED TO WILL DURANT

Morality in foreign policy: "Moral principles have their place in the heart of the individual and in the shaping of his own conduct, whether as a citizen or as a government official. . . . But when the individual's behavior passes through the machinery of political organization and merges with that of millions of other individuals to find its expression in the actions of a government, then it undergoes a general transmutation, and the same moral concepts are no longer relevant to it. A government is an agent, not a principal; and no more than any other agent may it attempt to be the conscience of its principal. In particular, it may not subject itself to those supreme laws of renunciation and self-sacrifice that represent the culmination of individual moral growth." —GEORGE F. KENNAN, 1954

Morality in foreign policy: "Our choice is not between morality and pragmatism. We cannot escape either, nor are they incompatible. This nation must be true to its beliefs or it will lose its bearings in the world. But at the same time it must survive in the world of sovereign nations with competing wills. We need moral strength to select among agonizing choices and a sense of purpose to navigate between the shoals of difficult decisions."
—HENRY A. KISSINGER

Morality in foreign policy: "The policymaker must be concerned with the best that can be achieved, not just the best that can be imagined. He has to act in the fog of incomplete knowledge without the information that will be available later to the analyst. He knows—or should know—that he is responsible for the consequences of disaster as well as for the benefits of success. He may have to qualify some goals, not because they would be undesirable if reached but because the risks of failure outweigh potential gains. He must often settle for the gradual, much as he might prefer the immediate. He must compromise with others, and this means to some extent compromising with himself."
—HENRY A. KISSINGER

Morality in foreign policy: "The only good principle is to have none."
—ATTRIBUTED TO TALLEYRAND

Morality in foreign policy: "No nation is fit to sit in judgment on any other nation."
—WOODROW WILSON, 1915

Most-favored-nation status: A principle of reciprocity in international relationships, generally applied to trade and tariff matters, that extends any benefits granted to a third party to all other states to which a state has agreed to accord most-favored-nation status.

Motivations: States seldom act from a single motive but from a combination of purposes. Yet the analyst who judges that the most important among these is the most selfish and self-interested of them will seldom be wrong.

Multilateral: Referring to interaction among more than three states (interaction between two or three states is referred to, respectively, as "bilateral" or "trilateral").

Multinational: Referring to organizations that comprise citizens or corporations from more than two states. See also *International* and *Transnational*. Contrast *Binational*.

N

Nation: A people, unified by a common history, language, culture, religion or ideology, or territory, considering themselves distinct from other peoples, and recognized by others as possessing distinctive traits as a people. See also *State*.

National: A citizen or subject of a state.

National interest: See *Interest, national*.

Nationalism: "All nations have present, or past, or future reasons for thinking themselves incomparable."
—PAUL VALÉRY, 1964

Negotiability: "Diplomacy is supposed to keep things in a negotiable state."
—A. WHITNEY GRISWOLD, 1960

Negotiability: "No power can agree to negotiate about what it considers the condition of its existence."
—HENRY A. KISSINGER, 1964

Negotiability: "What's mine is mine, what's yours is negotiable."
—ATTITUDE ATTRIBUTED TO SOVIET NEGOTIATORS

Negotiability: "Negotiation is necessary to solve a problem when both parties are equal, when each has the power to block the other's attainment of its goal, or when both parties' agreement is needed for a solution."
—I. WILLIAM ZARTMAN AND MAUREEN R. BERMAN, 1982

Negotiation, refusal of: Refusal to negotiate is often a form of negotiation. It should not be mistaken for unrealism or a refusal to compromise when circumstances change.

Negotiation, rejection of: Rejection of a proposal in principle means that the proposal, as composed, is not negotiable. A shift to rejection on grounds of impracticality signals willingness to bargain.

Negotiating objectives, elegance of conceptualization and: Success in a complex negotiation is most likely to come from a clear expression of simple and precise objectives, consonant with the fundamental national interests of the parties, whether or not they initially recognize them. "Elegance" of conceptualization, in the mathematical sense of a lucidly simple and precisely formulated equation of trade-offs between the parties, can beat a murky or one-sided proposal every time. If a negotiator has an "elegant" formula, in this sense, with the logic of national interests behind it, he is well advised to stick with it. He should be patient. Its time will come.

Negotiating objectives, need to limit: A negotiator must resist the temptation to solve too much. Trying to solve too much is a recipe for solving nothing. A negotiator should define the problem he is trying to solve and avoid being distracted by the possibility of solving other problems until he has solved the one he set out to solve.

Negotiating objectives, realism in: It is folly to define success in a negotiation in terms of an outcome one could not hope to impose by other means if the negotiation were to fail.

Negotiating record: "The true diplomatist [is] aware of how much subsequently depends on what clearly can be established to have taken place. If it seems simple in the archives, try it in the maelstrom."
—Daniel Patrick Moynihan, 1978

Negotiating record, keeping: Preparation of accurate minutes of each negotiating session should be a matter of priority for a negotiator. He will need such records whether the negotiations succeed or fail. If they succeed, accurate records will be essential to interpretation of what has been agreed. If the negotiations fail, they will be essential to their successful resumption at a later date. An accurate record is also an invaluable basis for assessment of the other side's position and planning for subsequent sessions by the negotiator and his team.

Negotiating record, knowing the: A negotiator must have a mind well marinated in the record, a prepared mind that cannot be taken by surprise and is ready to react intelligently to unexpected turns in the course of the discussions in which he is engaged. No one can foresee all the possibilities in an effort to compose differences with others, but a man who has ruminated on these possibilities is better able to cope with them than one who has not.

Negotiating record, knowing the: Master the record of a negotiation and you can both deter your opponent from misrepresenting it to his advantage and enhance your ability to build on what may have been implicitly accomplished in previous discussions.

Negotiating strategies, formulation of: Governments are wise to recall their ambassadors and to include them in the formulation of negotiating strategies and objectives and the drafting of instructions for a negotiation. This ensures that their principal representative in the capital of the opponent state has a full understanding of the interests and rationale behind their posture in the negotiating process. It commits ambassadors to the objectives set by their capital and inhibits their seduction by the other side. It facilitates use of their special insights into the national interests, obsessions, and negotiating style of the opponent. It can help to assure that a government's negotiating strategy and objectives are realistic and best fitted to be crowned with success.

Negotiating strategy: "A negotiator will maximize his gains (or be 'successful') if he starts with high requests, has a small rate of concession, has a high minimum level of

expectation, and is very perceptive and quite unyielding."
—MICHAEL BLAKER, 1977, CITING SIEGEL AND FOURAKER,
BARGAINING AND GROUP DECISION-MAKING (NEW YORK, 1960)

Negotiating teams, composition of: When negotiations are complicated or politically controversial, they are best conducted by a delegation rather than a single envoy. Both the leadership and the composition of such a delegation are critical elements in its success. It need not be led by its most technically well-versed member, but its leader should be a person of presence and confidence who is more concerned about being respected than being liked. He should be polite but direct in speech, neither deferential nor diffident, judicious but decisive, of strong convictions but pragmatic, undeterred by setbacks and willing to accept responsibility for necessary but unpopular compromises. The delegation leader must be capable both of concerting the different viewpoints of its members and of drawing fully on their expertise to maintain a disciplined and coherent team approach. His team should contain representatives of the major concerned bureaucracies of his government, including those who, lacking a direct interest in most details of the agreement being negotiated, are both skeptical about it and in a position to savage it in domestic debate over ratification and implementation if they do not feel committed to supporting an agreement they played a role in achieving. The delegation must not be so large as to be unmanageable but should include members with special expertise on the issues, who know the country (or countries) involved and speak their languages. The head of delegation should strive for a rational division of labor among the members of his delegation, each of whom should attempt to cultivate a specific counterpart in the opposing delegation.

Negotiating teams, composition of: "A team sent . . . to negotiate in another capital or at an international conference . . . is likely to be made up of three elements. The delegation will, often but not always, be led by a political representative of the government of the day . . . whose job is to provide a general sense of direction and to exercise the authority entrusted to him by his governmental colleagues to conclude certain bargains, though he may not be there all the time. He will have with him a small personal staff. Then there will be professional diplomats, experts on the foreign countries involved and in negotiating with other governments, including the ambassador accredited to the state or international body in question, who is (or ought to be) the specialist on dealing with it. Thirdly there will be the technical experts on dealing with the various aspects of the subject in question. Their principal roles will be to serve on technical committees and to help shape the negotiating position of the delegation; and to do this most of them will normally maintain close direct links with their own government department or other institution, as well as conform in their dealings with other delegations to the decisions of the minister in charge of the negotiation."
—ADAM WATSON, 1983

Negotiating teams, division of labor in: Anyone entering a negotiation must know the issues in detail and be prepared to discuss them unencumbered by the presence of experts and assistants. Breakthroughs in negotiation are most likely to occur in private discussion between the heads of delegation in the absence of advisers. It is, however, unwise for the heads of delegation to attempt to settle technical issues or to agree on details; they may make their most effective contribution to the success of a negotiation by setting a framework within which the experts must find agreement on precise language to embody a mutually satisfactory resolution of issues of detail.

Negotiating teams, linguistic qualifications of: A well-built negotiating team should include at least one member able to understand what is said by the members of the opposing delegation to each other but not perceived by them as being able to do so.

Negotiating teams, management of: "A large negotiating team . . . requires a great deal of managerial skill. The head of delegation, apart from preparing himself for his mission, must see to it that the . . . objectives in the negotiation are fully understood by all members of the team; that information on the progress of the talks is promptly and adequately disseminated to those members of the delegation directly concerned; that there is full and prompt reporting to [the Foreign Ministry] on the progress, problems and prospects of the negotiation, including where necessary requests for supplementary instructions; that there is continuing liaison between his delegation and all other participating delegations; that satisfactory administrative arrangements exist to insure that his delegation can be reached at any hour of the day or night; that the whereabouts of the principal negotiator and his deputies are constantly known to the administrative staff of his delegation; wherever possible, that equitable time-off arrangements are made for the delegation's secretarial staff; and, in summary, that all of the members of the delegation come to feel that they are valued members of the same team and all are contributing to the mission's success."
—Unidentified diplomat quoted by John St. G. Creaghe, 1965

Negotiation: See also *Prenegotiation.*

Negotiation: The object of negotiations is not necessarily to achieve a resolution of a dispute; it may simply be to put an idea before the public.

Negotiation: "Negotiations are not exercises in charity. Their purpose is to produce a clearly advantageous result for the side the negotiator represents. . . . But there is more to it than that. They should also produce a result which will last."
—William Macomber, 1975

Negotiation: "For men to live together in a state of society, implies a kind of continuous negotiation. . . . Everything in life is, so to say, intercourse and negotiation, even between those whom we might think not to have anything to hope or fear from one another."
—Antoine Pecquet, 1737

Negotiation, criteria for: "Two elements must normally be present for negotiation to take place: there must be both common interests and issues of conflict. Without common interests there is nothing to negotiate for; without conflict there is nothing to negotiate about." —FRED C. IKLÉ, 1964

Negotiation, defined: "The term 'negotiation' means the art of handling the affairs of state as they concern the respective interests of the great and supposedly independent societies interacting in a free state of nature. . . . However, negotiation is not limited to international affairs. It takes place everywhere where there are differences to conciliate, interests to placate, men to persuade, and purposes to accomplish. Thus, all life could be regarded as a continual negotiation. We always need to win friends, overcome enemies, correct unfortunate impressions, convince others of our views, and use all appropriate means to further our projects." —FORTUNE BARTHÉLEMY DE FELICE, 1778

Negotiation, diplomatic: Diplomatic negotiation is the course of bargaining entered into by two or more states to achieve a mutual resolution of the matters at issue between them.

Negotiation, flexibility in: "[Negotiators] . . . must design opening and fallback positions with great care, to build both mobility and flexibility into the negotiating process, if this should be needed to avoid sterility and stalemate, and to assure that this flexibility will never go beyond the point where national interests are disadvantaged." —WILLIAM MACOMBER, 1975

Negotiation, functions of: "Negotiation has three main objectives, namely: 1) to formulate by expressing agreements or disagreements in a manner that does not open unbridgeable schisms; 2) to perpetuate by providing a forum for making concessions; and 3) to persuade by stating a plausible reason for settlement. These are the normal functions of negotiation." —HENRY A. KISSINGER, 1956

Negotiation, power and: "When a prince or a state is powerful enough to dictate to his neighbors, the art of negotiation loses its value." —FRANÇOIS DE CALLIÈRES, 1716

Negotiation, purpose of: "One does not negotiate to conclude something, but to ensure the triumph of the interests in one's charge." —MAURICE-JACQUES COUVE DE MURVILLE

Negotiation, resort to force and: "The in-built bias of diplomacy towards settling issues between states by negotiation presupposes that such negotiations and the settlements achieved will reflect the power of the parties and does not therefore exclude the possibility of the coercive use of power." —ADAM WATSON, 1983

Negotiation, state of mind: "You cannot shake hands with a clenched fist." —INDIRA GANDHI

Negotiation, time and: "Only time resolves conflicts, but time needs help."
—I. WILLIAM ZARTMAN, 1985

Negotiation, with revolutionary powers: "Negotiation today means war carried on
by other means and does not mean bargaining between parties both wanting to reach
agreement."
—DEAN ACHESON, 1966

Negotiation, with revolutionary states: "When two sides take positions, each unacceptable to the other, it is said that the solution lies somewhere in between. These maxims,
unobjectionable in themselves, reflect . . . experience . . . with negotiations . . . in the
commercial field. In commercial negotiations, the rules of the game are known. Usually, there is an implicit understanding that an agreement will be reached. Restraints are
imposed by the need for a continuing relationship. Both sides generally are in accord on
what constitutes a 'reasonable' argument. When each party believes it has gained some
advantage both will settle. The courts will interpret the agreement and enforce it. Most of
these factors are lacking to a greater or lesser degree in negotiations with . . . [revolution-
ary] states. In contrast with most . . . domestic experience, what . . . [is] at issue . . . [is] not
the adjustment of disputes within a framework which [can] be taken for granted, but the
framework itself."
—HENRY A. KISSINGER, 1960

Negotiations, ad referendum: "Regardless of a negotiator's ability, the best guarantee
that a calm and measured judgment will be applied to major developments in a negotiation is the requirement that they be referred to higher authority before being finally
agreed to. Such a process provides time for the negotiator and his staff, and his higher authorities, to have a last careful review of critical steps before they are finally and formally
agreed to."
—WILLIAM MACOMBER, 1975

Negotiations, antidote to weakness: "Some powers, with very mediocre forces, win support and rid themselves of the most troublesome difficulties. They owe their success to
their prudence, to their care in accommodating themselves to conditions around them, to
their sharp grasp of occasions favorable to their interests, and to a wise observation of the
maxim that it is always best to submit to negotiation those things that one cannot contest
by arms. Such conduct depends on continual negotiations and on friends and allies; it is
the unique but sure resource of the weak, and it is most useful for tempering the excessive force of the powerful."
—FORTUNE BARTHÉLEMY DE FELICE, 1778

Negotiations, by democracies: "If agreement is usually found between the two starting points, . . . good bargaining technique would suggest a point of departure far more
extreme than what one is willing to accept. The more outrageous the initial proposition,
the better . . . the prospect that what one 'really' wants will be considered a compromise.
Such a method of negotiation is particularly difficult for a democracy. When the negotiators adhere to a maxim which makes compromise desirable in itself, effectiveness at the
conference table depends on overstating one's demands. Yet extreme proposals make
it difficult to muster public support. The dilemma is real. . . . To be perfectly flexible,

we should start with a maximum program and offer 'concessions' in the course of the conference. On the other hand, if we make proposals in which we really believe, we must inevitably be somewhat rigid about them. . . . The emphasis on compromise for its own sake brings about an atmosphere of 'damned if you do and damned if you don't.'"
—HENRY A. KISSINGER, 1960

Negotiations, conduct of: "Even if you know your destination in negotiations, you must choose the route carefully, avoiding potholes and pitfalls. You travel by tortoise and not by hare when the nitty gritty must be worked out."   —MAX M. KAMPELMAN, 1987

Negotiations, documents in: "[Never] . . . allow any opponent to carry away any official document, under the pretext that he wishes 'to study it more carefully'; let him read it as often as he wishes, and, if it is necessary, allow him to take minutes of it, but both in your presence."
—LORD MALMESBURY, 1813

Negotiations, domino effect: "One hallowed bargaining precept is that chances of reaching agreement on major issues are improved if the sides first come to terms over less significant problems. This is the 'domino' effect—each bargain that is struck, however unimposing in and of itself, bolsters mutual trust, enlarges expectations, and raises prospects of securing an overall agreement. As a tactical matter, it may be profitable for a negotiator to concede on relatively insubstantial problems at the beginning and then to use these previous concessions later as proof of 'good faith,' to shift the initiative for compromise to the opponent, and to extract counterconcessions on more critical items."
—MICHAEL BLAKER, 1977

Negotiations, durable outcomes of: When you negotiate an agreement, you must remember that you are also negotiating a relationship.

Negotiations, duration of: "A good negotiation takes about as long as it takes an elephant to have a baby."
—HAROLD NICOLSON, 1960

Negotiations, during war: "One can never foresee the consequence of political negotiations under the influence of military eventualities."   —NAPOLEON

Negotiations, events: Events force tactical decisions. Some events force reevaluation of policy and strategy by the parties. The side in a position to create such forcing events has a controlling advantage in negotiations.

Negotiations, flexibility in: "Be not so soft as to be squeezed dry, nor so stiff as to be broken."
—ARAB PROVERB

Negotiations, implementation: The effective negotiator regards implementation not as the result of the negotiating process, but as its final phase.

Negotiations, national styles of: All nations do not negotiate alike. There are distinctive patterns of bargaining style that characterize the behavior and expectations of the representatives of each state and people. The study of national negotiating styles is an important element in the training of professional diplomats.

Negotiations, objectives in: "The object of any successful negotiator is knowing in advance what the absolute minimum is that you can accept, where you are prepared to walk out and have the negotiation fail completely if you can't maintain your minimum position. And then in the process, in the opening moves of the negotiations, to try to set your position outposts far enough in advance so that you've got concession room if you are backed down to your minimum position by . . . [domestic political decisions], or by your allies. If you are engaged in an alliance negotiation, you are in a much more constricted position from the opening right to the conclusion."
—LIVINGSTON MERCHANT, QUOTED BY I. WILLIAM ZARTMAN AND MAUREEN R. BERMAN

Negotiations, objectives of opponents: The best time to affect the other side's negotiating position to one's advantage is at the prenegotiation stage, before its instructions have been formulated or its objectives hardened through approval by higher authority.

Negotiations, opening position in: "[As a negotiator, you should] . . . make a firm resolute stand in the first offer you are instructed to make, and, if you find this nail will not drive, . . . bring forward your others most gradually and not, either from an apprehension of not succeeding at all, or from an eagerness to succeed too rapidly, injure essentially the interests of your Court."
—LORD MALMESBURY

Negotiations, outcome of: "A hard bargain is always a bad bargain."
—DWIGHT MORROW, QUOTED BY HAROLD NICOLSON, 1935

Negotiations, peace: Peace negotiations are the war after the war.

Negotiations, peace: "The only alternative to war is peace. The only road to peace is negotiation."
—GOLDA MEIR

Negotiations, power and: "Every negotiation which does not have power behind it . . . [is] ridiculous and fruitless."
—ADOLF HITLER, 1924

Negotiations, propitious moment for: "The moment is propitious for negotiation when both sides perceive that they may be better off with an agreement than without one . . . [or] when power relations shift toward equality: when the former upper hand slips, or the former underdog improves his position."
—I. WILLIAM ZARTMAN AND MAUREEN R. BERMAN, 1982

Negotiations, publicity about: "If the good of the State requires that current business be carried on silently for some time, there comes however a time when mystery is not only unnecessary but even criminal." —Francisco de Almeida, 1826

Negotiations, publicity about: "A negotiation is like a conversation: none of the participants is free to publish any part of it without thereby harming or offending the other participant. To show the public the adversary's hesitations, transactions, strokes and counterstrokes is to blow bridges behind him and often behind yourself as well and to expose yourself, surely, to a total collapse of the process." —Jules Cambon, 1926

Negotiations, publicity about: "If there is secrecy in negotiation, this secrecy ends in the very hour when these negotiations lead to an agreement; all things considered, there is no truly secret diplomacy." —Jules Cambon, 1926

Negotiations, publicity about: "The most momentous transformation of all [is] the invasion of diplomacy by the mass media. What used to be a compact and reticent exercise cut off from public knowledge is now breached in almost every sector. The media will not accept any compromise; they insist on being present, even at primary and intermediate stages of negotiation. They assert that the right to know belongs to the public in every phase of the tactical negotiation process. Every tentative idea, every trial balloon, every proposal presented for the sake of evoking a response, has to be made known to the public immediately. This is a vast change, and it makes agreements very hard to achieve.
"Agreements require compromise. What do we mean by compromise? Compromise means that you accept today that which you swore the day before that you would always refuse to accept. In order to achieve compromise it is necessary to make concessions. To your adversary you must say that the concession you offer him is so painful that it is almost beyond endurance. In the meantime, you whisper to your domestic constituency that your concession is really quite trivial, and only your own skill and your neighbor's gullibility have given it a certain importance. The trouble is that the wind carries your words in each direction; your adversary and your constituency each hears what you intend for the other." —Abba Eban, 1985

Negotiations, publicity about: "Diplomats and scholars with a professional approach have usually regarded the intrusion of the media into negotiations as a major disruption of the diplomatic process. They argue that 'negotiation' can never break from the mercantile context implied in the word itself. Negotiation presupposes bargaining. A negotiator must be prepared to come out of the bargaining process with positions different from those which he espoused in the beginning. If initial positions are widely published the negotiator is inhibited in his capacity to move to other proposals. The legitimate mobility of negotiation becomes interpreted in the public mind as a failure of credibility." —Abba Eban, 1983

Negotiations, publicity about: "Nobody can challenge the need to present agreements to public scrutiny before they are put into force. It is quite another thing, however, when negotiators have to present to their constituencies not only the agreement for which they seek approval but every tactical phase, trial balloon or tentative proposal, including those submitted for the purpose of provoking a response. . . . International agreements have been endangered through premature exposure to domestic scrutiny." —ABBA EBAN, 1983

Negotiations, publicity about: "The best results of negotiation cannot be achieved in international life any more than in our private world in the full glare of publicity with current debate of all moves, unavoidable misunderstandings, inescapable freezing of positions due to considerations of prestige and the temptation to utilize public opinion as an element integrated into the negotiation itself." —DAG HAMMARSKJLD

Negotiations, publicity about details of: Information about what is happening in negotiations must be carefully husbanded. It is useful for a negotiator to provide background information to the media before and after each negotiating session; this can disarm critics and set a context favorable to his objectives. But access to detailed information on the negotiations themselves must be tightly controlled by him if it is not to leak out and to be interpreted, or misinterpreted, to his possible disadvantage. What is put on paper may be readily copied and disseminated; what is conveyed by a negotiator orally to individuals in private has a chance of remaining confidential and between them.

Negotiations, publicizing success in: "A diplomat must, of course, seek to succeed but he will do well not to do so with a bang. Success is sometimes touchy. Nothing is more dangerous than provoking the vanity of an adversary, and there is no lasting success other than one accepted by both sides. An ambassador must know how to stay in the background. The government to which he is accredited will appreciate his reserve and his own government be perhaps even more grateful to him. There is great power in modesty." —JULES CAMBON, 1926

Negotiations, publicizing success in: "No nation is much offended by its being shewn that they have concluded a negotiation with another and with a stronger power by a treaty in all respects to their advantage." —PALMERSTON

Negotiations, secrecy in: "In the free market no seller will carry on public negotiations with a buyer, no landlord with a tenant, no institution of higher learning with its staff. No candidate for public office will negotiate in public with his backer, no public official with his colleagues, no politician with his fellow politicians. . . . How, then, are we to expect that nations are willing to do what no private individual would ever think of doing?" —HANS MORGENTHAU

Negotiations, secrecy in: "Unless covenants are arrived at secretly, there will be none to agree to openly." —RICHARD M. NIXON, 1992

Negotiations, secrecy in: In negotiation between states, secrecy is essential to facilitate necessary concessions and to save the face of those making them. It may well be appropriate for there to be full disclosure of the results of such a negotiation; it can never be anything other than injurious both to a negotiator's reputation for discretion and to the prospects for subsequent negotiations for the details of how agreement was reached to be revealed.

Negotiations, secrecy in: Secrecy is essential, above all, in discussion of territorial issues. Governments find it almost impossible to retreat from positions on territorial questions that have become public. They therefore lack flexibility to negotiate seriously. The public airing of positions on boundary matters is a familiar prelude to the outbreak of war.

Negotiations, unilateral gestures in: "In most negotiations, unilateral gestures remove a key negotiating asset. In general, diplomats rarely pay for services already rendered—especially in wartime. Typically, it is pressure on the battlefield that generates . . . negotiation. Relieving that pressure reduces the enemy's incentive to negotiate seriously, and it tempts him to drag out the negotiations to determine what other unilateral gestures might be forthcoming."
—HENRY A. KISSINGER, 1994

Negotiators, assessment of opponents: "Good negotiators have in common an ability to assess their opponents—that is what their adversaries' real objectives are, how they think, what agreements will appeal to them, what will not, how their confidence and respect can be gained if they are decent men, and how the latter can be accomplished even if they are not."
—WILLIAM MACOMBER, 1975

Negotiators, authority of: "What gives a negotiator his chance of success is not so much his skill or sincerity as his visible authority. A negotiator of limited skill and wisdom who can commit his government is likely to be more effective than a man of great virtuosity who lacks that mandate."
—ABBA EBAN, 1983

Negotiators, character of: "The compleat negotiator, according to seventeenth- and eighteenth-century manuals on diplomacy, should have a quick mind but unlimited patience, know how to dissemble without being a liar, inspire trust without trusting others, be modest but assertive, charm others without succumbing to their charm, and possess plenty of money and a beautiful wife while remaining indifferent to all temptations of riches and women."
—FRED C. IKLÉ, 1964

Negotiators, cordiality between: "If you had very friendly relations with your opposite number, if he had instructions he might be able to tell you that those were his instructions and personally he disagreed, but this is different from assuming that just by being nice you are going to get the fellow over to your side."
—GERALD FORD, QUOTED BY I. WILLIAM ZARTMAN AND MAUREEN R. BERMAN

Negotiators, inability to make concessions: "The power of a negotiator often rests on a manifest inability to make concessions and to meet demands. . . . It may be a strategic advantage to relinquish certain options deliberately, or even to give up all control over one's future actions and make his responses automatic." —THOMAS C. SCHELLING, 1960

Negotiators, instructions to: To be fully effective, a negotiator must enter a negotiation with a clear-headed appreciation of what elements must be present in an agreement to make it acceptable and what elements are desirable but not essential. The best way to ensure this understanding by a negotiator is to have him participate in drafting his own instructions. He should not be left in the position of guessing what elements in a lengthy draft proposal fall into which category.

Negotiators, intelligence agencies and: For a negotiator, the major tasks are to know what he wants and how to create facts to achieve it, not to accept as given the facts as they are. Intelligence agencies attempt to understand and explain reality; diplomats seek to change it. Intelligence agencies can provide invaluably timely insights into changing situations; they seldom succeed in illuminating the probable shape of the future the statesmen they serve are trying to mold.

Negotiators, interest in success of: "Negotiators almost always abandon the interest of their principals for that of the success of the negotiation, which gives them credit for having succeeded in their undertaking." —FRANÇOIS DE LA ROCHEFOUCAULD, 1665

Negotiators, listening by: "One of the most necessary qualities in a good negotiator is to be an apt listener; to find a skillful yet trivial reply to all questions put to him and to be in no hurry to declare either his own policy, still less his own feelings; and on opening negotiations he should be careful not to reveal the full extent of his design except as far as it is necessary to explore the ground; and he should govern his own conduct as much by what he observes in the faces of others as by what he hears from their lips." —FRANÇOIS DE CALLIÈRES, 1717

Negotiators, modesty in: On the whole, it is better for a negotiator to be underestimated than it is for him to be regarded with apprehension. A negotiator should therefore take care to adopt a modest demeanor and to appear less authoritative, competent, and effective than he believes himself to be.

Negotiators, objectivity in: Excessive objectivity is the negotiator's Achilles' heel; a negotiator must understand his opponent's viewpoint and logic but he must always remember that he is, first and last, an advocate of the interests of his own state.

Negotiators, personality of: "Any negotiator who seduces himself into believing that his personality leads to automatic breakthroughs will soon find himself in the special purgatory that history reserves for those who measure themselves by acclaim rather than achievement." —HENRY A. KISSINGER

Negotiators, private meetings between: The head of a negotiating team should consider arranging an early private meeting with his chief opponent. This can help him add to his government's understanding of the other party's perspective and enhance his ability to articulate his nation's interests in a manner calculated to appeal to it. By affirming, however disingenuously, his confidence in his opponent's realism and good faith, he can encourage him to be embarrassed about adhering to extreme or one-sided positions at the formal negotiating table. He can even assist the other party to rearticulate his nation's interests in ways that facilitate agreement. Such dialogue, moreover, can provide a natural opportunity for a negotiator to emphasize points in common between the parties and to restate his nation's interests in terms calculated to reassure the other side.

Negotiators, probity of: "The qualities of the heart in every profession, and especially that of the negotiator, are the most important. His success chiefly depends upon the confidence he inspires; sentiments of candor, truth, and probity are indispensable to him. One may seduce men by the brilliancy of one's talents, but if these are not guided by probity, they become useless and even dangerous instruments. Men do not forgive having been deceived."
—Antoine Pecquet, 1737

Negotiators, qualities of: "The public negotiator should have the necessary qualities for the conduct of affairs to a much higher degree than one who deals with private matters. Along with the intelligence necessary to his calling, he needs a deep knowledge of men and their affairs, a rare talent for exploiting the sentiments of others and controlling his own, an art of speaking and writing agreeably, forcefully, and easily, and indomitable courage tempered by a gentleness without condescension, an open appearance accompanied by noble and endearing manners, a superior wisdom, a sharply discerning mind, an enlightened honesty, consummate prudence untrammeled by trickery, an inventive spirit through difficulty, and finally an elevation of heart and mind to keep him out of trivia. Such spiritual superiority is required by public affairs where the taste for trivia that characterizes small minds has most dangerous consequences."
—Fortune Barthélemy de Felice, 1778

Negotiators, rank of: The importance of a negotiation is, for better or worse, often judged by the rank and title of the negotiators, In general, it is best to commence negotiations at the level of ambassador or special envoy, rather than at a lower level. It is often easier politically to downgrade the level of a negotiation than to upgrade it.

Negotiators, representation back home of: A negotiator should be represented in his capital at all times by someone who can accurately and effectively explain his actions at the negotiating table to his superiors and sustain their support; he must be prepared to confide in and trust the discretion and political skills of this person. Success in negotiation involves striking a balance between the interests and demands of the parties to it; this reflects judgments about the relative priority to be accorded to these interests. Those in his capital with special interest in the outcome of the negotiation but remote from its realities can be expected to carp at any compromises a negotiator advocates and to seek to discredit him. No reputation can long withstand such abuse from the confidants of his superiors without constant, stalwartly loyal, informed, and direct espousal of his views to them.

Negotiators, selection of: "If you want to come to an agreement, you want to pick a fellow who has a reputation on the other side—it may not have to be very publicly known—of being fair and wanting to reach agreements. Whereas if you appoint a man who does not have this fair reputation, you may sacrifice progress in the negotiation."
—W. Averell Harriman, quoted by I. William Zartman and Maureen R. Berman

Negotiators' opponents: The less you know about your opponent in a negotiation, the more likely you are inadvertently to offend him and the less likely you are to persuade him to accept your point of view.

Negotiators' opponents: "If you would work any man, you must either know his nature and fashions, and so lead him; or his ends, and so persuade him; or his weakness and disadvantages, and so awe him; or those that have interest in him, and so govern him. In dealing with cunning persons, we must ever consider their ends, to interpret their speeches; and it is good to say little to them, and that which they least look for. In all negotiations of difficulty, a man may not look to sow and reap at once; but must prepare business, and so ripen it by degrees."
—Francis Bacon

Neighbors: "Every power has an interest in seeing its neighbors in a state of weakness and decadence."
—Stendhal (Henri Beyle), 1818

Neutrality: A status of declared aloofness and noninvolvement by a state in actual or potential hostilities between other states, asserted because the state declaring neutrality considers that its interests are not engaged in their struggle or that these interests would be better served by remaining outside the realm of contention. See also *Nonalignment*.

Neutrality: "Even to observe neutrality you must have a strong government."
—Alexander Hamilton, 1787

Neutrality, armed: "When a country abjures its intention of exploiting a conflict between two other parties, it is in fact signaling that it has the capacity to do so and that both parties would do well to work at preserving that neutrality. So too, when a nation expresses its 'deep concern' over a military contingency, it is conveying that it will assist—in some as yet unspecified way—the victim of what it has defined as aggression."
—Henry A. Kissinger, 1994

Neutrality, great powers: Great powers cannot be genuinely neutral in great conflicts. Their reluctance to decide, as much as any decision they make, affects the outcome of the struggle.

Neutrality, nonintervention in internal affairs and: "I have always given it as my decided opinion that no nation had a right to intermeddle in the internal concerns of another; that every one had a right to form and adopt whatever government they liked best to live under themselves; and that, if this country could, consistently with its engagements, maintain a strict neutrality and thereby preserve peace, it was bound to do so by motives of policy, interest, and every other consideration." —GEORGE WASHINGTON, 1796

Neutrality, virtues of: "It rarely pays to get between a dog and a lamp-post."
—ATTRIBUTED TO CORDELL HULL

New diplomacy: "New diplomacy, old diplomacy are words that correspond to nothing real. What tends to change is the exterior, the attire of diplomacy, if you will. But the substance will always be the same because human nature does not change, nations will continue to have but one way to resolve their differences, and the word of an honest man will ever be the best tool available to a government to defend its point of view."
—JULES CAMBON, 1926

New diplomacy: "The new diplomacy is an old art practiced under new conditions. . . . The new diplomacy deals formally with governments but actually with the peoples that control governments."
—CHARLES EVANS HUGHES, 1925

NGO: A nongovernmental organization is "a private, self-governing, not-for-profit organization dedicated to alleviating human suffering; and/or promoting education, health care, economic development, environmental protection, human rights and conflict resolution; and/or encouraging the establishment of democratic institutions and civil society."
—U.S. ARMY FIELD MANUAL

NGO, single interest: Nongovernmental organizations, with their characteristic focus on a single issue, seek to score points for their cause without regard to other, perhaps more important national interests. But, very often, progress on the issue of concern to them cannot occur without the progress on other issues that they are, in effect, undermining.

Nonalignment: A national policy repudiating entangling alliances, political identification, or military cooperation with one great power or bloc against another.

Nonalignment: Refusal to join in coalitions or entangling alliances with other states, especially with major power contenders, in the interest of avoiding embroilment in their quarrels, struggles, and wars; a frequent stance of newly independent, precariously established, or weak nations. See also *Neutrality.*

Nongovernmental organization: See *NGO.*

Nonintervention: "Nonintervention is a metaphysical and political term meaning almost the same thing as intervention."
—TALLEYRAND, 1832

Non-paper: A very informal means of conveying written information, especially the summary of points that have been made (or will be made) in oral representation by a diplomat to officials of the host government, intended to aid the memory but not for quotation or attribution as an authoritative statement of the position of the diplomat's government.

Nonviolence: A technique of struggle that transforms weakness into strength by provoking the authorities to use morally offensive forceful measures against a passively resistant, unarmed populace, building sympathy for the oppressed and ultimately shaming their oppressors into policy change.

Note, circular: A diplomatic communication from an ambassador to his colleagues, the ambassadors and chiefs of mission of the diplomatic corps, collectively.

Note, collective: A joint diplomatic communication from two or more ambassadors to one or more addressees, containing identical texts.

Note, diplomatic: A formal communication between an ambassador and a minister (usually the foreign minister) of his host government or another ambassador.

Note, identic: A coordinated diplomatic communication from two or more ambassadors to one or more addressees, conveying similar but not identical message texts.

Note verbale: Unsigned, but initialed, diplomatic communication, written in the third person, between an ambassador and a minister (usually the foreign minister) of his host government.

Notes: "Diplomats write Notes, because they wouldn't have the nerve to tell the same thing to each other's face."
—WILL ROGERS, 1949

Notes, exchange of: An agreement recorded in the form of an offer reciprocated by an acceptance of this offer.

Nuance: "Truth and wisdom lie in nuances."
—ERNEST RENAN

Nuclear war: See *Annihilation*.

Nuclear war: Nuclear war is a fatal hazard to the health of its participants and, one must therefore hope, an anachronism.

Nuclear proliferation: "Acquiring nuclear capability is a statement of a lack of confidence in all alternative security arrangements."
—LAWRENCE FREEDMAN

Nuncio: The title carried by the ambassadors of the Vatican.

Objectives: "We are unlikely to get what we want unless we know what that is."

—Roger Fisher

Objectives: "If a man does not know to what port he is steering, no wind is favorable."

—Seneca

Objectives, declaring: It is foolish to declare an intention to achieve a particular objective unless one is confident one has both the means and the political will to accomplish it.

Objectives, national: "Nations, like individuals, have to limit their objectives, or take the consequences."

—James Reston, 1967

Objectives, unrealistic: The first rule of diplomacy or war is never to declare objectives that one does not have the means or the will to achieve, and never to issue threats that one has no intention of enforcing.

Objectives and power: Objectives and power must be commensurate. If your objectives exceed your power, you must either increase your power or curtail your objectives.

Obstacles: Never mistake an obstacle for the end of the road.

Occupation: "One can do everything with bayonets except sit on them."   —Talleyrand

Offense, defense: "I would rather be the hammer than the anvil."   —Erwin Rommel

Old diplomacy: "The old-world diplomacy of Europe was largely carried on in drawing rooms, and, to a great extent, of necessity still is so. Nations touch at their summits."

—Walter Bagehot, 1867

Opinion: "The world is ruled by force, not by opinion, but opinion uses force."

—Blaise Pascal

Opinion, foreign: "An attention to the judgment of other nations is important to every government for two reasons. The one is that, independently of the merits of any particular plan or measure, it is desirable that it should appear to other nations as the offspring of a wise and honorable policy. The second is that, in doubtful cases, particularly where the national councils may be warped by some strong passion or momentary interest, the presumed or known opinion of the impartial world may be the best guide that can be followed."

—James Madison

Opportunities: "Strike while the iron is hot." —GEORGE FARQUHAR, 1707

Opportunities: "He who seizes the right moment is the right man."
—JOHANN WOLFGANG VON GOETHE, 1808

Opportunities: "Take time by the forelock." —PROVERB

Opposition parties: "Always be in with the outs." —ELLIS BRIGGS, 1968

Optimism: "Optimism is to a diplomat as courage is to a soldier."
—ADLAI E. STEVENSON, JR.

Oratory: "[An ambassador's] way of speaking will be grave, brief and weighty, not interspersed with many quotations . . . or with rare words, and antiquated."
—HOTMAN DE VILLIERS, 1603, CITED BY J.J. JUSSERAND

Oratory: "No one can be a perfect ambassador who is not at the same time a good orator." —TORQUATO TASSO, 1582

Order: "International relations is not a scene of utter chaos; it is a realm of unique kaleidoscopic order." —PETER LYON, 1973

Order, justice and: "Order precedes justice in the strategy of government; but only an order which implicates justice can achieve a stable peace." —REINHOLD NIEBUHR, 1944

Order, legitimizing principle: "International order expresses the need for security and an equilibrium . . . [and] is constructed in the name of legitimizing principle. [Negotiations transform] force into acceptance . . . [and] must attempt to translate the requirements of security into claims and individual demands into general advantage. It is the legitimizing principle which establishes the relative 'justice' of claims and the mode of their adjustment."
—HENRY A. KISSINGER, 1964

Order, new: "There is nothing more difficult to carry out, nor more doubtful of success, nor more dangerous to handle, than to initiate a new order of things. For the reformer has enemies in all those who profit by the old order, and only lukewarm defenders in all those who would profit by the new order, this lukewarmness arising partly from fear of their adversaries, . . . and partly from the incredulity of mankind, who do not truly believe in anything new until they have had actual experience of it. Thus it arises that on every opportunity for attacking the reformer, [as] his opponents do so with the zeal of partisans, the others only defend him half-heartedly, so that between them he runs great danger." —NICCOLÒ MACHIAVELLI

Order, revolution and: "Revolutions are temporary disturbances in the life of states. Order always ends up by reclaiming its own; states do not die like individuals, they transform themselves. It is the task of statesmanship to guide this transformation and to supervise its direction."

—METTERNICH

Order, revolutionary challenge to: "Whenever there exists a power which considers the international order or the manner of legitimizing it oppressive, relations between it and other powers will be revolutionary. In such cases, it is not the adjustment of differences within a given system which will be at issue, but the system itself. Adjustments are possible, but they will be conceived as tactical maneuvers to consolidate positions for the inevitable showdown, or as tools to undermine the morale of the antagonist."

—HENRY A. KISSINGER, 1964

Order, stable: "The foundation of a stable order is the relative security—and therefore the relative insecurity—of its members. Its stability reflects, not the absence of unsatisfied claims, but the absence of a grievance of such magnitude that redress will be sought in overturning the [existing order] rather than through an adjustment within its framework. The security of a domestic order resides in the preponderant power of authority, that of an international order in the balance of forces and in its expression, the equilibrium."

—HENRY A. KISSINGER, 1964

Order, vulnerability of established: "Revolutionaries almost always start from a position of inferior strength. They prevail because the established order is unable to grasp its own vulnerability."

—HENRY A. KISSINGER, 1994

Orders: Never give an order unless you have reason to believe it can and will be obeyed.

Ostracism: Ostracism breeds resentment; resentment sustains recalcitrance.

Overbidding, in negotiations: A state competing with other nations whose interests are less intense or more time-constrained than its own for concessions from a second state may offer more than it will actually be prepared to give. This classic negotiating strategy can make what the others are offering seem unattractive. It may delay acceptance of less generous but more realistic offers until those making them lose patience and abandon the field. The sole remaining bidder can then be in a position to make its own bargain.

P

p.c.: An abbreviation of the French phrase *pour condoler,* written in the lower left corner of a calling card to express condolences upon a death or calamity.

p.f.: An abbreviation of the French phrase *pour féliciter,* written in the lower left corner of a calling card to convey congratulations—for example, upon a national holiday, promotion, engagement or marriage.

p.p.c.: An abbreviation of the French phrase *pour prendre congé,* written in the lower left corner of a calling card to say goodbye before departure from a post of diplomatic assignment.

p.r.: An Abbreviation of the French phrase *pour remercier,* written in the lower left corner of a calling card to express thanks—for example, for a party or a gift.

Pacification: "You may spread fire and desolation, but that will not be government!"
—CHARLES LENNOX, 3RD DUKE OF RICHMOND AND LENNOX

Pacification: "Who overcomes by force hath overcome but half his foe." —JOHN MILTON

Pacifism: "Like a snake devouring a mouse, the Earth devours a king who is inclined to peace."
—ARTHASASTRA OF KAUTILYA

Pacifism: "Virtue, stripped of force, reveals its own weakness. . . . A state which only defends itself against its powerful neighbors with justice and moderation will be defeated sooner or later."
—ABBOT MABLY, 1757

Paranoia: By making it impossible for others to be their friends, the paranoid transform potential allies into actual enemies.

Partisans of good relations: In every society there are natural partisans of good relations with a particular foreign country. These include graduates of study programs in that country, admirers of its culture, institutions, and artifacts, spouses of its nationals, speakers of its language, adherents to its predominant religion, and others. Such people constitute a reservoir of affection for an ambassador's country and a source of potential understanding and support for his government's perspective on troublesome bilateral and international issues. This reservoir needs continuous refreshment, however, in the form of a flow of contact and information, if it is not to dry up. Facilitating such renewal of goodwill on the part of old friends in his host country is among an ambassador's most enjoyable—and essential—duties.

Partition: The division of a state into two or more states or its division into regions to be incorporated into neighboring states. Sometimes partition occurs as a result of civil war; sometimes it is the product of collusion between adversaries seeking to preempt unilateral action by each other and to ensure that neither gains undue strategic advantage.

Passport: A travel identity document, officially issued to a citizen or national by his government, that attests to his nationality and date and place of birth, gives him a right of return to his homeland, and requests that other governments afford him prompt and unhindered passage and, where needed, aid and protection.

Patience: The capacity to outsit the other side at the table is one of the key attributes of successful negotiators in conference diplomacy.

Patience: "Everything comes to those who wait." —PROVERB

Patience: "States, like individuals, which have a future are in a position to be able to wait." —LORD SALISBURY, 1878

Patriotism: The sense by individual members of a nation that it is worth sacrificing some significant portion of their personal interests to defend the common interests and well-being of their nation against challenges from others.

Patriotism: "He who denies his heritage is not worthy of one." —ARAB PROVERB

Peace: "Peace is liberty in tranquility." —CICERO, 43 B.C.

Peace: "Peace is at best a truce on the battlefield of Time." —J.A. CRAMB, CITED BY SIR VICTOR WELLESLEY

Peace: "Peace itself is war in masquerade." —JOHN DRYDEN, 1682

Peace: "Peace is tranquil freedom, and is contrary to war, of which it is the end and destruction." —HUGO GROTIUS, 1625

Peace: "Only rulers who have no other remedy should seek peace." —ARTHASASTRA OF KAUTILYA

Peace: "The mere absence of war is not peace." —JOHN F. KENNEDY, 1963

Peace: "Peace as the term is commonly employed is nothing more than a name, the truth being that every state is by law of nature engaged perpetually in an informal war with every other state." —PLATO

Peace: "Peace, like war, can succeed only where there is a will to enforce it, and where there is available power to enforce it." —Franklin Delano Roosevelt, 1944

Peace: "Peace . . . does not mean a condition in which there are no conflicts between the needs, demands and goals of states, for these are always present. It means—in the United Nations Charter, for instance, and in common usage—a condition where states and political entities do not use violence against one another in pursuit of their incompatible goals." —Adam Watson, 1983

Peace: "It must be a peace without victory. . . . Victory would mean peace forced upon the loser, a victor's terms imposed upon the vanquished. It would be accepted in humiliation, under duress, at an intolerable sacrifice, and would leave a sting, a resentment, a bitter memory upon which terms of peace would rest, not permanently, but only as upon quicksand. Only a peace between equals can last." —Woodrow Wilson, 1917

Peace, absence of war: "Peace seldom reigns over all Europe, and never in all quarters of the world." —Carl Maria von Clausewitz

Peace, as primary policy objective: "Whenever peace—conceived as the avoidance of war—has been the primary objective of a power or group of powers, the international system has been at the mercy of the most ruthless member of the international community. Whenever the international order has acknowledged that certain principles could not be compromised even for the sake of peace, stability based on an equilibrium of forces [has been] at least conceivable." —Henry A. Kissinger, 1964

Peace, bad: "There never was a good war or a bad peace." —Benjamin Franklin, 1773

Peace, bad: "A bad peace is even worse than war." —Tacitus, c. 110

Peace, defined: Peace is restrained tolerance of the status quo by those with the capability to alter it by violence. Contrast *Concord*.

Peace, disadvantageous: "The most disadvantageous peace is better than the most just war." —Erasmus, 1508

Peace, durability of: "No one can have peace longer than his neighbor pleases." —Dutch proverb

Peace, duration of: "What we dignify with the name of peace is really only a short truce, in accordance with which the weaker party renounces his claims, whether just or unjust, until such time as he can find an opportunity of asserting them with the sword." —Vauvenargues, 1746

Peace, effects of: "Peace is a very apoplexy, lethargy; mulled, deaf, sleepy, insensible; a getter of more bastard children, than war is a destroyer of men."
—WILLIAM SHAKESPEARE, CORIOLANUS, 1607

Peace, eternal: "Mankind has grown strong in eternal struggles and it will only perish through eternal peace." —ADOLF HITLER, 1924

Peace, eternal: "Eternal peace is a dream, and not even a beautiful one."
—HELMUTH VON MOLTKE ("THE ELDER"), 1880

Peace, eternal: "Eternal peace lasts only until the next war." —RUSSIAN PROVERB

Peace, interests: "Though peace be made, yet it is interest that keeps peace."
—OLIVER CROMWELL, 1654

Peace, justice: The end of injustice marks the beginning of peace.

Peace, justice and: "If peace were to be the supreme goal of all states, and there were to be no recourse to war or other forms of violence in order to right wrongs or to change the world, then only those wrongs could be righted and only those adjustments made which a state could be induced to accept without the use of force. It is true that the values of states change; and that a state may sometimes be persuaded to yield by argument, because its government and people acknowledge the justice of the case brought against it. For instance, imperial states may freely, and without the use of force, grant independence to colonies. . . . Or a state may be induced to give way by other member states of the international system applying pressure short of force, such as economic sanctions. But in practice such changes are limited. The renunciation in advance of the use of force in order to right a proclaimed 'injustice' is recognized in practice as a diplomatic formula weighted heavily in favour of the status quo. So peace, the exclusion of violence by one political entity against another, it essentially the policy of satisfied states, weak states and states which consider that the changes they really care about can be achieved by diplomacy and the help of their friends without recourse to violence." —ADAM WATSON, 1983

Peace, making: "It's easier to make war than to make peace." —GEORGES CLEMENCEAU

Peace, object of war: "The legitimate object of war is a more perfect peace."
—WILLIAM TECUMSEH SHERMAN, 1882

Peace, opposite of: "The opposite of peace is not merely war but all political violence."
—ALEKSANDR SOLZHENITSIN

Peace, price for: "There is a price which is too great to pay for peace, and that price can be put in one word. One cannot pay the price of self-respect." —WOODROW WILSON, 1916

Peace, purpose of war: "The purpose of all war is peace."

—St. Augustine

Peace, reconciliation with enemies: "We become reconciled with our enemies because we want to improve our situation, because we are weary of war, or because we fear defeat."

—François de la Rochefoucauld, 1665

Peace, security of: Peace is secure only when there is no obvious profit in war.

Peace, terms of: War subdues peoples but does not capture their hearts; it is a principal task of diplomacy to reconcile the vanquished to their defeat.

Peace, treaty of: "The first object of a treaty of peace should be to make future war improbable."

—Lord Salisbury, 1870

Peace, vindictive: "There can be no greater fault of statesmanship than to impose a vindictive peace upon a fallen yet potentially powerful enemy." —Victor Wellesley, 1944

Peace, war: When peace is seen as more likely to prove injurious than war, nations will choose war.

Peace, war termination: "As a general rule, countries striving for stability and equilibrium should do everything within their power to achieve their basic peace terms while still at war. . . . If this principle is neglected and the key issues are left unresolved until the peace conference, the most determined power [in a coalition] ends up in possession of the prizes and can be dislodged only by a major confrontation."

—Henry A. Kissinger, 1994

Peace and war: It sometimes happens that statesmen are unable to make peace, because they are too weak at home, and unable to make war, because the risks are too great.

Peace and war: "Peace is the dream of the wise; war is the history of man."

—Richard Burton, 1865

Peace and war: "Peace is the daughter of war."

—French proverb

Peace and war: "Civilized mankind has always desired peace and, in spite of its civilization, has always made war. Mankind, however, is perfectible, and its aspirations, its attempts at suppressing wars or at least diminishing the occasions for them, have . . . long been represented, to some extent at least, by the institution of the diplomatic service."

—J.J. Jusserand

Peace and war: "Of all the unhappy conditions to which princes or republics can be reduced, the most unhappy is when they are unwilling to accept peace and incapable of sustaining war; and to this condition those are reduced who consider themselves op-pressed by the terms of peace, and who, if they wished to make war, would have to yield themselves a prey to their allies, or victims to their enemies. And all this results from following evil counsels, and from taking a wrong course because of not having estimated their forces correctly." —Niccolò Machiavelli

Peace and war: "It is expedient for the victor to wish for peace restored; for the van-quished it is necessary." —Seneca

Peace Process: A protracted course of negotiation that, by allowing the parties to play for time and maneuver for advantage, becomes a substitute for peace and an excuse for its continuing absence rather than a means to achieve it.

Peacekeeping: If an agreement needs to be enforced by an outside party, it is not really agreed and is unlikely to survive the withdrawal of those enforcing it. The peacekeep-ers are therefore hostage to the future willingness of the quarreling parties to advance toward a settlement of differences through mutual concessions and compromise. But pro-tracted outside enforcement of a truce can easily come to be seen by these parties as less costly to them than the political sacrifices needed to achieve reconciliation. So peacekeep-ing operations tend to be protracted and, paradoxically, often become a potent obstacle to real peace between the parties.

Peacemakers: "Blessed are the peacemakers: for they shall be called the children of God." —Matthew

Peacemaking: "It is diplomacy, not speeches and votes, that continues to have the last word in the process of peace-making." —Dag Hammarskjld, 1958

Peacemaking, need for discretion in: "How is the task of peacemaker . . . to be pursued if you shout your grievances from the housetop whenever they occur? The only result is that you embitter public feelings, that the differences between the two States suddenly attain a magnitude they ought never be allowed to approach, that the newspapers of the two countries have their passions set on fire, and great crises arise, which may end, have ended sometimes in international castastrophes. . . . I do not hold the view that antique methods are pursued by diplomatists which no man of common sense adopts in the ordinary work of everyday life." —Arthur James Balfour

Peacemaking, reconciliation with enemies: "An impotent enemy is a fact; a reconciled enemy a conjecture. A territorial accretion represents the surety of possession; to integrate an opponent into the community of nations through self-restraint is an expression of faith. It is no accident that the advocates of 'absolute security' always have popular sup-port on their side. Theirs is the sanction of the present, but statesmen must deal with the future." —Henry A. Kissinger, 1964

Peacemaking, statecraft in: "[It may be necessary for a peacemaker to rely] less on the application of raw power than on a determined statecraft deriving its leverage from others, from the regional balance of power itself, and from the logic of the concepts to which [he is committed]."
—CHESTER A. CROCKER, 1992

Peacemaking, verification, guarantees: "Warring parties are unlikely to take possibly irreversible steps toward military disengagement until they have come to grips with the basic deal. Nor are they likely to hammer out the specifics of essential trade-offs on the key issues until (a) the basic parameters of the deal are agreed, and (b) a climate of greater confidence exists and no side feels that it is negotiating at gunpoint. Efforts to negotiate . . . language relating to verification or guarantees make the most sense once it is reasonably clear what is to be verified or guaranteed. Institutionalized mechanisms for implementation and follow-up come at the end, when the sides have acquired a substantial stake in the success of their own efforts."
—CHESTER A. CROCKER, 1992

Perception management: "Actions to convey and/or deny information . . . to foreign audiences to influence their emotions, motives and objective reasoning as well as to intelligence systems and leaders . . . ultimately resulting in foreign behaviors and official actions favorable to [our] objectives. In various ways, perception management combines truth projection, operations security, cover and deception and psychological operations."
—UNITED STATES DEPARTMENT OF DEFENSE

Permission: It is much easier to gain forgiveness for unauthorized action that has succeeded than to get permission to do something that might fail.

Perseverance: "The simple truth is that perseverance in good policies is the only avenue to success, and that even perseverance in poor ones often gives the appearance of being so."
—DEAN ACHESON

Persona non grata: A declaration that a specifically named individual diplomat is no longer welcome on the territory of his host nation and must leave or may not return.

Personal relations, summits: Mutual familiarity and trust in each other's integrity undergird the subtle links of understanding and common interest that give leaders the confidence to do business at a distance or through diplomatic agents. Thus, the greatest value of summits lies in opportunities for leaders to form first-hand impressions of each other's character and modes of reasoning.

Personnel: "Let me control personnel, and I will ultimately control policy. For the part of the machine that recruits and hires and fires and promotes people can soon control the entire shape of the institution, and of our foreign policy."
—GEORGE F. KENNAN, 1970

Personnel: "The skillful employer of men will employ the wise man, the brave man, the covetous man, and the stupid man. For the wise man delights in establishing his merit, the brave man likes to show his courage in action, the covetous man is quick at seizing advantages, and the stupid man has no fear of death." —Du Mu

Personnel: "Hard though it is to know people, there are ways. First is to question them concerning right and wrong, to observe their ideas. Second is to exhaust all their arguments, to see how they change. Third is to consult with them about strategy, to see how perceptive they are. Fourth is to announce that there is trouble, to see how brave they are. Fifth is to get them drunk, to observe their nature. Sixth is to present them with the prospect of gain, to see how modest they are. Seventh is to give them a task to do within a specific time, to see how trustworthy they are." —Zhuge Liang

Persuasion: "On the whole, the difficult thing about persuading others is not that one lacks the knowledge needed to state his case nor the audacity to exercise his abilities to the full. On the whole, the difficult thing about persuasion is to know the mind of the person one is trying to persuade and to be able to fit one's words to it. . . . The important thing in persuasion is to learn how to play up the aspects that the person you are talking to is proud of and to play down the aspects he is ashamed of. Thus, if the person has some urgent personal desire, you should show him that it is his public duty to carry it out and urge him not to delay. If he has some mean objective in mind and yet cannot restrain himself, you should do your best to point out to him whatever admirable aspects it may have and to minimize reprehensible ones. If he has some lofty objective in mind and yet does not have the ability needed to realize it, you should do your best to point out to him the faults and bad aspects of such an objective and make it seem a virtue not to pursue it. If he is anxious to make a show of wisdom and ability, mention several proposals which are different from the one you have in mind but of the same general nature in order to supply him with ideas; then let him build on your words, but pretend that you are unaware that he is doing so, and this way abet his wisdom. If you wish to urge a policy of peaceful coexistence, then be sure to expound it in terms of lofty ideals, but also hint that it is commensurate with the ruler's personal interest. If you wish to warn the ruler against dangerous and injurious policies, then make a show of the fact that they invite reproach and moral censure, but also hint that they are inimical to his personal interests."

—Han Feizi, as translated by Burton Watson

Persuasion, bargaining and: Persuasion generally precedes bargaining in negotiations. Persuasion differs from bargaining in that it represents an effort to bring the other side to an acceptance, through appeals to reason or emotion, of the reasons that your demands are so important to you and of your views of why their demands are excessive, unacceptable, and contrary to their own interest. Bargaining is characterized by conditional offers, threats, and inducements intended to promote acceptance of proposals for compromise and a trade-off between competing interests.

Phrasing: "Use soft words and hard arguments." —English Proverb

Planning: "Plans are useless but planning is indispensable." —Dwight D. Eisenhower

Placement: The art of seating guests in such a manner as to recognize their status and order of precedence, and to please rather than enrage or bore them.

Places, strategic: "I would not be too much impressed by what the soldiers tell you about the strategic importance of . . . places. If they were allowed full scope they would insist on the importance of garrisoning the moon in order to protect us from Mars."
—Lord Salisbury

Plan:

"In the beginning was the plan,
And then came the assumptions,
And the assumptions were without form,
And the plan was completely without substance,
And the darkness was on the face of the workers,
And they spoke to their Deputy-Directors saying:
'It's a crock, and it stinketh.'
And the Deputy-Directors went unto their Director, and sayeth:
'It's a pail of dung, and none may abide the odor thereof.'
And the Directors went unto their Directors-General and sayeth unto them:
'It's a container of excrement, and it is very strong such that none may abide by it.'
And the Directors-General went unto their Assistant Deputy Minister, and sayeth to him:
'It's a vessel of fertilizer, and none may abide by its strength.'
And the Assistant Deputy Ministers went to the Executive Committee and sayeth:
'It contains that which makes plants grow, and it is very strong.'
And the Executive Committee went unto the Under Secretary and sayeth unto him:
'This powerful new plan will actively promote the growth and efficiency of the department, and this area in particular.'
And the Minister looked upon the Plan, and saw that it was good.
And the Plan became Policy."
—Benoît Plamandon, 1994

Planning: "Planning, simply defined, should be the place where the political leader is faced with an awareness of the consequences of his decisions before he makes them instead of afterwards. It should be the means by which the lines of communication are kept open between those who make decisions, those who illuminate them, and those who carry them out. Whatever form planning takes, if it does not keep these lines of communication open, there will be a mess."
—Eugene Black

Planning: "Planning is a waste of time unless it is done by the people who have got to execute it."
—Henry A. Kissinger, 1970

Planning, contingency: Contingency planning is the preparation of plans to apply the power of the state, primarily its military power, to scenarios and situations that have not occurred and may never do so. It sets objectives and defines the courses of action, patterns of organization, and logistical requirements that would best accomplish them, if so directed.

Planning, contingency, civilians and: Decisions affect interests, organizations, and individuals, rewarding some and inflicting loss on others. They entail political costs. This is a major reason civilian leaders resist military contingency planning. From their point of view, contingencies are hypothetical situations that posit policy failures. They see no benefit in accepting that their policies might fail. Nor do they wish to foreshadow, still less make, politically costly decisions before it is imperative to make them.

Planning, diplomats and: "In every foreign service officer there is a foreign policy planner, struggling to be free. . . . Scratch a liberal, and you'll find a socialist; scratch a diplomatist, and you'll find the frustrated artist of some grand design." —JAMES EAYRS, 1971

Planning, futility of: "About politics one can make only one completely unquestionable generalization which is that it is quite impossible for statesmen to foresee, for more than a very short time, the results of large-scale political action." —ALDOUS HUXLEY, 1941

Planning, futility of: "Men fight and lose the battle, and the thing they fought for comes about in spite of their defeat, and when it comes, turns out to be not what they meant, and other men have to fight for what they meant under a different name."
—WILLIAM MORRIS

Planning, operational vs. policy: Operational planning, as practiced mainly by the military, manages discrete segments of events. It aims to organize courses of action that have a beginning, a middle, and an end. The objective of operational planning is the attainment of a predefined end state. Policy planning, as practiced by statesmen and diplomats, deals with a kaleidoscopic reality that is ceaselessly evolving. It strives to guide responses to events that it does not create and often cannot anticipate. The objective of policy planning is to make gains and to minimize setbacks in a world in which every success gives birth to new problems and every setback opens new opportunities. Given the differences between operational and policy planning, it is hardly surprising that their practitioners find it difficult to understand each other or the requirements of their respective crafts.

Planning, operations: Operations planning is the preparation, in detail, of schemes for specific military operations in a hostile environment, including the manner and means of initiating and carrying on with military action, the composition and deployments of the forces necessary to do so, and the logistics and mobilizations necessary to achieve a predefined end state.

Planning, profitability of: "The truth is that in foreign affairs manhours spent in thinking and planning on future action are by far the most profitable investment. The thundering present becomes so soon the unchangeable past that seizing it at any moment of its acceleration is as dangerous as mounting a train gathering speed. . . . Every bird-shooter knows that you must lead your bird and swing with its flight. . . . The true problem lies in determining the emerging future and the policy appropriate to it."   —DEAN ACHESON

Plans: When the devil's grandmother begins to mess with your plans, you better make new ones.   —RUSSIAN PROVERB

Poise: "Discipline, self-restraint, caution, and poise of manner (which became impassiveness when it was overdone) were qualities of the traditional diplomatist." —R.B. MOWAT

Polemics: Moral and ideological argumentation intended to reassure the populace of one's own state of the justice of their cause and to sow doubt among the people of hostile or neutral states about the justice of the opposing cause, thereby dividing them, undermining their will to resist, and sapping their morale.

Policy and bureaucracy: "The spirit of policy and that of bureaucracy are diametrically opposed. The essence of policy is its contingency; its success depends on the correctness of an estimate which is in part conjectural. The essence of bureaucracy is its quest for safety; its success is calculability. Profound policy depends on perpetual creation, on a constant redefinition of goals. Good administration thrives on routine, the definition of relationships which can survive mediocrity. Policy involves an adjustment of risks; administration an avoidance of deviation. Policy justifies itself by the relationship of its measures and its sense of proportion; administration by the rationality of each action in terms of a given goal. The attempt to conduct policy bureaucratically leads to a quest for calculability which tends to become a prisoner of events. The effort to administer politically leads to total irresponsibility, because bureaucracies are designed to execute, not conceive.

"The temptation to conduct policy administratively is ever present, because most governments are organized primarily for the conduct of domestic policy, whose chief problem is the implementation of social decisions, a task which is limited only by its technical feasibility. But the concern with technical problems in foreign affairs leads to a standard which evaluates by mistakes avoided rather than by goals achieved, and to a belief that ability is more likely to be judged by the pre-vision of catastrophes than the discovery of opportunities."   —HENRY A. KISSINGER, 1964

Policy, defensive: "Limited policies inevitably are defensive policies, and defensive policies inevitably are losing policies."   —JOHN FOSTER DULLES, 1950

Policy and diplomacy: "The art of diplomacy consists of making the policy of one government understood and if possible accepted by other governments. Policy is thus the

substance of foreign relations; diplomacy is the process by which policy is carried out."
　　　　　　　　　　　　　　　　　　　　　　　　　　　—J. Rives Childs

Policy and diplomacy: "Diplomacy is not policy but the agency for giving effect to it. Both are complementary to each other since the one cannot act without the cooperation of the other. Diplomacy has no separate existence from foreign policy, but the two together form one executive policy—policy determining the strategy, and diplomacy the tactics."
　　　　　　　　　　　　　　　　　　　　　　　　　　—Victor Wellesley

Policy, imposing: In practice, policies cannot be imposed on other countries without their assent. Short of their capitulation at gunpoint, their assent must be obtained by negotiation, and negotiation is the opposite of dictation; it always involves a measure of mutual accommodation.

Policy, imprecision: "An imprecise policy means no policy at all. It means aspiration only."
　　　　　　　　　　　　　　　　　　　　　　　　　　—Harold Nicolson

Policy, national security: Diplomacy is the form which national security policy takes in normal times; it is the silent, bloodless stuff of strategy.

Policy, source of mistaken: "The temptation to tell a chief in a great position the thing that he most likes to hear is one of the commonest explanations of mistaken policy."
　　　　　　　　　　　　　　　　　　　　　　　　　　—Winston Churchill

Policy, wrong: "The pursuit of wrong policies provokes external enemies; immoderation provokes anger in one's own people; both are diabolic practices."
　　　　　　　　　　　　　　　　　　　　　　　—Arthasastra of Kautilya

Policymaking: "Never fall victim to the black magic of specialist infallibility."
　　　　　　　　　　　　　　　　　　　　　　　—Violet Bonham-Carter

Policymaking: "The commonest error in politics is sticking to the carcasses of dead policies. When a mast falls overboard, you do not try to save a rope here and a spar there, in memory of their former utility; you cut away the hamper altogether. And it should be the same with a policy. But . . . we cling to the shred of an old policy after it has been torn to pieces, and to the shadow of the shred after the rag itself has been torn away. And therefore it is that we are . . . in perplexity."
　　　　　　　　　　　　　　　　　　　　　　　　　　　—Lord Salisbury

Politeness: "To speak kindly does not hurt the tongue."　　　　—French proverb

Politeness: "The language of diplomacy may often . . . simply [cover] a mailed fist with a velvet glove; but so long as forms of courtesy [are] preserved and naked force . . . not openly threatened, passion [is] restrained; the sang froid upon which peace depends in critical negotiations [is] preserved. Politeness between international competitors or antagonists is not a 'false' thing, any more than between people who disagree with each other in private life."

—R.B. Mowat

Politeness: "With a smile on the lips and a brow of bronze one can get by everywhere."

—Talleyrand

Politeness, case for: "The great art of living easy and happy in society is to study proper behavior, and even with our most intimate friends to observe politeness; otherwise we will insensibly treat each other with a degree of rudeness, and each will find himself despised in some measure by the other."

—James Boswell, 1762

Politeness, function of: "The aim of the diplomat is to get as much as he can for his country while giving as little as he can. His unfailing courtesy in this process is not the result of a spineless desire to make himself agreeable to foreigners or to bargain away his country's good name for good will. It is rather grounded upon a mutual recognition that current negotiation is a mere incident in a continuing relationship, that both parties will have an unending series of matters to settle in the future, and that any agreement will be facilitated through maintenance of objectivity, good will, and good temper."

—Kenneth W. Thompson, 1962

Politeness, in diplomacy: "Be polite. Write diplomatically. Even in a declaration of war one observes the rules of politeness."

—Otto von Bismark

Politeness, in diplomacy: "To be a diplomat, it is not enough to be an ass, you must also be polite."

—Attributed to Talleyrand

Political appointees: See *Appointees, political.*

Political section: The section of an embassy, usually headed by a counselor or first secretary, that is responsible for liaison with working levels of the receiving state's foreign ministry on international developments of mutual concern. It has primary responsibility for collecting, analyzing, and reporting information on developments in the foreign and domestic policies and politics of the receiving state of interest to the sending state.

Political warfare: "Mental confusion, contradiction of feeling, indecisiveness, panic: these are our weapons."

—Adolf Hitler, 1939

Politicians, as ambassadors: "A quiet legation is the stuffed mattress which the political acrobat wants always to see ready under him in case of a slip."

—John Hay

Politicians, as ambassadors: "Diplomacy is the sewer through which flows the scum and refuse of the political puddle. A man not fit to stay at home is just the man to send abroad."

—New York Herald Tribune, 1857

Politician, statesman: "A politician is a man who understands government, and it takes a politician to run a government. A statesman is a politician who's been dead 10 or 15 years."
—HARRY S. TRUMAN

Politics: All politics is personal. To gain the day, address the politician.

Politics: "Politics is the art of the possible."
—ATTRIBUTED TO OTTO VON BISMARCK

Politics, foreign policy: In foreign affairs, domestic politics drives posture, but only until reality forces reassessment of risks and costs.

Politics, military actions: "Military actions are the most extreme form of politics."
—WILLIAM E. ODOM

Politics, nature of: "Politics depend above all else upon the power of persuading others to accept ideas."
—VIOLET BONHAM-CARTER

Politics, rules of: "In politics nothing is contemptible."
—BENJAMIN DISRAELI

Politics, warfare: "Politics is warfare without bloodshed, and warfare is politics with bloodshed."
—MAO ZEDONG

Polity: A society that has established institutions through which it makes decisions regarded by its members as binding upon them and as entitled to legitimacy in the eyes of others. See also *Society, Nation, State,* and *Community.*

Posture: Sit to ingratiate them. Stand to lead them.

Pouch, diplomatic: A sealed container used to transport privileged communications, publications, and the like between embassies and foreign ministries that is immune from search by foreign officials. Pouches containing especially sensitive material are usually escorted by a diplomatic courier.

Poverty: Those who cannot live by their wallets must live by their wits.

Power: Power is the capacity to influence, perhaps even determine, the course of events.

Power: "The three components of power —esprit, military might, and genius [capacity for analysis and judgment]—are in ascending order of importance. A king who is superior, as compared to his enemy, in an item later in the list outmaneuvers his adversary."
—ARTHASASTRA OF KAUTILYA

Power: "Distance weakens power. Great distance weakens power greatly."
—THOMAS A. BAILEY, 1968

Power: "Power, in whatever hands, is rarely guilty of too strict limitations on itself."
—EDMUND BURKE, 1777

Power: "Power consists in having things your way." —JAMES EAYRS, 1967

Power: "If you have no power, you are a conquered king." —ARTHASASTRA OF KAUTILYA

Power: "Power is the ultimate aphrodisiac." —HENRY A. KISSINGER

Power: "The statesman, who means to maintain peace, can no more ignore the order of power than an engineer can ignore the mechanics of physical force."
—WALTER LIPPMANN, 1943

Power: "International politics, like all politics, is a struggle for power. Whatever the ultimate aims of international politics, power is always the immediate aim. Statesmen and peoples may ultimately seek freedom, security, prosperity, or power itself. They may define their goals in terms of a religious, philosophic, economic, or social ideal. . . . But whenever they strive to realize their goal by means of international politics, they do so by striving for power." —HANS J. MORGENTHAU, 1948

Power, arbitrary: "Arbitrary power is the natural object of temptation to a prince as wine or women to a young fellow, or a bribe to a judge, or avarice to old age, or vanity to a woman." —JONATHAN SWIFT

Power, balance of: "The balance of power is a system of alliances; and alliances may very easily vary, be mixed up like a pack of cards, provided a certain equality is the result. The object is peace, not any high ethical purpose." —LORD ACTON

Power, balance of: "The balance of power is easy to calculate when the elements of a nation's power remain reasonably constant. But if power factors change rapidly, uncertainty is introduced into relationships between potential adversaries. This, in turn, can make miscalculation and hostilities more likely." —ABBA EBAN, 1983

Power, balance of: "Each nation is . . . under the necessity of incessant watchfulness to prevent the excessive aggrandizement of one of its neighbors, . . . for the aggrandizement of a nation beyond a certain limit changes the general system of all the nations that have relation to it. . . . Everything which changes or alters this general system . . . is dangerous and entails infinite evils." —FÉNELON

Power, balance of: "To establish an equilibrium between the powers of such a kind as to prevent the union of many in a single one, so that the balance of equality, which it is desired to assure, could not incline to the advantage of one of these powers to the risk and injury of the others." —CHARLES J.B. GIRAUD, 1847

Power, balance of: "The management of a balance of power is a permanent undertaking, not an exertion that has a foreseeable end." —HENRY A. KISSINGER, 1979

Power, balance of: "Those who scoff at 'balance of power diplomacy' on the world scene should recognize that the alternative to a balance of power is an imbalance of power—and history shows us that nothing so drastically escalates the danger of war as such an imbalance." —RICHARD M. NIXON, 1972

Power, balance of: "'Balance of power' means only this—that a number of weaker states may unite to prevent a stronger one from acquiring a power which should be dangerous to them, and which should overthrow their independence, their liberty, and their freedom of action. It is the doctrine of self-preservation." —PALMERSTON, 1854

Power, balance of: "The balance of power is a system designed to maintain a continuous conviction in every state, that if it attempted aggression it would encounter an invincible combination of the others." —QUINCY WRIGHT, 1942

Power, balance of, conditions for: "The balance of power works best if at least one of the following conditions pertains. First, each nation must feel itself free to align with any other state, depending on the circumstances of the moment. . . . Second, when there are fixed alliances but a balancer sees to it that none of the existing coalitions becomes predominant. . . . Third, when there are rigid alliances and no balancer exists, but the cohesion of the alliances is relatively low so that, on any given issue, there are either compromises or changes in alignment. When none of these conditions exists, diplomacy turns rigid. A zero sum game develops in which any gain of one side is conceived as a loss for the other. Armaments races and mounting tensions become inevitable." —HENRY A. KISSINGER, 1994

Power, balance of, diplomacy in: An international state system composed of many states of approximately equal strength allows subtlety of diplomatic maneuver to substitute for military strength. As long as no nation is strong enough to eliminate all the others, a state can use shifting coalitions to exert pressure against others or to marshall support for its position; its bargaining position depends on maintaining its potential availability to any and all other states as a partner. In such a state system, no relationship is considered permanent and no conflict will be pushed to an extreme; rather disputes will be limited by the tacit understanding that maintenance of the existing order is at least as important as the outcome of any specific disagreement among two or more states. In these circumstances of equilibrium in the distribution of power, diplomacy is truly a substitute for war. Wars are not absent, but they are limited in scope and objectives; they do not risk national survival and can be ended through the settlement of the specific issues that provoke them.

Power, confidence: "Power without a nation's confidence is nothing."
—CATHERINE THE GREAT

Power, corruption by: "Power tends to corrupt; absolute power corrupts absolutely."
—ATTRIBUTED TO LORD ACTON

Power, distribution of: The phrase "balance of power" sometimes refers to the distribution of power in a state system. The way power is distributed determines the risk of a major war breaking out. The distribution of power may, at any given moment, be one of equilibrium, in which power is possessed in roughly the same measure by potential adversaries, or one of imbalance, in which one state or coalition enjoys a preponderance of power over others. Equilibrium can be a relatively stable state when the states participating in it adhere to common rules of conduct, facilitating the adjustment of disputes by diplomacy rather than war. If there is no such consensus, equilibrium can quickly decay into war. When the distribution of power is in imbalance, the risk of war is determined by whether the preponderance of power rests with states committed to the status quo or with those dedicated to establishing a new order in its place.

Power, economic: Economic power resembles a string connecting two nations; it is something with which one can pull but with which one cannot usefully push. The threat to sever economic ties exerts pressure that can add to a bargaining process that has other, more positive elements, but the actual severance of economic relations releases both parties to fly off in opposite directions.

Power, economic, and war: "Everyone may begin a war at his pleasure, but cannot so finish it. A prince, therefore, before engaging in any enterprise should well measure his strength, and govern himself accordingly; and he must be very careful not to deceive himself in the estimate of his strength, which he will assuredly do if he measures it by his money, or by the situation of his country, or the good disposition of his people, unless he has at the same time an armed force of his own. For although the above things will increase his strength, yet they will not give it to him, and of themselves are nothing, and will be of no use without a devoted army. Neither abundance of money nor natural strength of the country will suffice, nor will the loyalty and goodwill of his subjects endure, for these cannot remain faithful to a prince who is incapable of defending them. Neither mountains nor lakes nor inaccessible places will present any difficulties to an enemy where there is a lack of brave defender. And money alone, so far from being a means of defense, will only render a prince the more liable to being plundered. There cannot be a more erroneous opinion than that money is the sinews of war."
—NICCOLÒ MACHIAVELLI

Power, hard: "Smart statecraft does not dispense with hard power; it uses hard power intelligently, recognizing the limits as well as the potential of purely military power, and integrating it into an overarching political strategy." —CHESTER A. CROCKER

Power, measuring: "The power of a state is made up of a number of elements, some of which cannot be exactly measured. What a state's neighbors perceive to be its power takes into account such things as the numbers and skills of its population, the extent, resources and strategic location of its territory, its wealth and productive capacity, including the sources from which it derives its wealth and how it controls them, its internal organization, public attitudes and the competence of its government, its existing and potential military capacity, and other more intangible but essential factors like its international aims and the degree of its determination to achieve them." —ADAM WATSON, 1983

Power, morality: "Power always thinks it has a great soul and vast views beyond the comprehension of the weak; and that it is doing God's service when it is violating all His laws." —JOHN ADAMS

Power, national: "National power is the sum total of the capabilities of the nation—both persuasive and coercive, peaceful and forceful, actual and potential—to preserve its interests, attain its goals and objectives, and promote its policies and strategies in its relations with other nations." —ELMER PLISCHKE, 1988

Power, neighboring states and: "Among the many . . . indications by which the power of a republic may be recognized is the relation in which they live with their neighbors; if these are tributary to her by way of securing her friendship and protection, then it is a sure sign that that republic is powerful. But if these neighboring states, though they may be more feeble than herself, draw money from her, then it is a sure sign of great weakness on the part of the republic. —NICCOLÒ MACHIAVELLI

Power, persuasiveness of: Military power, no matter how immense, is without persuasive force if adversaries disbelieve it will be applied.

Power, persuasiveness of: "A man-of-war is the best ambassador." —OLIVER CROMWELL

Power, policy and: "Very near the heart of all foreign affairs is the relationship between policy and military power." —MCGEORGE BUNDY, 1951

Power, policy and: "In foreign relations, as in all other relations, a policy has been formed only when commitments and power have been brought into balance." —WALTER LIPPMANN, 1943

Power, policy and: "Policy which is not supported by commensurate power is inoperative." —WILLIAM MACOMBER, 1975

Power politics: "Power politics is the diplomatic name for the law of the jungle." —ELLY CULBERTSON, 1946

Power, reliance on: "To rely on the efficacy of diplomacy may lead to disaster; but to rely on power with insufficient means is suicide."
—HENRY A. KISSINGER, 1964

Power, reputation for: "Nothing is so weak and unstable as a reputation for power not based on force."
—TACITUS

Power, size: In international relations, size does not equate to power, nor energy to strength.

Power, soft: See *Influence*.

Power, source of: "Political power issues from the barrel of a gun." —MAO ZEDONG, 1937

Power of the weak: The greatest power of the weak is their capacity to shame their oppressors or to impose on them a crisis of conscience. To accomplish this, the weak must contrast their own unthreatening behavior and status as victims with the aggressive inhumanity of their opponents. They must provoke the strong to do their worst and be prepared to suffer it without loss of resolve. The highest form of such a strategy is non-violence.

Powerful nations lead: "When negotiations are on foot between two sovereigns, one the greater and the other the less, the more powerful of the two should make the first advance."
—FRANÇOIS DE CALLIÈRES, 1716

Power projection: The capacity to conduct expeditionary warfare in areas distant from the homeland.

Practicality: "Nothing is unreasonable if it is useful."
—THUCYDIDES

Precedence: The protocol order in which members of a diplomatic or consular corps are ranked or in which the individual members of a diplomatic or consular missions are ranked. Precedence is fixed by the Vienna Conventions on diplomatic and consular relations. In the diplomatic corps, it is as follows: (1) ambassadors extraordinary and plenipotentiary; (2) envoys extraordinary and ministers plenipotentiary; (3) ministers resident; (4) chargés d'affaires ad hoc; (5) chargés d'affaires ad interim. Precedence among representatives of the same rank is according to the date of the official notification of their arrival to the host government or organization.

Precedents, bad: "All bad precedents begin as justifiable measures." —JULIUS CAESAR

Precision: "Understandings have to be very precise. You can't make a deal unless you can carry it out."
—W. AVERELL HARRIMAN

Precision: "Diplomacy, if it is ever to be effective, should be a disagreeable business. . . . It would be interesting to analyse how many false decisions, how many fatal misunderstandings, have arisen from such pleasant qualities as shyness, consideration, affability or ordinary good manners." —HAROLD NICOLSON

Precision: "If truthfulness is the first essential in the ideal diplomatist, surely the second is precision." —HAROLD NICOLSON

Precision: "There is nothing more important in negotiation than to make it perfectly clear what was agreed upon. . . . The lines should be made so clear that little or nothing can be read between or behind them." —LESTER B. PEARSON, 1959

Precision: "In diplomacy, many problems are solved by not being too precise and public about the solutions." —GEORGE P. SHULTZ, 1993

Predictions: Most predictions are worthless; to ensure that they are valued, one should therefore demand a high price for making them.

Preemption: "Preemption is the right of any nation in order to preserve its National Security; however, preemptive war is a tactic, not a strategy. When used as a strategy preemption dilutes diplomacy, creates an atmosphere of distrust, and promotes regional instability." —ELLEN TAUSCHER

Preemption: "He who takes the initiative asserts control over the enemy; he who acts later is subject to control by the enemy." —XIANG YU

Prejudice: "The basic rule is that neither admiration of his host country nor lack of it must ever be allowed to color a diplomat's judgment respecting his own country's interest. Nor must it disfigure in any other way the objectivity and professional character of his performance." —WILLIAM MACOMBER, 1975

Prenegotiation: Negotiation about negotiation; the process of bargaining and maneuver that precedes decisions by two or more parties to pursue or reject negotiations to resolve some or all of their differences.

Prenegotiation: "A . . . way of bringing about negotiations is to show the amount of agreement that exists and narrow the subjects of disagreement. In this case, the perception of the other party is manipulated by showing him the many—even if minor—areas of agreement and by isolating the few—albeit major—areas of disagreement. . . . By looking for areas where agreement already exists, the parties may find that less separates them than they thought; they may also discover that the gap is greater, but at least they have begun provisionally the negotiating process. Usually in the process they will want to establish a third category of issues, where neither agreement nor disagreement will be established for the moment, the parties reserving these items for possible bargaining when the topics of disagreement are discussed."

—I. WILLIAM ZARTMAN AND MAUREEN R. BERMAN, 1982

Prenegotiation: "Negotiations can be brought about by convincing the other party that only worse alternatives exist in the absence of a joint solution. By showing that a stalemate does exist, that there is no way out in the absence of talks, or that things will (or can be made to) get worse as time goes on without a settlement, the party [seeking a negotiated solution] is able to put teeth in its demand for negotiations."

—I. WILLIAM ZARTMAN AND MAUREEN R. BERMAN, 1982

Prenegotiation, reframing questions and: "Find a way to frame a question to which it is almost impossible to say no. There is likely to be some hypothetical bargain that would attract even the most reluctant party. [This] 'flypaper principle' is used with the party whose current position is perceived by everyone else to be the 'main obstacle' to negotiations."

—CHESTER A. CROCKER, 1992

Prenegotiation, tasks of: "The peacemaker requires a strategy for the 'pre-negotiation' phase which includes everything that must occur before a formal negotiation can begin. In [Harold L.] Saunders's terms, the tasks of pre-negotiation include (a) achieving a common definition of the problem; (b) producing a shared commitment to a negotiated settlement; and (c) arranging agreed procedures, formats, and terms of reference for the formal negotiations themselves. The second of these occurs only after the parties are convinced that the status quo is unacceptable. They must also see that a fair deal is available."

—CHESTER A. CROCKER, 1992

Preparedness: "An aggressor often decides on war before the innocent defender does, and if he continues to keep his preparations sufficiently secret, he may well take the victim unawares. Yet such surprise has nothing to do with war itself, and should not be possible. War serves the purpose of defense more than that of the aggressor. It is only aggression that calls forth defense, and war along with it. The aggressor is always peace-loving . . . ; he would prefer to take over our country unopposed. To prevent his doing so one must be willing to make war and be prepared for it. In other words, it is the weak, those likely to need defense, who should always be armed in order not to be overwhelmed. Thus decrees the art of war." —CARL MARIA VON CLAUSEWITZ, 1832

Preparedness: "It is late to begin digging a well when feeling thirsty."—FRENCH PROVERB

Preparedness: "Without adequate preparedness . . . diplomacy becomes weak and ineffective. If . . . diplomacy abroad is to achieve favorable results, [the nation] should be constantly prepared to meet all eventualities." —JOSEPH C. GREW, 1945

Preparedness: "If you want peace, prepare for war." —LATIN PROVERB

Preparedness: "A prepared ability to fight dissuades attack that weakness could invite, thereby averting war. It is just as true that a prepared ability to fight can ensure peace in quite another way, by making war unnecessary as the weak are induced to give way to the strong without a fight." —EDWARD N. LUTTWAK, 1987

Preparedness: "Preparation for war is a constant stimulus to suspicion and ill will." —JAMES MONROE, 1818

Presence: The demonstration of the interest, commitment, and capacity speedily to apply power, especially military or economic power, through the placement of armed forces or official representatives in or near a country or region of concern.

Press: "In his dealings with the press, the diplomat cannot, if he is a responsible operative, retreat from its members, nor ignore their key role in a free society. Nor can he forget the conflict of interest which prevails. He must learn to be frank, helpful, and accurate—but never careless and never indiscreet. In his dealings with both the press and other diplomats, he must also remember always that indiscretions come about in part, as well as in whole—that a fragmentary indiscretion can be as damaging as whole in the hands of an adroit recipient whose business it is to collect and piece together many parts from many sources, thus coming to understand the whole." —WILLIAM MACOMBER, 1975

Press attachés: See *Attachés, press.*

Press, good: "My advice to any diplomat who wants to have a good press is to have two or three kids and a dog." —CARL ROWAN, 1963

Press, government and the: "The responsible government official and the responsible reporter when they do their best work are allies with one another."—JAMES RESTON, 1967

Press, responsibilities of the: "The Press engages in Diplomacy; and Diplomacy exerts influence through the Press. The people, exposed to this double impact, is unconsciously guided in various directions; or else, if it tries to think for itself, falls into error. The responsibility of the Press is so great that wars, in so far as they are not made by Governments, are made by the Press." —R.B. MOWAT, 1936

Pressure, public: "Quiet pressure does not make leaders of the target nation respond in the midst of public uproar, while public pressure can. Publicity generated, strong popular sentiment, nearly always defiantly against the foreign 'bully,' may be a bargaining advantage for the target's leaders as it limits their range of options and, in effect, hardens their bargaining position; or it may be a disadvantage as it precludes negotiating a compromise when doing so is the smartest choice." —RICHARD J. ELLINGS, 1985

Pressure, rejection of: Warnings by a state that it will never yield to pressure are a standard diplomatic ploy by which it attempts to determine what concessions are required from it to reach a settlement.

Prestige: "Prestige is a shadow cast by power, which is of great deterrent importance."
—DEAN ACHESON

Prevention, rescue: One can never prove that one has prevented disaster. Not surprisingly, therefore, people seldom thank those who succeed in precluding adversity, though they are always grateful to those who save them from the disasters their rescuers have failed to prevent.

Pride: "Great nations are too strong to be destroyed by their foes. But they can easily be overcome by their own pride."
—REINHOLD NIEBUHR

Principle, agreement in: "Agreement in principle may mean disagreement in practice."
—THOMAS A. BAILEY

Principle, agreement in: "Principles are fine; they entail no commitment." —NAPOLEON

Principles: "A people that values privilege above its principles soon loses both."
—DWIGHT D. EISENHOWER, 1953

Principles: "The . . . diplomat must always seek to avoid disputes over principle. 'If you want a war, nourish a doctrine,' William Graham Sumner wrote years ago. It is a timeless truth. For when doctrine or principle enter the picture, the prospects for compromise and conciliation markedly decline."
—WILLIAM MACOMBER, 1975

Principles: "Diplomacy, like politics, is an area of give and take, of compromise with cherished principles, and of continued adjustment to practical possibilities. Both realms provoke the impatience of those who look for more clear-cut and less ambiguous choices. Principles in diplomacy and politics compete with one another, and the statesman more often than not must balance out the weight and force of contending objectives."
—KENNETH W. THOMPSON, 1962

Principles: "Principles, as statesmen conceive them, are threads in the labyrinth of circumstances. . . . Throw the conceiving mind, habituated to contemplating wholes, into the arena of politics, and it seems to itself to be standing upon shifting sands, where no sure foothold and no upright posture are possible."
—WOODROW WILSON, 1890

Principles: "Principles—such as self-determination, the inviolability of frontiers, or noninterference in internal affairs—are important legitimizers for political solutions and should be used as such, but should not dictate the choice of the solution. Principles are no guide to a choice among themselves; indeed, the cause of conflict can usually be traced to the parties' self-interested adherence to conflicting principles. It is better to seek a balanced distribution of power than to apply a pure principle. . . . Conflict resolution requires an outcome that has something for everyone. Parties cannot be expected to give up their claims without receiving compensation." —I. William Zartman, 1985

Privileges and immunities: Exemptions from the normal operation of the law of the host country granted to foreign diplomats in order to assure that their official duties will not be impeded. Among the most important of these are the inviolability of their persons and premises and exemption from the taxation and civil and criminal jurisdiction of the local authorities.

Privileges and immunities: "Unless accredited diplomats receive the protection of the host country, a foundation of international relations is destroyed. . . . The remedy is unhesitating, decisive retaliation, together with a readiness—unless reparation is made and assurance regarding future conduct is received—to penalize an offending regime by breaking relations with it." —Ellis Briggs, 1968

Privileges and immunities: "The inviolability of ambassadors is sacred and acknowledged as such by all civilized peoples." —Julius Caesar

Privileges and immunities: "Envoys are the mouthpieces of kings. They must carry out their instructions, and it would be wrong to put them to death even if they were outcastes." —Arthasastra of Kautilya

Privileges and immunities: "Whatever treatment is given to an ambassador, whether good or bad, it is as if it were done to the very king who sent them, and kings have always shown the greatest respect to one another and treated envoys well, for by this their own dignity has been enhanced. And if at any time there has been disagreement or enmity between kings, and if ambassadors have still come and gone as occasion requires, and discharged their missions according to their instructions, never have they been molested or treated with less than usual courtesy. Such a thing would be disgraceful, as God (to Him be power and glory) says (in the Quran 24.53), 'The messenger has only to convey the message plainly.'" —Nizam al-Mulk Tusi

Probity: "No quality [is] more important for an ambassador than probity." —Rousseau de Chamoy, 1697, cited by J.J. Jusserand

Procès-verbal: Summary minutes of a conference, or notice of a proposed treaty modification.

Processes, diplomatic: Diplomatic processes can serve as shock absorbers when bilateral interests collide. They have a tendency, however, to become ends in themselves. Preserving the means by which conflict is avoided may come to replace resolution of conflict and its causes as the objective of the participants' diplomacy.

Productive: When used to describe a meeting, generally indicates that, while some progress was made, the issues under discussion were not resolved.

Profession of diplomacy: Diplomacy is more than a profession; it is a way of life.

Profession of diplomacy: "Diplomacy is a profession by itself which deserves the same preparation and assiduity of attention that men give to other recognized professions. The qualities of a diplomatist and the knowledge necessary to him cannot, indeed, all be acquired. The diplomatic genius is born, not made. But there are many qualities which may be developed with practice, and the greater part of the necessary knowledge can only be acquired by constant application to the subject. In this sense diplomacy is certainly a profession itself capable of occupying a man's whole career, and those who think to embark upon a diplomatic mission as a pleasant diversion from their common task only prepare disappointment for themselves and disaster for the cause which they serve. The veriest fool would not entrust the command of an army to a man whose sole badge of merit was his eloquence in a court of law or his adroit practice of the courtier's art in the palace. All are agreed that military command must be earned by long service in the army. In the same manner it should be regarded as folly to entrust the conduct of negotiations to an untrained amateur." —FRANÇOIS DE CALLIÈRES, 1716

Profession of diplomacy: "What a hard trade is the diplomatist's! I know of none which demands so much abnegation, so much readiness to sacrifice one's interests for the sake of duty, so much courage. The ambassador who properly discharges his obligations, never betrays fatigue, boredom, disgust. He disguises the emotions which he feels, the temptations to succumb which assail him. He knows how to pass over in silence the bitter deceptions which are dealt to him, as well as the unexpected satisfactions with which fortune, though rarely, rewards him. Jealous of his dignity, he never ceases to be cautious, takes care to quarrel with nobody, never loses his serenity, and in all the great crises, when the question of war arises, shows himself calm, impassive, and sure of success." —COUNT HÜBNER

Profession of diplomacy: "Diplomacy, if it adheres to its proper objectives and most effective methods, is an honorable profession. To the degree it remains committed to the search for peace, it can be an exalted one as well." —WILLIAM MACOMBER, 1975

Profession of diplomacy: "Professional diplomacy is surely not the only career through which a citizen can participate in the dual effort to advance his nation's interests and to make the world a better and safer place for all its inhabitants. This can be done from every walk of life. But the diplomat's profession clearly places him at a unique advantage. It permits a lifetime devoted exclusively to these goals. And because he spends this lifetime where the action is, it ensures him a continuing opportunity, and a far better opportunity than most, to put forward his ideas where . . . they will count the most." —WILLIAM MACOMBER, 1975

Profession of diplomacy: "It is the duty of the diplomatic profession to work for a world which deals in negotiable, not nonnegotiable, demands." —WILLIAM MACOMBER, 1975

Profession of diplomacy: "Diplomacy is the profession par excellence: pure service, involving what the Middle Ages called a 'Mystery,' with the quality of performance utterly unmeasurable except by peer judgment." —MARTIN MAYER, 1983

Profession of diplomacy: "Always, men respond to the demands which their profession makes on them. The military men, the physicians, the clergy, conform to the high demands of their calling, even if they fall short of the ideal. So it is with the diplomatists; peace and good relations are the inexorable demands of their profession. It exacts qualities of temper, poise, judgment, and serious application, which they seldom fail to display. Because they are, first and last, reasonable people, conciliatory, unprejudiced, humane, with the art and habit of living together as colleagues in society, they have been called 'the most civilized portion of the human race.'" —R.B. MOWAT, 1936

Promises: Promises bind those who accept and rely upon them more than those who make and can always break them.

Promises: "Promises, like piecrusts, are made to be broken." —ATTRIBUTED TO V.I. LENIN

Promises: "There is no disgrace in disregarding promises that have been exacted by force. Promises touching public affairs, and which have been given under the pressure of force, will always be dishonored when that force no longer exists, and this involves no dishonor." —NICCOLÒ MACHIAVELLI

Pro-Nuncio, Apostolic: The formal title of an ambassador of the Holy See (Vatican) in capitals where the papal nuncio is not automatically the dean of the diplomatic corps, equivalent to "Ambassador Extraordinary and Plenipotentiary." See also *Nuncio.*

Propaganda: An aspect of political warfare consisting of the public dissemination of information, whether truthful or deceptive, intended to promote strategic or ideological objectives. Propaganda may be attributed, that is, acknowledged to be the product of the state that authored it; unattributed; or attributed to a source other than its true one.

Propaganda: "In war, truth is the first casualty." —AESCHYLUS

Propaganda: "Vilify! Vilify! Some of it will always stick." —BEAUMARCHAIS

Propaganda: "Propaganda is that branch of the art of lying which consists in nearly deceiving your friends without quite deceiving your enemies." —F.M. CORNFORD, 1978

Propaganda: "Not all propaganda is deceptious—though much of it is. But all propaganda is tendentious. Governments do not wish to tell the world of their shortcomings. In deciding what to tell the world—the truth as one sees it, part of that truth, what is known to be untrue—expedience prevails over ethics. What matters is not the truth of the message but the credibility of the message. And the estimate of the credibility of the message is determined by the estimate of the gullibility of the masses." —James Eayrs, 1965

Propaganda: ". . . the people can always be brought to do the bidding of the leaders. That is easy. All you have to do is tell them they are being attacked and denounce the pacifists for lack of patriotism and exposing the country to danger. It works the same way in any country." —Herman Goering

Propaganda: "Propaganda, as inverted patriotism, draws nourishment from the sins of the enemy. If there are no sins, invent them! The aim is to make the enemy appear so great a monster that he forfeits the rights of a human being. He cannot bring a libel action, so there is no need to stick at trifles." —Ian Hamilton, 1921

Propaganda: "No amount of genius spent on the creation of propaganda will lead to success if a fundamental principle is not forever kept in mind. Propaganda must confine itself to a very few points, and repeat them endlessly. Here, as with so many things in this world, persistence is the first and foremost condition of success." —Adolf Hitler, 1924

Propaganda: "The great mass of the people . . . will more easily fall victim to a big lie than to a small one." —Adolf Hitler, 1924

Propaganda: "Propaganda is emotional engineering." —Attributed to Aldous Huxley

Propaganda: "Regular diplomatic officials tend everywhere to view propaganda with distaste and scepticism. The profession of diplomacy induces a weary detachment, foreign to all political enthusiasm and ex parte pleas." —George F. Kennan, 1958

Propaganda: "Propaganda should be based on a national policy, it should encompass allies and adversaries, and it should always remain cognizant of long-term objectives." —Paul A. Smith, Jr., 1989

Propaganda: "Propaganda must be two-edged. It must cut through obstacles on the home front while it cleaves the mental armour of the enemy on the outer front. Next to the work of physical fighting no work is more urgent than this. . . . It must fit policy as a sabre fits the scabbard." —Wickham Steed

Propaganda: "A thorough understanding of the limitations of the propaganda gun is as essential as knowing the range of a piece of artillery is to its firing. . . . Propaganda can enhance the results of good policies and diplomacy and can mitigate the effects of bad policies and poor diplomacy, but it cannot be a substitute for either policy or diplomacy or indeed exist without them." —CHARLES W. THAYER, 1959

Propaganda, diplomacy and: "Alone, propaganda has no creative force. It cannot forge alliances with our friends or spark revolutions to annihilate our enemies. But as the handmaiden of diplomacy, as an extension of the diplomat's arm, it can . . . significantly [further] . . . international interests." —CHARLES W. THAYER, 1959

Propaganda, foreign policy and: "Good foreign policy and good propaganda go hand in hand." —GEORGE VENABLE ALLEN, 1958

Prophesies, self-fulfilling: Fear and the response of others to it are the usual causes of self-fulfilling prophesies.

Prosperity: Changes in financial well-being alter calculations and call commitments into question. Prosperity and poverty both change men's minds. Take no alliance with a rising or declining power for granted!

Protecting power: The state and embassy that have been designated as the diplomatic custodian of the interests of another state that has severed relations with a third nation. The protecting power is responsible for maintaining the property of the state whose interests it is protecting and representing its diplomatic interests, inter alia by facilitating communication between the two states without relations, as requested and required. See *Interests section.*

Protectionism: "Economic protectionism is not only an anomaly, but it is a ridiculous and ignominious expedient for a nation of . . . economic vigor and stature. What was right and necessary for a struggling underdeveloped country can be a form of infantile escapism for a strong and ostensibly mature one." —GEORGE F. KENNAN, 1954

Protest: An official, diplomatic notice of objection to a policy, practice, or action by a government or international organization.

Protocol: An agreement or an amendment to a preexisting agreement.

Protocol: Many rules of protocol, like the "order of precedence" for the diplomatic corps, represent the stilling of ancient preoccupations and the settlement of quarrels best left unrenewed.

Protocol: "There must be rules of procedure and a technical language in any Service, business undertaking, academic institution, trade union—or indeed family. An internationally accepted code to which all subscribe is immensely helpful to members of the group and to others prepared to submit to it while they are living in that environment. . . .

Protocol does more to glue people together than it does to gum up the works."
—DOUGLAS BUSK, 1967

Protocol: "Protocol . . . provides a framework in which diplomatic contacts can be carried out in an orderly fashion."
—ERIC CLARK, 1973

Protocol, blunders of: "It is not always easy to avoid making mistakes in precedence and protocol generally in a foreign country. A diplomat who considers himself the victim of such a one and attempts to make a scene renders himself, more often than not, ridiculous. . . . Such mistakes are seldom made of malice aforethought."
—ERNEST SATOW

Protocol, defined: "Protocol is a form of hierarchical order, the expression of good manners among nations, and just as politeness is one of the basic rules for everyday life, so protocol is the set of rules of conduct for governments and their representatives on official and on private occasions."
—JOHN R. WOOD AND JEAN SERRES, 1970

Protocol, insistence upon: A rigid insistence on protocol by an ambassador is a sure sign that he has little, if anything, of importance to accomplish.

Psychological operations: Actions, including propaganda, on the eve of or during hostilities, directed specifically at undermining the morale and softening the will to fight of hostile military personnel and their civilian support.

Public appearances: "Only two rules really count: never miss an opportunity to relieve yourself; never miss an opportunity to rest your feet."
—DUKE OF WINDSOR

Public opinion: "What we call public opinion is generally public sentiment."
—BENJAMIN DISRAELI, 1880

Public opinion: "The Government cannot act in advance of public opinion."
—DAVID LLOYD GEORGE

Public opinion: "Public opinion compels governments which usually know what would be wiser or more necessary or more expedient to be too late with too little or too long with too much, too pacifist in peace or too bellicose in war, too appeasing in negotiation or too intransigent. Mass opinion has a growing power . . . but it has shown itself to be a dangerous master of decisions when the stakes are life and death."
—WALTER LIPPMANN, 1955

Public opinion: "In ninety-nine cases out of a hundred what is called 'public opinion' is mere forgery."
—NICHOLAS II (OF RUSSIA), 1909

Public opinion, foreign policy and: "Public opinion is always wrong, much too intransigent in war, much too yielding in peace, insufficiently informed, lacking the specialized knowledge upon which lucid judgments can be based." —WALTER LIPPMANN

Public opinion, policy recommendations and: Diplomats face a dilemma in the need to take account of the domestic public opinion of their own nation as they consider how to advance its interests abroad. If they ignore public opinion completely, their recommendations will strike their leaders as unrealistic and infeasible but, if they defer to it too diffidently, they will have failed to contribute the expertise they alone possess with respect to foreign realities. In either case, they may justly be charged with dereliction of professional responsibility.

Public opinion, power of: "Public opinion is one of the most powerful weapons, which like religion penetrates the most hidden corners where administrative measures lose their influence; to despise public opinion is like despising moral principles." —METTERNICH, 1808

Public relations: "Confused leaders have a tendency to substitute public relations maneuvers for a sense of direction." —HENRY A. KISSINGER, 1994

Publicity: In many situations between states, what can be accomplished is inversely proportional to the publicity attached to it.

Publicity: "It is obvious that much . . . diplomatic work, particularly those efforts that are classed as preparatory toward the reaching of agreements, [must] be conducted in confidence . . . premature disclosure of positions and arguments could very well bar the attainment of any reasonable solution." —DWIGHT D. EISENHOWER, 1954

Publicity: "In the main, our acts are public, because that is the way a democracy moves. But diplomacy cannot always be so, or else it would be little more than debate, adding its fuel to the very fires it hopes to quench." —DEAN RUSK, 1961

Publicity: "Publicity is often a deterrent to the reconciliation of conflicts, [so] the diplomat attempts to conceal what the journalist strives to reveal." —CHARLES W. THAYER, 1960

Publicity: "Open covenants of peace, openly arrived at, after which there shall be no private international understandings of any kind but diplomacy shall proceed always frankly and in the public view." —WOODROW WILSON, FIRST OF THE "FOURTEEN POINTS," 1918

Publicity: See also *Negotiations, publicity about*.

Purpose: "Pursue one great decisive aim with force and determination."

—CARL MARIA VON CLAUSEWITZ

Purpose, importance of: "However brilliant an action may be, it should not be accounted great when it is not the result of a great purpose."   —FRANÇOIS DE LA ROCHEFOUCAULD

Purposes, national: A nation's purposes must be proportional to its capabilities.

Purposes, national: "The nation's purposes always exceed its means, and it is finding a balance between means and ends that is the heart of foreign policy and that makes it such a speculative, uncertain business."

—ADLAI E. STEVENSON, JR., 1954

Quarrels: "Every government is in some respects a problem for every other government, and it will always be this way so long as the sovereign state, with its supremely self-centered rationale, remains the basis of international life."   —GEORGE F. KENNAN, 1961

Quarrels: "The same reason that makes us wrangle with a neighbor, causes a war between princes."   —MICHEL DE MONTAIGNE

Quarrels: "There is nothing more likely to start disagreement among people or countries than an agreement."   —E.B. WHITE, 1944

Quarrels, of friends: "The quarrels of friends are the opportunities of foes."   —AESOP

Questions: Never ask a question unless you're sure the answer will help your cause.

Raison d'état: "Reason of state," the principle that the interests of the state are exempt from or assume precedence over all considerations of private morality.

Raison d'état: "Everything that falls under the heading of unselfishness is inappropriate to the action of a state. No one has a right to be unselfish with other people's interests." —Hugh Cecil

Rapporteur: One who is charged with preparing a summary report of the proceedings of a committee or multilateral meeting.

Rapprochement: The process of restoration or establishment of improved relations between states and governments that were previously estranged. A phase in the spectrum of international relations lying between Détente and Entente.

Rapprochement: "Those who want to be loved should do something lovable." —ʿAbdullah bin ʿAbd Al-Aziz Al-Saʿud

Rapprochement: "[Rapprochement is the process begun when] one or both sides express a desire to search for agreements. It is a condition antecedent to entente and applies only to the beginnings of conflict reduction and agreement between previously hostile nations." —Alexander L. George, 1993

Ratification: Agreement by a state, in accordance with its constitutional processes, to be bound by a bilateral or multilateral treaty.

Readiness: "There is no record in history of a nation that ever gained anything valuable by being unprepared to defend itself." —H.L. Mencken, 1926

Readiness: "If we desire to avoid insult, we must be able to repel it. If we desire to secure peace, it must be known that we are at all times ready for war." —George Washington

Reality, intentions: Reality cannot be prevented from intruding on the best of intentions.

Reason of relationship: The professional ethic of diplomacy that dictates a continuing effort to buttress relations with allies and friends, while avoiding severing communication or precluding rapprochement with enemies.

Reason of state: See *Raison d'état*.

Reason of system: The ethical principle underlying the duty of diplomats to defend and act to improve an international order that enhances prospects for the nonviolent resolution of disputes and expanded cooperation among states.

Reassignment: See *Postings.*

Rebellion: "The only justification of rebellion is success."   —Thomas B. Reed

Recall, letters of: The official document, presented by a new ambassador to a chief of state along with his credentials, that formally terminates the appointment of his predecessor and recalls him.

Recall of ambassador: A step short of severance of diplomatic relations, involving the temporary suspension of representation at the ambassadorial level in a foreign capital to signal serious concern about the policies, practices, or public pronouncements of the receiving state's government.

Receiving state: The state to which a diplomat is sent and/or accredited. Also referred to as the "host government."

Receptions, diplomatic: A diplomatic reception is like a mousetrap, baited with big cheeses, cigars, and canapés. When you are outside you want to get in; and when you are inside the mere sight of the other mice makes you want to get out. Still, the purpose is to trap mice; and it works.

Reciprocity, principle of: The principle of treating the diplomatic representatives of another state in the same manner as it treats one's own, often invoked to retaliate against practices in a receiving state regarded as prejudicial or contrary to international norms of diplomacy.

Recognition, criteria for diplomatic: "The three standard criteria for recognition are effective control of the instrumentalities of government, absence of resistance to the new regime, and professed intention to abide by international commitments."
                                                                                      —Ellis Briggs, 1968

Recognition, diplomatic: The notion that diplomatic recognition is a favor to be withheld from those judged to be unworthy makes the government that espouses it a licensing agency rather than the responsible custodian of its state's interests in a world of diversity.

Record, off the: An agreed basis for a discussion between an official and a journalist that allows the journalist to use the information provided by the official for planning purposes but prohibits the journalist from publishing it in any form.

Record, on the: An agreed basis for a discussion between an official and a journalist that permits the journalist to quote information directly and attribute it to the official who provided it by name and title.

Reform, perils of: "Experience suggests that the most dangerous moment for an evil government is usually when it begins to reform itself. Only great ingenuity can save a prince who undertakes to give relief to his subjects after long oppression. The sufferings that are endured patiently, as being inevitable, become intolerable the moment it appears that there might be an escape. Reform then only serves to reveal more clearly what still remains oppressive and now all the more unbearable." —Alexis de Tocqueville

Refoulement: The forcing back of a person seeking sanctuary as a refugee.

Refugee: A person seeking asylum in another country on the basis of a well-founded fear of persecution in his or her homeland.

Refugee: A person who, "owing to well-founded fear of being persecuted for reasons of race, religion, nationality, membership of a particular social group or political opinion, is outside the country of his nationality and is unable, or owing to such fear, is unwilling to avail himself of the protection of that country; or who, not having a nationality and being outside the country of his former habitual residence as a result of such events, is unable or, owing to such fear, is unwilling to return to it." —United Nations Convention relating to the Status of Refugees

Regime installation: "No people can ever be made to submit to a form of government they say they will not receive." —Charles Lennox, 3rd Duke of Richmond and Lennox

Regionalism: A concept of cooperation and combination for common purposes between neighboring states, generally to promote their defense against a potentially hegemonic power or to enhance their economic competitiveness vis-à-vis a dominant economic power.

Reinforcement, diplomatic: Hold something in reserve, not just to shore up a failing strategy while you consider alternatives but to be able to reinforce a winning strategy in time to magnify its gains.

Rejection: The act of refusing to accept a diplomatic note or other formal statement of position of a foreign state or government because of its offensive contents.

Relations, ambassadorial: The conduct of diplomatic relations at the level of ambassadors rather than ministers or chargés d'affaires.

Relations, breaking diplomatic: "Diplomats . . . resent the degree to which the word 'diplomacy' is equated in the public mind with the external forms rather than with the living content of their craft. . . . [This] applies to one of the oldest and most fallacious habits of the diplomatic system: the habit of treating diplomatic relations as a grace to be awarded or withheld rather than as a convenience to be universally employed. Nothing could be more full of anomaly than the 'breaking off' of diplomatic relations in moments of crisis. It is precisely when there is conflict that there is most need of such relations, and it is in such conditions that they are often eroded. This [reflects] the erroneous belief that diplomatic relations have a moral rather than a utilitarian significance."

—ABBA EBAN, 1983

Relations, breaking diplomatic: "Severing relations is like playing the Ace of Spades in bridge. You can only use it once. When you play it, you haven't got any more, so your hand is considerably weakened. Breaking relations has the direct disadvantage of some-times redounding to your own discomfort, because the maintenance of relations between governments has been found to be generally advantageous to both parties. If you break off relations with another government, the chances are, over the next few years, you are going to find you need relations with that country. Now the other fellow, as the ag-grieved party, is usually not in a position to take the initiative in resuming relations, and that means you have to swallow your pride and go to him on your hands and knees and say, 'Come on old fellow. Let's make up.' That is not anything a government likes to do."

—GEORGE F. KENNAN, 1946

Relations, close: "Unhappily, amity is not the inevitable result of close relations between either people or peoples. Marriage and war lock both into close embrace. Sometimes the parties live happily ever after; sometimes they don't. So it is with allies."

—DEAN ACHESON, 1963

Relations, consular: An official relationship between two states below the diplomatic level, intended to facilitate travel and trade between them and to assure protection for the nationals of each in the territory of the other. Establishment of consular relations, in the absence of diplomatic relations, confers de facto but not de jure recognition of a government.

Relations, diplomatic: An official relationship between the chiefs of state and govern-ment of two states, conducted through agents who have been publicly designated and accredited for this purpose. If such agents reside in the capital of foreign state, they constitute an embassy.

Relations, diplomatic: The exchange of envoys symbolizes and embodies a process of continuous bargaining between states. The purpose of diplomatic relations is to influence a foreign capital and its policies, not to confer a favor on it.

Relations, establishing: "The reason for having diplomatic relations is not to confer a compliment, but to secure a convenience."   —WINSTON CHURCHILL, 1949

Relations, friendly: Ceaseless attentiveness and tact are the price of sustained good relations with both individuals and nations.

Relations, managing: "Should there be but one hair linking me and the others, I would not have it cut: for if they slacken it I would pull, and if they pull it I would slacken it."
   —MUAAWIYA

Relevance: The extent to which a capability can be brought to bear on the issues in dispute and those who can decide them. Capabilities, however impressive, that cannot be applied to an opponent to influence the resolution of a particular issue are irrelevant with respect to that issue. Capabilities that do not touch an opponent's interests at stake in a dispute or that do not correlate to its decisions on the matters in dispute are either ineffectual or provocative, risking a widening and deepening of the contention between the parties.

Reliability: In foreign relations, reliability is a moral imperative.

Religion: An ideology premised on the existence of supernatural or superhuman forces and characterized by a distinctive body of ritual. See also *Ideology*.

Religion: Religion scoffs at sovereignty.

Religion, influence on diplomatic theory: "The worst kind of diplomatists are missionaries, fanatics and lawyers; the best are the reasonable and humane skeptics. Thus it is not religion which has been the main formative influence in diplomatic theory; it is common sense."   —HAROLD NICOLSON, 1939

Religion, utility of: "Religion becomes a dangerous arm when one knows how to make use of it."   —FREDERICK THE GREAT, 1747

Remarks, public: "A Foreign Secretary . . . is always faced with this cruel dilemma. Nothing he can say can do very much good, and almost anything he may say may do a great deal of harm. Anything he says that is not obvious is dangerous; whatever is not trite is risky. He is forever poised between the cliché and the indiscretion."
   —HAROLD MACMILLAN, 1955

Reparations: Compensation for war damage by a defeated state.

Repetition: Unembarrassed repetition of negotiating positions is part of the art of diplomatic attack. Many demands that are judged unreasonable at first come to seem less unacceptable when heard many times.

Reporting: "The best dispatches are those written in a clear and concise manner, unadorned by useless epithets or by anything that may becloud the clarity of the argument. Simplicity is the first essential and diplomats should take the greatest care to avoid all affectations such as a pretense of wit or the learned overweight of scientific disquisitions."
—FRANÇOIS DE CALLIÈRES, 1716

Reporting: "Never report what you said and you'll never get into trouble."
—ADVICE FROM AN OLD DIPLOMAT, QUOTED BY CHARLES W. THAYER, 1959

Reporting, brevity in: Reports that remain unread by those with the capacity to act on them might just as well not have been written. The shorter the report and the more lively its style, the more likely it is to attract attention from busy decisionmakers in the capital. If the subject does not lend itself to brief treatment, it is wise to parallel a lengthy report with a much briefer summary report that persuasively calls attention to more detailed analysis.

Reporting, brevity in: "Brevity, consistent with both clarity and accuracy, is a virtue devoutly to be sought by all diplomats. Where achieved, it earns undying gratitude in a profession where eye strain is an enduring occupational hazard. As in anything else in diplomacy, it takes practice, for it is easier to draft a long report than a good short one."
—WILLIAM MACOMBER, 1975

Reporting, criticism in: "Do not compromise others in your reports. It is neither decent nor clever. Do not write ab irato. Indignation and rancor are conceptions foreign to diplomacy. The diplomat is neither a preacher of penitence, nor a judge in a criminal case, nor a philosopher. His sole and exclusive interest must be the real and downright interest of his country."
—HEINRICH VON BÜLOW

Reporting, economic: To promote exports, governments need to understand the general economic and financial circumstances and trends in foreign markets, and they need to make this information available to potential exporters. Collection of such information has long been one of the primary duties of diplomats and consuls.

Reporting, exactitude in: "The most essential care of the envoy should be exactitude in the facts he reports; he must neither weaken them nor change their hue, but distinctly state which are in his eyes certain, and which doubtful . . . He must not flatter his master by his selection of the facts he narrates or by his way of narrating them. The object of his mission is not to lead his chief astray, but to enlighten him."   —ANTOINE PECQUET, 1737

Reporting, honesty in: Ingratiating as it may be for a diplomat to report what is agreeable to his government, it is his duty to report only what is true.

Reporting, honesty in: "Hold it as a maxim that displeasing things must be sent as well as pleasing ones, and the prince, in the end, if he is a man of wisdom and understanding, will be better satisfied with the ambassador who will not have concealed from him any item he may have learnt where he is stationed, than with the one who, to spare him annoyance, will have abstained from writing unpleasant things but which it would have been of interest for him to know in time." —Bishop Danès, 1561, cited by J.J. Jusserand

Reporting, memoranda of conversation: "No one ever lost an argument in his own memorandum of conversation."
—Dean Acheson

Reporting, political: To understand local politics, frequent the taverns. That's where bastards, political movements, and legislation are usually conceived.

Reporting, purpose of: The purpose of diplomatic reporting is not just to anticipate and analyze events. It is to point out the implications of trends for national interests and to enable governments to act to shape events to their advantage and to the disadvantage of their adversaries.

Reporting, reward for honest: The rewards for diplomats who report honestly and forthrightly on foreign developments that contradict the convictions of their leaders at home have been well established by history. They will first be ignored, then charged with disloyalty, and, finally, dismissed. Diplomatic reporting is therefore always a contest between the professional integrity of those doing it abroad and the prejudices of those who read it at home.

Reporting, style of: Diplomatic reports are useful only if read by those with the capacity to address the problems they identify and the solutions they propose.

Reporting, style of: "The zeal and efficiency of a diplomatic representative is measured by the quality and not by the quantity of the information he supplies. He is expected to do a great deal of filtering for himself, and not simply to pour out upon us over these congested wires all the contradictory gossip which he hears." —Winston Churchill

Reporting, style of: "Draft telegrams as if you were going to have to take them to the local post and pay for them yourselves."
—Lord Trevelyan

Representivity: It is desirable for an army to be drawn from and to be broadly representative of all ranks and classes of the nation it is created to defend. This binds the army to the people and assures it a measure of political support it would not otherwise enjoy. In the end, however, the purpose of armies is to fight. Their ability to do so is determined by the quality of their organization, leadership, and discipline; the fitness of their doctrine for dealing with potential enemies; the quality of their equipment; the adequacy of their training; and their morale. Their success is not determined by the extent to which they mirror the diversity of their nation. Similarly, it is desirable for a diplomatic service to be broadly representative of the people of the state it represents to the governments of other states. In the end, however, the purpose of a diplomatic service is skillfully to identify and advance the interests of its state in competition with other states. The capacity of a diplomatic service to do so is determined by the quality of its leadership, professionalism, intelligence, and morale, not by the origins or appearance of its members.

Repression, resistance: Repression empowers resistance.

Reprisal: "If the enemy fights deceitfully he should be paid in his own coin."
—The Mahabharata

Reputation: One's reputation is as valuable as a sack of gold and, unlike a sack of gold, if lost, it cannot be replaced.

Reputation, honor: "Reputation is what other people know about you. Honor is what you know about yourself." —Lois McMaster Bujold

Reservation: A formal stipulation of an interpretation, limitation, or qualification to obligations under a treaty asserted in connection with its ratification.

Residence, ambassador's: The soul of an ambassador's residence is in the guests who animate it.

Residence, ambassador's: "The expenditure of the house must be well regulated, yet splendid in every respect, chiefly for the table and cooking, to which foreigners . . . pay more attention than to any other item."
—Hotman de Villiers, 1603, cited by J.J. Jusserand

Respect: Respect and influence are commodities of value on the international scene. They should not be needlessly squandered.

Respect: "While the wise diplomat seeks to win for his country the admiration and respect of others, he will not waste his time trying to inspire the deeper emotion of affection."
—Charles W. Thayer, 1959

Restraint: "Of all manifestations of power, restraint impresses men most."
—Thucydides

Results: "Results test actions." *[Exitus acta probat.]* —Ovid

Retreat: Some battles are won only after a retreat to more advantageous ground.

Reunification: The reintegration of a nation divided by civil war or foreign intervention.

Revanchism: The desire of a state to regain portions of its original territory lost to annexation, secession, or treaties signed under duress.

Revolution: "A revolutionary movement always starts from a position of inferior strength. It owes its survival to the reluctance of its declared victims to accept its professions at face value. It owes its success to the psychological advantage which single-minded purpose confers over opponents who refuse to believe that states or groups may prefer victory to peace."   —HENRY A. KISSINGER, 1960

Revolutionary states: See *States, revolutionary.*

Rewards: "It is good to be able to say to one's self that . . . one deserve[s] to be well treated. It is in itself a recompense, to be worthy of [a reward]. . . . Every man owes himself to the service of his country without any title to exact rewards. We are born in a country and partake in her glory, splendor, and safety; we owe to her the goods and fortune inherited from our fathers; we therefore owe a service to her of one sort or another."   —ANTOINE PECQUET, 1737

Risks: "No course is ever completely free from hazard; but the greatest of all risks is when risk is shirked."   —VICTOR WELLESLEY, 1944

Rudeness, utility of: It can pay to be rude. Anger your opponents in a negotiation and you confuse and distract them. In their rage, they may be goaded to reveal objectives they had been concealing from you.

Rulership: "Only a hand that can grasp a sword may hold a scepter."   —TIMUR (TAMERLANE)

Ruthlessness: Ruthlessness breeds savagery in one's enemies.

S

Salutes: Military honors accorded diplomatic and consular officers in the form of the flying of flags and the firing of artillery. Diplomatic and military protocol stipulates the number of rounds.

Sanctions: Military cowardice tarted up as moral outrage. See also *Isolation*.

Sanctions, boycott: Sanctions against imports from a foreign nation can usefully reduce pressure on a government for military intervention there. They let the government do something seemingly risk-free to express popular outrage. Such boycotts may accomplish nothing at all, but they make the public feel better and benefit domestic agricultural and industrial producers at the immediate expense of morally objectionable foreigners.

Sanctions, boycott: "A nation that is boycotted is a nation that is in sight of surrender. Apply this economic, peaceful, silent, deadly remedy and there will be no need for force. It is a terrible remedy. It does not cost a life outside the nation boycotted, but it brings a pressure upon the nation which, in my judgment, no modern nation could resist."
—Woodrow Wilson, 1919

Sanctions, economic: Economic sanctions are trade or financial penalties imposed by a state or group of states on another state or states.

Sanctions, economic: "Economic sanctions are delusory. The longer they are continued, the more irritation is caused, and the more heavily the burden of them falls where you do not wish it to fall."
—Dean Acheson, 1969

Sanctions, economic: "To determine the pattern of rulership in another country requires conquering it. . . . The idea of using commercial restrictions as a substitute for war in getting control over somebody else's country is a persistent and mischievous superstition in the conduct of foreign affairs."
—Dean Acheson, 1969

Sanctions, economic, accompanying measures: "Covert action, mounted by the intelligence forces, often accompanies the imposition of economic sanctions when the destabilization of a target country is sought. In destabilization cases and in other episodes where major policy changes are sought, the sender state may also invoke quasi-military force— for example, massing troops at the border or stationing war vessels off the coast. Finally, sanctions may precede or accompany actual armed hostility."
—Gary Clyde Hufbauer et al.

Sanctions, economic, adverse consequences of: Economic sanctions, particularly embargoes of exports, more often than not backfire. They stimulate a drive for self-sufficiency and consequent artificial prosperity in the target nation or induce still other nations to develop the capacity to meet the unmet demand in the target nation. Those who impose the sanctions may end up hurting themselves more than they hurt those at whom they are aiming.

Sanctions, economic, duration of: Once economic sanctions are imposed, they seldom continue to be evaluated and justified in terms of progress toward the political objectives that inspired them. Their effectiveness comes to be measured solely by the extent to which they restrict trade and inflict economic hardship. With the passage of time, vested interests in the continuation of sanctions strengthen. Their removal comes to be seen as entailing economic as well as political costs. So the rationale for sanctions evolves and they stay in place long after the circumstances that originally justified them have changed.

Sanctions, economic, timing of: Sanctions usually come too late to deter the misbehavior of the nations on which they are targeted but just in time to save the domestic reputations of the governments that impose them.

Sanctions, economic, and military: "Sanctions can have only one purpose, and that is to coerce the transgressor into submission. If economic pressure fails, to refrain from proceeding to military sanctions is the height of absurdity and can obviously only court . . . discomfiture. . . . There is in fact a point where the distinction between economic and military sanctions disappears and the only consideration that matters is effectiveness or ineffectiveness." —Victor Wellesley, 1944

Sanctions, efficacy of: Sanctions tend to create their own antidotes.

Sanctions, influence: To apply pressure commensurate with one's influence, one must be sufficiently engaged to have influence. Disengagement and ostracism free a state from the vital connections that give it a reason to heed the views of foreign states. Attempts to isolate and shun thus reduce rather than enhance leverage.

Sanctions, motivation for: "[Leaders may] . . . feel compelled to dramatize their opposition to foreign misdeeds, even when the likelihood of changing the target country's behavior seems remote. In these cases sanctions . . . are imposed because the cost of inaction—in terms of lost confidence at home and abroad in the ability . . . to act—is seen as greater than the costs of sanctions." —Gary Clyde Hufbauer et al.

Sanctions, purpose of: "Sanctions always accomplish their principal objective, which is to make those who impose them feel good." —Douglas Paal

Sanctions, revolutionary states: Sanctions and other measures to reduce engagement with a country in revolution are often secretly welcomed by its leaders. Sanctions provide the evidence of foreign hostility revolutionary leaders need to harness the spirit of nationalism to their cause. Sanctions also help them to rid their country of objectionable foreign influences, and justify their speedy reorientation of foreign relations toward the enemies of those imposing the sanctions.

Sanctions, targets of: Economic sanctions are most likely to be imposed on enemies but are, seemingly paradoxically, more effective against allies and the like-minded. Those who desire to preserve a cooperative relationship with the nation imposing the sanctions have a much greater incentive to bend on specific issues than those who do not.

Sanctions, war: One argument for sanctions is that they are better than going to war. Often, however, the interests at stake cannot justify war and sanctions are not in fact an alternative to it. They are instead an expression of the dubious supposition that the only way to influence foreigners is by coercion. In this context, sanctions are an alternative to the persuasive engagement of diplomacy, not to the use of force.

Sarcasm: Sarcasm is the last way station on the route to despair.

Secession: Withdrawal by a portion of a nation from union with the rest in an effort to establish itself as a separate state.

Secrecy: Secrecy is necessary to enable governments that have taken extreme positions in public to compromise in private and to be protected against the consequences of disclosure until the terms of agreement are final and can be defended successfully against domestic critics.

Secrecy: "A useful rule is that if you cannot afford to be found out, do not engage in activity that will cover you with shame when it comes to light."
—Thomas A. Bailey, 1968

Secrecy: "Secrecy is the very soul of diplomacy."   —François de Callières, 1716

Secrecy: "The day secrecy is abolished, negotiation of any kind will become impossible."
—Jules Cambon

Secrecy: "Do not tell secrets to those whose faith and silence you have not already tested."
—Queen Elizabeth I

Secrecy: "Secrecy is the first essential in affairs of the state."   —Cardinal Richelieu

Secrecy, intelligence services: "It is the lot of those in our intelligence agencies that they should work in silence—sometimes fail in silence, but more often succeed in silence. Unhappily, . . . it is sometimes they must suffer in silence. For, like all in high public position,

they are occasionally subject to criticism which they must not answer. . . . Achievements and triumphs can seldom be advertised. Shortcomings and failures often are advertised. The rewards can never come in public acclaim, only in the quiet satisfaction of getting on with the job and trying to do well the work that needs to be done in the interests of your Nation."
—LYNDON B. JOHNSON, 1966

Secrecy, military: "Whether it be treason or not, it does . . . just as much harm for military secrets to be made known to potential enemies through open publication, as it does for military secrets to be given to an enemy through the clandestine operations of spies."
—HARRY S. TRUMAN, 1951

Secrecy, in politics and diplomacy: "The diplomatic dialogue of an international society is an aspect of politics. And all politics, even in the most open democracies, involves public debate and also private discussions, between members of governments and leaders of political parties, and also between executive governments and parliamentarians and between members of legislatures. All politics is concerned with conflicts and alliances of interests and personalities, even in countries where public debate over matters of principle is permitted as well."
—ADAM WATSON, 1983

Secrecy, protecting confidences: "States do not talk to one another only about their own intentions. They also exchange confidential views and guesses about . . . other states . . . and the intentions of those states—views and guesses which they do not want repeated to the others. Unless a state can keep to itself the confidences it learns in this way—and this involves not passing on these confidences to other states or to journalists or legislators who will make [them] public—it will soon find itself cut off from the confidence of other states, which will involve a serious loss of awareness of what is going on."
—ADAM WATSON, 1983

Secrecy, utility of: "If there are differences between us and friendly nations about one or another aspect of the passing parade of events, these are more likely to be resolved by quiet conversation than by a public quarrel. If two of our friends find themselves in difficulty with each other, it is not always conducive to agreement for it to be publicly known that we have been offering friendly counsel."
—DEAN RUSK, 1961

Secrecy during negotiations: "There is a great deal in foreign affairs which cannot be disclosed. Secrecy there must be up to a certain point because in foreign affairs we are dealing with the relations with other countries, the secrets of which do not belong to us especially but which we are sharing with one or more foreign Powers. . . . Very often at an early stage of negotiation to make a premature disclosure would result in the other Power desiring to break off relations altogether."
—LORD GREY OF FALLODON, CITED BY VICTOR WELLESLEY

Secrecy of communications: "A really effective cipher is literally worth far more than its weight in gold."
—FRANÇOIS DE CALLIÈRES, 1716

Secrecy of reporting: "Reporting between a . . . government and its embassies abroad needs to be confidential, in the same sort of way as between a lawyer and his clients, and is covered by the general recognition of the value of diplomatic immunity."

—Adam Watson, 1983

Secretariat: The substitute for thought at the top of a foreign ministry is its secretariat staff.

Secretary (diplomatic): One of six grades of diplomatic title—as in first, second, and third secretary, in that order of rank. In the traditional order of diplomatic precedence, secretaries follow counselors and outrank attachés.

Secrets: "The face is the mirror of the mind, and eyes without speaking confess the secrets of the heart."

—Saint Jerome

Security: "If you believe the doctors, nothing is wholesome; if you believe the theologians, nothing is innocent; if you believe the soldiers, nothing is safe." —Lord Salisbury

Security: "He passes through life most securely who has least reason to reproach himself with complaisance toward his enemies."

—Thucydides, 404 b.c.

Security, absolute: "Could a power achieve all its wishes, it would strive for absolute security, a world-order free from the consciousness of foreign danger and where all problems have the manageability of domestic issues. But . . . absolute security for one power means absolute insecurity for all others . . . and can be achieved only through conquest."

—Henry A. Kissinger, 1964

Security from enemies: The simplest way to secure oneself against enemies is to be careful not to make them.

Self-control: "[The diplomat must have] sufficient control over himself to resist the longing to speak before he has really thought what he shall say. He should not endeavor to gain the reputation of being able to reply immediately and without premeditation to every proposition which is made, and he should take special care not to fall into the error of . . . [so warming up to] controversy [that he reveals] important secrets in order to support his opinion."

—François de Callières, 1716

Self-control: "If we want to dominate the emotions of others, we must master our own. Otherwise we will always be off on false adventures; we will not be able to await the proper moment or seize the right occasion, because we have been carried away. We will not be able to use gentle insinuations and charming words. Our emotions will warn others to be wary of us, and will make us imagine interests that we do not have. They will blind us to the nature of the resources that we must use and to the ways of using them. Indeed, a man who wishes to succeed in negotiations must be able to hide his emotions to the point of appearing cold when he is overwhelmed with sorrow and calm when he is shaken with passion. . . . It is often useful to appear to be shaken with emotion but of a different kind than that which is actually at work. An impassioned man gives hope of being won over, whereas a reserved man puts others on guard. In fact, a man who feigns emotions distracts those who are trying to get the upper hand on him. Such acting is permitted and is in no way contrary to proper behavior."

—Fortune Barthélemy de Felice, 1778

Self-defense, justification: "There must be a necessity of self-defense, instant, overwhelming, leaving no choice of means, and no moment for deliberation."

—Daniel Webster

Self-interest, enlightened: "I think with others that nations are to be governed with regard to their own interests, but I am convinced that it is their interests in the long run to be grateful, faithful to their engagements even in the worst of circumstances, and honorable and generous always."

—Thomas Jefferson

Self-knowledge: A negotiator must know himself, his own weaknesses and vulnerabilities, in addition to knowing his opponent, in order to succeed.

Sending state: The state which sends a diplomatic mission to another state (the receiving state or host government).

Sentiment: "A sentimental policy knows no reciprocity."   —Otto von Bismarck

Sherpas: The tribe of bureaucrats who prepare summit meetings.

Silence: Silence is sometimes the most eloquent answer.

Silence: "The first qualification of a diplomat is to keep silent."   —Napoleon

Silence: "Even a fool, when he holdeth his peace, is counted wise."

—Proverbs, XVII, v. 28

Sincerity: "Sincerity greatly facilitates the conduct of affairs; dealings can be expedited when they involve people known for their truthfulness, and one can save the time that would be required to unveil the lies of those who do not have truth in their reputation. Honest parties do not have to waste time in soundings, in examinations, and in unmasking each other, and confidence smooths all difficulties. Truth is also most useful when one finds oneself before deceitful and suspicious characters with whom one has to deal. Such individuals judge others by the standards of their own corruption, hearing truth as falsehood and thus fooling their own selves. For this reason Sir William Temple always maintained that truthfulness was the only ruse that always worked."

—Fortune Barthélemy de Felice, 1778

Sincerity: "The sincerity of a government must never be called into question. Facts may be denied, deductions examined, disapproved and condemned, without just cause of offense; but no impeachment of the integrity of the government in its reliance on the correctness of its own views can be permitted." —John Bassett Moore

Skepticism, optimism: Skepticism and mental flexibility are as essential to success in analysis as optimism and perseverance are to the attainment of policy objectives.

Skills, bureaucratic and diplomatic, contrasted: The skills of courtiers and bureaucrats differ from those of diplomats and warriors. The capitals of great powers tend to be full of men who are as quick to sacrifice the reputations of their nations' diplomats as they are to sacrifice the lives of its soldiers. Those charged with affairs of state should be men tempered by experience in the difficulties of diplomacy and the horrors of war.

Small nations: Small nations have long memories and thin skins; only those large and self-confident enough to do so forget and forgive the humiliations of the past.

Small nations: "The paradox of power operates to the advantage of small states, as it does to the disadvantage of the great. Great powers may aptly be compared to the albatross in a poem by Baudelaire. The albatross is the most majestic of the birds. Well may it take a certain consolatory pride in its magnificent dimensions. The spread of its immense wings inspires awe and wonder. But its wings are too heavy for it to take to the air. It is immobilized by its own weight. And so it squats, sullen and disconsolate, less awesome than absurd, as all around it the smaller birds—puffins and gulls, cormorants and terns—wheel and dip with abandon, snatching food within its range, sometimes from its beak. The paradox of power has made small states into great states, middle powers into great powers." —James Eayrs, 1967

Small nations: "Powerful states need no ambassadors. Their force speaks for themselves. For small states, it matters how they express themselves." —Albert Einstein, quoted by Abba Eban

Small nations: "Small nations are like indecently dressed women. They tempt the evil-minded." —Julius K. Nyerere, 1964

Society: An association of individuals, families, and other social units that values the preservation or promotion of a sense of common identity and heritage, collective well-being, and mutual cooperation among its constituent elements.

Society of nations: "Wherever nations are fully reconciled to each other's existence and borders and status in the world, and wherever their relations are not seriously clouded by ulterior political involvements, there is room for . . . a framework of legal obligation, designed to prevent the minor disputes from becoming major ones. But it [is] important to bear in mind at all times the natural limitations which surround these principles, and

above all not to look to them as substitutes for diplomacy or as magic keys to world
peace." —GEORGE F. KENNAN, 1954

Soldiers: See *Warriors.*

Solutions, problems: A solution to one problem is the father of the next.

Sovereignty: The rights of exclusive authority, jurisdiction, control, and coercive application of violence asserted by a state over its territory and nationals in relation to the
actions of other states and their nationals.

Sovereignty: "Every independent commonwealth has a right to do what it pleases to
other commonwealths." —THOMAS HOBBES

Speech, a form of action: "A capacity to use words with precision and a highly developed sense of their potential effect on listeners are of substantive importance and are not
merely a matter of ritual elegance. The semantic obsessions of diplomats deserve more
respect than they generally receive. What statesmen and diplomats say is often as vital
as what they do. It would not be farfetched to go further and declare that speech is an
incisive form of action." —ABBA EBAN, 1983

Sphere of influence: See *Influence, sphere of.*

Spies, anonymity of: "The life of spies is to know, not to be known."
—GEORGE HERBERT, 1640

Spies, kinds of: "There are five kinds of spy: local spies, inside spies, reverse spies,
dead spies and living spies. When the five kinds of spies are all active, no one knows
their routes—this is the very essence of organizational genius, and gives leaders a major
advantage.
   "Local spies are hired from among the people of a locality. Inside spies are hired from
among enemy officials. Reverse spies are hired from among enemy spies. Dead spies
transmit false intelligence to enemy spies. Living spies come back to report."   —SUNZI

Spouses: An ambassador's residence is very likely to be treated by his compatriots,
especially visiting officials from his capital, as a sort of official hotel, in which food, drink,
accommodation, and laundry services are demanded as of right. The ambassador's wife
must not only be a gracious hostess, she must also be the skilled manager of a small inn
in which she and her husband, rather than her guests, foot the bills.

Spouses: The wives of resident compatriots look naturally to the wife of their ambassador for sponsorship and leadership of their community activities. An ambassador's wife
must have the grace, stamina, and political acumen to discharge this role in addition to

the many other duties which her husband's position has thrust on her: the emissary of her nation's women to the women where she resides, her husband's consort at diplomatic and official functions, the friend and confidante of the wives of senior officials and diplomatic colleagues, the manager and hostess of a great house, and the chief social worker concerned with the welfare and morale of her embassy's women and children. Like her husband, she cannot afford to forget that others see her always as a representative of her country. They also see her as an intimate of the ambassador with special insights to impart. She is never off duty.

Spouses: "Pay, pack, and follow."
—RICHARD BURTON: INSTRUCTIONS TO HIS WIFE ON BEING SUMMARILY RECALLED FROM A DIPLOMATIC POSTING TO DAMASCUS, 1870

Spouses: "In no profession can a wife play a more helpful and important role than in the Foreign Service." —JOSEPH C. GREW, 1956

Spouses: "Anyone who knows even the least about diplomacy knows what invaluable support an effective diplomatic wife can be to her husband, and how much the performance of any diplomatic institution depends on the cumulative contributions of its distaff side." —WILLIAM MACOMBER, 1975

Spouses: "Diplomats have known for many centuries . . . that wives are valuable auxiliaries." —CHARLES W. THAYER, 1959

Stability: "Stability . . . has commonly resulted not from a quest for peace but from a generally accepted legitimacy . . . , [meaning] an international agreement about the nature of workable arrangements and about the permissible aims and methods of foreign policy. It implies the acceptance of the framework of the international order by all major powers, at least to the extent that no state is so dissatisfied that . . . it expresses its dissatisfaction in a revolutionary foreign policy. A legitimate order does not make conflicts impossible, but it limits their scope. Wars may occur, but they will be fought in the name of the existing structure and the peace which follows will be justified as a better expression of the 'legitimate,' general consensus. Diplomacy in the classic sense, the adjustment of differences through negotiation, is possible only in 'legitimate' international orders." —HENRY A. KISSINGER, 1964

Staffing of embassies: "In diplomacy there is an inverse relationship between numbers and performance. . . . The envoy's is a one-man task; double the team and the results are halved." —JOHN LOMAX, QUOTED BY ELLIS BRIGGS, 1968

Stakes, high: The stakes can sometimes be too high for rational calculation.

Stalemate: "'Stalemate' exists when the circumstances prevent either party [to a dispute] from creating a solution alone. Each party has necessary but insufficient ingredients

of a solution; making this known to another party in the same position (assuming that together their ingredients are sufficient) can turn stalemate into agreement."
—I. WILLIAM ZARTMAN AND MAUREEN R. BERMAN, 1982

Stamina: "A negotiator must have stamina—physical and mental stamina. He has got to be physically prepared, since he cannot always control the time of negotiations because other people are involved. He must not tire easily."
—I. WILLIAM ZARTMAN AND MAUREEN R. BERMAN, 1982

State: A polity controlling fixed territory with defined borders. A nation state is a state embracing a single nation or people, unified by a common language and culture. A seminational (or "divided") state is one that embraces less than all the people of a given nation or people. A multinational state or empire is a state consisting of more than one nation and people, unified by a common ideology or by the power of a ruling elite.

State, revolutionary: "The distinguishing feature of a revolutionary power is not that it feels threatened—such feeling is inherent in the nature of international relations based on sovereign states—but that nothing can reassure it. Only absolute security—the neutralization of the opponents—is considered a sufficient guarantee, and thus the desire of one power for absolute security means absolute insecurity for all the others."
—HENRY A. KISSINGER, 1964

State, revolutionary: "No peace is possible with a revolutionary system."
—METTERNICH, 1807

State system: The mode of organization of the international community of states. A multistate system is one composed of states that are legally independent and theoretically equal in sovereignty, and among whom power is dispersed, permitting them to compete and cooperate as they perceive their national interests to dictate. A universal state is a world government or empire in which no nation is independent of a common central authority. A feudal state system is one in which the independence and authority of the component states are determined by the hierarchy of their relationships with an overlord or hegemon.

Statecraft: Statecraft is the art—consisting of doctrines, dispositions, policies, processes, and operations—that promotes the governance, security, and survival of a polity.

Statecraft: Statecraft is the art of advancing the interests of one's state and its people against those of others by either violent or non-violent means. The men and women who practice this subtle and dangerous art are known as statesmen. Those who implement the policies of statesmen by violence are soldiers; those who do so by peaceful means are diplomats.

Statecraft: Statecraft is the strategy of power.

Statecraft: "The winds and waves are always on the side of the ablest navigators."
—EDWARD GIBBON

Statecraft: "The key to running military and state affairs is to know people's thinking and to manage routine affairs. Give safety to those feeling danger; cheer up those in fear; return the rebels home; resolve grievances; investigate complaints; raise the status of humble people; suppress the strong; cause damages to hostile people; enrich greedy people; let people do what they want; hide those who are afraid; be close to those good at thinking; place under cover those who slander other people; restore what is destroyed; destroy those in opposition; subdue the truculent; frustrate the arrogant; recruit those who have come over; house those who submit; and please those who surrender."
—THREE STRATEGIES [SAN LUE]

Statecraft, decisionmaking in: "The statesman must cross the Rubicon not knowing how deep and turbulent the river is, nor what he will find on the other side. . . . He must face the impenetrable darkness of the future and still not flinch from walking into it, drawing the nation behind him."
—HANS J. MORGENTHAU, 1962

Statecraft, diplomacy as servant of: "Diplomacy, . . . insofar as it is the servant of statecraft, is the art of doing just enough and no more than is necessary to achieve possible national objectives, that must, in the nature of the case, be limited."
—SISLEY HUDDLESTON, 1954

Statecraft, foxes and lions: "A prince, being thus obliged to know how well to act as a beast, must imitate the fox and the lion. For the lion cannot protect himself from traps, and the fox cannot defend himself from wolves. One must therefore be a fox to recognize traps, and a lion to frighten wolves."
—NICCOLÒ MACHIAVELLI

Statecraft, intelligence as component of: Intelligence is a component of statecraft, meeting its need to have reliable information and knowledge about other states and peoples that can affect the well-being of the polity on whose behalf statesmen are acting.

Statecraft, mediocrity in: "It is the essence of mediocrity [in statecraft] that it prefers the tangible advantage to the intangible gain in position."
—HENRY A. KISSINGER, 1964

Statecraft, smart: "Smart statecraft is what you get when wits, wallets, and muscle pull together so that leverage in all its forms is harnessed to a realistic action plan or political strategy that can be set in motion by agile diplomacy."
—CHESTER A. CROCKER

Statements: "No nation's foreign policy can be ascertained merely from what its officials say. More important are the philosophy of its leaders and the actual manifestation of that philosophy in what is done."
—JOHN FOSTER DULLES, 1946

Statesman, defined: "A statesman is a successful politician who is dead."
—Thomas B. Reed

Statesmanship, defined: Statesmanship consists of farsightedness, wisdom, skill, and tactful conciliation in the conduct of government business.

Statesmen, advice to: "Keep strong, if possible. In any case, keep cool. Have unlimited patience. Never corner an opponent, and always assist him to save his face. Put yourself in his shoes—so as to see things through his eyes. Avoid self-righteousness like the devil—nothing is so self-blinding."
—Basil Liddell Hart, 1960

Statesmen, politicians: "Anyone who would be a statesman has to be a successful politician first."
—Richard M. Nixon, 1982

Stares, revolutionary: Revolutionary powers are those that regard the existing order of things as unjust and are prepared to act to overthrow it.

States, large and small: "Powerful states can maintain themselves only by crime; little states are virtuous only by weakness."
—Mikhail Bakunin

States, longevity: "If Sparta and Rome perished, what state can hope to endure forever?"
—Jean-Jacques Rousseau

States, revolutionary, appeasement of: "When an outlaw state not only rejects important norms of the international system but also seeks major changes in the status quo, appeasement of even its legitimate and seemingly reasonable demands is unlikely to contribute to resocializing it into accepting the norms of the international system. In fact, such a strategy is more likely to reinforce the rogue leader's ambitions and strengthen his predisposition to challenge the system. Nevertheless, limited appeasement may have to be resorted to occasionally as a time-buying strategy for determining the true character of the adversary, strengthening one's capabilities, or generating domestic and international support for resisting the outlaw more effectively later." —Alexander L. George, 1993

Statesmen: "Men who deal with international matters in a haggling spirit have missed their vocation, they are not meant for statesmanship, but for horse dealing."
—David Lloyd George

Statesmen, as strategists: "A good strategist . . . [cannot] be content merely with meeting and averting immediate dangers. To deal with such dangers when and as they arise often requires skill, nay, very great skill, but it belongs to the tactical and not to the strategic order. Good strategy implies something more than mere survival, something more than the discovery of expedients to meet sudden emergencies and to postpone the day of the decisive battle, something more than the invention of ingenious formulae to parade as an agreement in the absence of a settlement. Tactics without strategy lead only to temporary solutions which as often as not result in the creation of new problems and the perpetuation of a never-ending choice of evils. The power to sense the future, to live in it and act up to it is an essential part of the farsighted statesman. He must possess a fine perception of all the indications of coming change and the ability to divine the high import of things from the signs which to most are imperceptible and unintelligible."

—VICTOR WELLESLEY, 1944

Statesmen, diplomats and: Government is a contractual relationship, under which the people yield authority to their leaders to conduct foreign relations on their behalf. The universe of states is one of shifting constellations; statesmanship is a task that is never finished and that never lets its practitioners rest. The challenge to statesmen has always been to assure that international change occurs smoothly and results in the greatest possible advantage (or the least disadvantage) to their nation. Such leadership requires strategy, as the changes statesmen must deal with are beyond the capacity of any single government to control. The people have the legitimate right to expect, under their contract with their chief of government, that such a strategy will be formulated and pursued by him. They also have a right to expect that his diplomatic lieutenants will counsel him astutely in the crafting of a strategy for turning international change to their advantage, and that his diplomats will inform him honestly of events that bear on his adjustment of it as it is implemented. Sycophancy in reporting and analysis is therefore not just a breach of faith by a diplomat with his government; it is a fundamental lapse of his responsibility, as an officer of the state, to the people of his nation.

Statesmen, good intentions of: "We cannot conclude from the good intentions of a statesman that his foreign policies will be either morally praiseworthy or politically successful. . . . How often have statesmen been motivated by a desire to improve the world, and ended by making it worse?"

—HANS J. MORGENTHAU

Statesmen, politicians: "Anyone who would be a statesman has to be a successful politician first."

—RICHARD M. NIXON, 1982

Statesmen, politicians and: "The difference between a statesman and a politician is that the former looks to the next generation and the latter to the next election."

—ENGLISH PROVERB

Statesmen, politicians and: "The politician says: 'I will give you what you want.' The statesman says: 'What you think you want is this. What it is possible for you to get is that. What you really want, therefore, is the following.'"

—WALTER LIPPMANN, 1929

Statesmen, qualifications of: "No man can qualify for the duties of statesman until he has made a thorough study of the science of war in its broadest sense. He need not go to military school, much less serve in the army or in the militia. But unless he makes himself thoroughly acquainted with the methods and conditions requisite to success in war he is liable to do almost infinite damage to his country."

—JOHN MACALLISTER SCHOFIELD, 1897

Statesmen, task of: "The task of a statesman consists only in listening carefully whether he can catch an echo of the strides of the Almighty through the events of this world, and then to spring forward and seize the hem of his garment."   —Otto von Bismarck

Statesmen, task of: "It is the business of the statesman to provide a decent burial for the past and to facilitate the birth of the future."   —Cited by Victor Wellesley

Status quo: The present state of affairs.

Status quo ante bellum: The state of affairs that were obtained before the war.

Status quo, changing: Preserving the status quo is generally easier than changing it, and deterrence is therefore less demanding than compellence.

Status quo, moral consensus and: "The only [means] by which a state, aware of its weakness, can preserve the status quo without exhausting its resources . . . [is] the creation of a moral consensus."   —Henry A. Kissinger, 1964

Strangers, courtesy to: "If a man be gracious and courteous to strangers it shows he is a citizen of the world."   —Francis Bacon, 1612

Strangers, politeness of: "A stranger is always polite."   —Arab proverb

Strategy: A strategy is a direct or indirect course of action, consisting of a series of maneuvers, to reach an objective at a cost that is significantly less than the benefits to be gained. A strategy is defined by judgments about what to do, how to do it, what to do it with, and how to limit both the costs and adverse consequences of doing it. Tactics apply strategy to the circumstances of the moment.

Strategy: "The best strategy is always to be strong."
      —Carl Maria von Clausewitz, 1832

Strategy: "Strategy is the art of controlling and utilizing the resources of a nation—or a coalition of nations—including its armed forces, to the end that its vital interests shall be effectively promoted and secured against enemies, actual, potential, or merely presumed."
      —Edward Mead Earle, 1943

Strategy, components of: "Insofar as states act to prepare or to avoid war, or use a capacity for warmaking to extort concessions by intimidation without any actual use of force, the logic of strategy applies in full, just as much as in war itself and regardless of what instruments of statecraft are employed. Thus, except for their purely administrative aspect, diplomacy, propaganda, secret operations, and economic controls are all subject to

the logic of strategy, as elements in the adversarial dealings of states with one another."
—EDWARD N. LUTTWAK, 1987

Strategy, critieria for effectiveness: "To be effective, a strategy must . . . be able to win a domestic consensus, both among the technical and the political leadership. It must be understood by the opponents to the extent needed for . . . deterrence. It must receive allied endorsement if alliances are to remain cohesive. It must be relevant to . . . problems in . . . uncommitted areas so as to discourage international anarchy."
—HENRY A. KISSINGER, 1964

Strategy, deterrence: Deterrence may be a prerequisite for strategy, but deterrence is not itself a strategy. It is directed at preventing injury to the national interest; strategy aims to advance it.

Strategy, diplomacy and: "The distinction between diplomacy and strategy is an entirely relative one. These two terms are complementary aspects of the single art of politics—the art of conducting relations with other states so as to further the 'national interest.' If, by definition, strategy, the conduct of military operations, does not function when the operations do not take place, the military means are [yet] an integral part of diplomatic method. Conversely, words, notes, promises, guarantees, and threats belong to the chief of state's wartime panoply with regard to allies, neutrals, and even today's enemies, that is, to the allies of yesterday or tomorrow."
—RAYMOND ARON

Strategy, diplomacy and: "Diplomacy is strategy's twin." —ANTHONY EDEN, 1965

Strategy, grand: Grand strategy integrates intelligence, diplomacy, military measures, and propaganda in a manner calculated to produce a desired set of political results.

Strategy, grand: "Grand strategy cannot wait for the right conditions to emerge; it must focus on those things that can be controlled, or at least influenced."
—CHESTER A. CROCKER

Strategy, grand: "The highest type of strategy—sometimes called grand strategy—is that which so integrates the policies and armaments of the nation that resort to war is either rendered unnecessary or is undertaken with the maximum chance of victory."
—EDWARD MEAD EARLE, 1944

Strategy, grand: "The student of grand strategy needs to take into consideration . . . the vital role of diplomacy, in both peacetime and wartime, in improving the nation's position—and prospects of victory—through gaining allies, winning the support of neutrals, and reducing the number of one's enemies (or potential enemies)."—PAUL KENNEDY, 1991

Strategy, grand: "Grand strategy has a higher purpose than the mere planning of campaigns in time of war. It must aim at the elimination of war by the planning of the peace."
—VICTOR WELLESLEY, 1944

Strategy, logic of: "Within the sphere of strategy, where human relations are conditioned by armed conflict actual or possible, [a] logic is at work [which] violates ordinary linear logic by inducing the coming together and even the reversal of opposites, and [which] tends to reward paradoxical conduct while confounding straight-forwardly logical action, by yielding results ironical if not lethally self-damaging." —EDWARD N. LUTTWAK

Strategy, negotiating: Refusal to negotiate is, not infrequently, the best negotiating strategy.

Strategy, status quo: It is an entirely understandable strategy for a well-established power to seek to preserve the status quo, to prevent any power from becoming so strong that it might pose a threat, to prevent the outbreak of major wars that might involve it and weaken it, to obtain any incidental advantages that might happen to become available from a passing situation, and to protect the lives and property of its citizens throughout the world. Such a strategy is best conducted as a series of tactical improvisations, opportunistically, and with as much freedom from sentimental entanglements as history and domestic politics will allow.

Strategy, tactical sacrifice essential to: "Petty geniuses attempt to hold everything; wise men hold fast to the most important resort. They parry the great blows and scorn the little accidents. There is an ancient apothegm: he who would preserve everything, preserves nothing. Therefore, always sacrifice the bagatelle and pursue the essential." —FREDERICK THE GREAT

Strategy, tactics: An accumulation of tactical maneuvers is not a strategy but a muddle.

Strategy, victory: The essence of strategy is not to choose a path that leads to victory but to position oneself so that most paths lead to victories.

Strategy, victory: "The true aim is not so much to seek battle as to seek a strategic situation so advantageous that if it does not of itself produce the decision, its continuation by a battle is sure to achieve this." —BASIL LIDDELL HART, 1954

Strength: Strong states do what they will; the weak do what they must.

Strength: The stronger the state, the gentler should be its diplomats. Power should speak for itself; when flaunted, strength arouses resentment.

Strength: "As important as having strength is being known to have it." —MCGEORGE BUNDY, 1964

Strength: "No state is forever strong or eternally weak." —HAN FEIZI

Strength: "True strength restrains itself; true greatness sets its own limits."
—Attributed to Talleyrand

Strength: "While affability and good nature . . . are generally recognized as invaluable to the diplomat, they must be tempered with dignity. The picture of his government that the professional diplomat seeks to convey is one not only of friendship but of strength."
—Charles W. Thayer, 1959

Strength: "It is said that God is always for the big battalions." —Voltaire, 1770

Strength, national: Sound policy, astute diplomacy, and military power are the sources of national strength.

Strength, success: "Strength is power, success is happiness." —Arthasastra of Kautilya

Subjugation: "When you cannot withstand the upper hand, kiss it and wish it broken!"
—Arab proverb

Subjugation: See also *Force, subjugation by.*

Subversion: Covert action through secret agents, front groups, or indigenous resistance forces intended to sap the strength and weaken the will to resist, carried out by a regime that is an opponent or potential adversary, to create internal diversion, and to bolster the determination and power of internal enemies.

Subversion: "Miraculous results can be achieved by practicing the methods of subversion."
—Arthasastra of Kautilya

Success: Success in statecraft is the product of the intelligent application of power through a strategy that is sustained by conviction, applied with skill, and backed by strength.

Success, diplomatic: "A diplomatic success is highly prized by every Government, for it means something gained in the world of great affairs, and gained without cost, without war, even without having to engage extra staff; for the diplomatist works quietly and economically—tongue, pen, and brain are all that he requires. The value of a diplomatic success is enhanced in the eyes of the Government which achieves it, if there is something sudden and dramatic about it. This arouses general interest and pleases the people. Governments and ministers are prone to attempts at 'sudden' diplomacy if they are actuated by vanity . . . , or if they are weak at home, or if they are not very sure of their ground abroad. Vain ministers . . . [try] to 'bring off' a sudden success, because it proclaims their cleverness to all the world, and means that they have outwitted somebody. Weak Governments do it, because it strengthens their domestic position; Governments uncertain of their ground abroad, because they trust that foreign Powers, which might reject a proposal, will accept an 'accomplished fact.' Nevertheless, sudden diplomacy is the worst that can be practised. It always offends somebody, some state or states; and every offense has to be paid for some time or another. It is always tactless; it is generally maladroit and, owing to changing circumstances, ill-timed. If it is done in order to discount foreign opposition and to face possible opponents with a fait accompli, it is dishonest. And although one or two instances of apparently successful villainy can be adduced in diplomatic history, nobody will hold this up as a model. Indeed, if an act or a scheme is dishonesty, it is not diplomacy, which is essentially a peaceful thing; dishonesty and peace never go together for long."　　　　　　　　　　—R.B. Mowat, 1936

Success, publicity about: "Successful diplomacy, like successful marriage, is not much publicized."　　　　　　　　　　　　　　　　—John Paton Davies, 1965

Succession: "Any system is inherently unstable that has no peaceful means to legitimize its leaders."　　　　　　　　　　　　　　　　　—Ronald W. Reagan

Sucker: If you look around the poker table and can't spot the sucker, the sucker is you.

Summit meetings: The fanfare accompanying meetings at the summit advertises failure as well as success. Such meetings, if undertaken for domestic political advantage, as often diminish the reputation of a head of government as enhance it.

Summit meetings: "The idea that only chiefs can talk to other chiefs keeps them rushing about so much that they do not have the time to devise and execute the policies which would make these frantic and repeated journeys unnecessary. The time which the highest echelons need to think is not for brooding in isolated detachment; it is needed to devise the action to meet the exigencies of our times, to bring conviction of the need of that action to the . . . people . . ., and to explain it to the world."　　　　—Dean Acheson

Summit meetings: "When a chief of state or head of government makes a fumble, the goal line is open behind him."　　　　　　　　　　　　　　　—Dean Acheson

Summit meetings: "Two great princes who wish to establish good personal relations should never meet each other face to face but ought to communicate through good and wise ambassadors."　　　　　　　　　　　　　　—Philippe de Commines

Summit meetings: "The advantage of a summit meeting is that the participants possess the authority to settle disputes. The disadvantage is that they cannot be disavowed. A summit conference can make binding decisions more rapidly than any other diplomatic forum. By the same token, the disagreements are liable to be more intractable and the decisions more irrevocable. The possibility of using summit conferences to mark a new departure in the relations of states should not be underestimated. At the same time, it would be foolish to deny the perils of having as principal negotiators the men who make the final decision [about peace and war]. . . . Frustration or humiliation may cause them to embark on an irrevocable course. A summit conference may contribute to clarification of the opposing points of view. But this is helpful only if the original tension was caused by misunderstanding. Otherwise, clarifying the opposing points of view may only deepen the schism. In short, the same factors which make for speed of decision also increase the risks of disagreement." —HENRY A. KISSINGER, 1960

Summit meetings: "When a head of government becomes directly involved in summit negotiations he violates one of negotiating's more useful rules. The rule is that the official with final authority should not be the negotiator who is in the room and at the table." —WILLIAM MACOMBER, 1975

Summit meetings: "Creation of a willowy euphoria is one of the dangers of summitry." —RICHARD NIXON

Summit meetings: "The direct confrontation of the chiefs of government of the great powers involves an extra tension because the court of last resort is in session." —DEAN RUSK

Summit meetings, agreements at: "Experience teaches us that the higher the summit the flimsier the agreements. Top-level politicians are much too impatient to watch details, important as they may be, and are always in a hurry to shake hands to mark a 'rapprochement' or other agreement. As one American diplomat once said to me: On an icy summit there grows only what you have carried up there. So it is wise to send conscientious, publicity-shy individuals ahead to prepare the texts and give the top officials concise information about the points especially to be watched." —KARL GRUBER, 1983

Summit meetings, case for: "Solution [of exceptionally difficult international problems] frequently requires resources beyond those of the most competent and qualified diplomatist. Such questions can only be settled in Conference by persons who have their hand on the pulse of the political conditions and currents of thought in their respective countries, who have at immediate disposal all the technical knowledge which Governments possess; who know how far they can persuade their fellow-countrymen to go in the direction of compromise; and who, insomuch as they have to defend their policy before their respective parliaments, are alone in a position to make real concessions. In former days, when the final responsibility rested with a sovereign or a government these matters could be entrusted to an ambassador. Nowadays, when governments are often responsible to Parliaments elected on the widest franchise, it is no longer advisable to rely entirely on intermediaries." —LORD HANKEY, 1946

Summit meetings, defects of: What is wrong with summits is insufficient preparation, lack of clear purpose, inflated expectations, and too much ballyhoo. In short, summits are magnificent entertainment; but are they diplomacy?

Summit meetings, drawbacks: "A summit conference combines the risk of such misunderstandings as are likely to arise between people who are meeting for the first or second time and have only a few hours in which to discuss weighty and often appalling problems through interpreters, with the most sensational publicity. It is a cross between secret and open diplomacy, and ends by accumulating the drawbacks of both."

—Domenico Bartoli, 1961

Summit meetings, justification for: "The favorite cliché of those who advocate summit talks regardless of the circumstances is, 'Talking is always better than fighting.' This, however, is not the only choice. Talking is not better than not talking when you do not know what you are going to talk about." —Richard M. Nixon, 1960

Summit meetings, negotiations at: "It is almost always a mistake for heads of delegation to undertake the details of a negotiation. They are then obliged to master specifics normally handled by their foreign offices and are deflected onto subjects more appropriate to their subordinates, while being kept from issues only heads of state can resolve. Since no one without a well-developed ego reaches the highest office, compromise is difficult and deadlocks are dangerous. With the domestic positions of the interlocutors so often dependent on at least the semblance of success, negotiations more often concentrate on obscuring differences than they do on dealing with the essence of a problem."

—Henry A. Kissinger, 1994

Summit meetings, preparation of: "If discretion is the better part of valour, preparation is undoubtedly the best part of summitry." —Geoffrey Jackson, 1981

Summit meetings, purpose of: "When the primary purpose of summit meetings is thought to be the fostering of good will, they become not a forum for negotiations but a substitute for them; not an expression of policy but a means of obscuring its absence. The constant international travels of heads of government without a clear program or purpose may be less an expression of statesmanship than a symptom of panic."

—Henry A. Kissinger, 1960

Superpower: An extremely powerful nation to whose leadership a bloc of less powerful nations habitually defers.

Support, unconditional: To offer to support a nation regardless of its circumstances or its government's role in creating them is to license it to act without regard for one's views or one's interests.

Surprise: More often than not, surprise results from reluctance to acknowledge events or trends that are contrary to what dogma, past experience, or wishful thinking predict. The most common, but least acknowledged, cause of surprise is inattentiveness to what was, in retrospect, obvious to an alert few whose views were dismissed as implausible.

Surprise: "It is a diplomat's first duty not to be taken by surprise. Politics are dominated by constant change. All things flow. Do not let your imagination run wild. Do not make an elephant out of every gnat. But look upon almost everything as possible and little as certain. Above all, don't let yourself be hurried. The deep secret of our life lies somewhere between excessive haste and lost opportunities." —HEINRICH VON BÜLOW

Survival: "Having extensive territory and a large population is not enough to constitute strength. Having strong armor and sharp weapons is not enough to win victory. Having high walls and deep moats is not enough to comprise security. Having strict orders and penalties is not enough to be authoritative. Those who carry out policies conducive to survival will survive even if small; those who carry out policies conducive to destruction will perish even if large. A small country that actually practices culture and virtue reigns; a large country that is militaristic perishes. An army that remains whole goes to battle only after it has already won; an army doomed to defeat is one that fights first and then seeks to win. When virtues are equal, the many prevail over the few. When powers are comparable, the intelligent prevail over the foolish."
—HUAINANZI, AS TRANSLATED BY THOMAS CLEARY

Suspicion: Ignorance is the mother of suspicion.

Sustainability: The extent to which the application of a capability can be continued over time.

Syllogisms: Syllogisms are substitutes for reality-based analyses; they explain the world through a chain of superficially persuasive assertions that are often catastrophically false.

Sympathy, empathy: "Sympathy for the other . . . [side's] position . . . [weakens] a negotiator's ability to speak for his own side, but empathy means that he knows how his position looks from the other fellow's shoes, as well as how it feels to be in them."
—I. WILLIAM ZARTMAN AND MAUREEN R. BERMAN, 1982

Tact: "Tact is the capacity of doing spontaneously what is suitable."

—Armand von Dumreicher

Tact: "What is of paramount necessity for a diplomat is tact. Tact requires the respect for form that a mediocre mind alone despises. The more society is civilized, the more form is respected as a wholesome barrier to the inevitable antagonisms to which incompatibility of character and birth give rise. Politeness is not an untruth. It merely reminds us of the justice and inner moderation which ought to guide us. It is only in bad company that we have to scream to make ourselves heard." —Charles de Martens, 1866

Tactics, strategy: An accumulation of tactical responses to opportunities, no matter how brilliant, does not add up to a strategy.

Tactics, strategy: Bad tactics annul good strategy.

Talk: "When statesmen want to gain time, they offer to talk."—Henry A. Kissinger, 1994

Targeting: A hammer is useless unless you know where the nails you want to strike are.

Tariffs: "It is often maintained that Protection is useful as a bargaining weapon for breaking down the economic nationalism of other countries and thus serves to promote freer trade. But experience has shown that tariff wars have generally ended in higher tariffs. Is it not far more probable that the real bargaining power lies in the threat to introduce Protection and that once in being that power is largely lost?" —Victor Wellesley, 1944

Taste, tact and: A diplomat must have both taste and tact. Taste is a feeling for beauty; tact, for what is fitting.

Technology: "Radio enables people to hear all evil, television enables them to see all evil, and the jet plane enables them to go off and do all evil."

—Kojo Debrah, quoted by Martin Mayer

Technology: "The tuth is that all the inventions of recent years have tended the same way; to narrow the world, to bring us closer together and sharpen the reactions before the shock absorbers are ready." —Anthony Eden, 1945

Technology, proliferation of: Conflict, or the anticipation of it, drives the development of military technology. New technology also spreads across national boundaries in response to military demands engendered by the ceaseless, competitive search for national security. Efforts to halt such transfer of technology may briefly retard it, but, in the absence of the removal of the sources of tension that motivate it, nothing can stop it for long.

Tensions: The effect of rising tensions between nations is to inflame resentments and to harden positions on both sides. An effort to lower tensions may well have the opposite effect.

Territory: A ceded territory on a nation's borders is a constant memorial to its humiliation.

Terror, banditry: From the point of view of the ruling authorities, bandits and terrorists look much the same. But bandits are motivated by greed; terrorists by political ambition. The difference is decisive. Bandits can be eliminated by force alone but terrorists cannot be suppressed without the skillful use of propaganda, political action, and cooption as well as the use of force.

Terror, insurrection: Terror is a classic opening phase of insurgency. It aims to discredit the authorities and weaken their capacity to govern as part of a strategy directed at displacing and delegitimizing them.

Terrorism: Asymmetric warfare through dramatic acts of violence against targets conventionally considered to be off limits, e.g., innocent civilians or noncombatants. Terrorism seeks to influence political behavior by unnerving public opinion and stimulating opposition to the authorities, by calling attention to grievances, or by provoking retaliatory action to trigger a wider or more savage conflict that will draw recruits to its cause.

Terrorism: Terrorism is the pursuit of political goals by criminally violent means.

Terrorism: The use of violence against noncombatants, civilians, or other persons normally considered to be illegitimate targets of military action for the purpose of attracting attention to a political cause, forcing those aloof from the struggle to join it, or intimidating opponents into concessions.

Terrorism: Terrorism is "any action intended to cause death or serious bodily harm to civilians or noncombatants, when the purpose of such an act, by its nature or context, is to intimidate a population or compel a government or an international organization to carry out or to abstain from any act."
—Kofi Annan (as Secretary-General of the United Nations)

Terrorism: "Terrorism is a technique of warfare—political intimidation through the killing of unarmed noncombatants."
—Zbigniew Brzezinski

Terrorism: "Terrorism is simply a term for the murder of noncombatants for political ends." —Patrick J. Buchanan

Terrorism causes: Terrorism begins as the desperate reaction of the powerless to humiliating injustice; the power it gains for its practitioners then addicts them to it.

Terrorism, poverty: "Terrorism is the war of the poor; war is the terrorism of the rich." —Hannah Arendt

Terrorism, purpose: "The purpose of terrorism is to terrorize." —V.I. Lenin

Theory, plan: A theory about what will happen is not a plan and should not be confused with one.

Third world: A loose grouping of states standing between two competing power blocs and politically affiliated with neither.

Third world: An unmodernized region or country often admired for its handicrafts but held in poverty by an intrusive, incompetent, and venal bureaucracy, usually under the political direction of a sanctimonious political movement, demagogue, or dictator.

Threat: Anticipated harm. In diplomacy, a threat is the menace of damage to national interests arising from hostile intentions on the part of a foreign nation. If the foreign nation is not hostile or antagonistic, it is no threat. In military science, a threat is the possibility of harm or humiliation arising from the exercise of the military capabilities of a potential adversary, without regard to his intentions. To the military, any nation with the capacity to harm one's own, even a friendly nation, poses a possible threat.

Threats: Before you make a threat, consider what you will do if it becomes public or the other side rejects it. Will you be prepared to make good on it? If not, how will you slide gracefully off your bluff?

Threats: "Threats without power are like powder without ball." —Nathan Bailey

Threats: "I hold it to be proof of great prudence for men to abstain from threats and insulting words to anyone, for neither diminishes the strength of the enemy; but the one makes him more cautious, and the other increases his hatred of you, and makes him more persevering in his efforts to injure you." —Niccolò Machiavelli

Threats, credibility of: A threat may be made more credible by the taking of some much more limited action that implies seriousness of purpose and a willingness to sacrifice to realize national interests.

Threats, credibility of: The threats of those notorious for unpredictable behavior and rash actions are much more likely to be believed than those of men admired for their statesmanship and prudence. A reputation for willfulness and even irrational risk-taking, even though acquired in games and on other matters of small import, can therefore be an asset when major interests are at stake.

Threats, empty: The only thing worse than empty threats is empty threats followed by generous concessions.

Threats, enemies: Threats unite enemies; conciliatory gestures divide them.

Threats, enemies: "The best enemies are those that make threats."   —GERMAN PROVERB

Threats, implied: "You will get more with a kind word and a gun than with a kind word alone."   —AL CAPONE

Threats, phases of military: Threats of military action move through stages. Efforts to reveal (or exaggerate) the extent of one's manpower, war industries, military traditions, internal fervor on the issue at hand, and international backing, all can constitute a reminder to another state that one retains the capacity to use forceful rather than peaceful means to resolve disputes.

Timing: "One should proceed against one's enemy whenever, by so doing, the enemy can be weakened or crushed."   —ARTHASASTRA OF KAUTILYA

Toasts: "The ability to give a good toast, when the occasion requires, is one of the minor but important skills which marks the professional diplomat. Toasts can be a useful tool in the diplomatic trade because they are delivered before listeners of influence. Too often, however, the opportunity is wasted in graceful words that have no substance. Good toasts should be gracious, of course, and gracefully delivered, but they should also get across a useful point—one which the diplomat-speaker believes is important to convey at that particular time. They should also be brief."   —WILLIAM MACOMBER, 1975

Tour d'horizon: A diplomatic discussion that roams the subjects of common concern.

Tour of duty: The projected period of assignment of a diplomat to his post.

Tour of duty: "One usually has to be at a post at least a year before one has gotten one's bearings, and established one's relationships, and sensed the important people that you want to cultivate and develop, and established your own rating system for the validity of the information and the soundness of the judgments that you extract, and learned the country and its problems."   —LIVINGSTON MERCHANT, 1983

Trade, free: "Free trade! What is it? Why, breaking down the barriers that separate nations; those barriers behind which nestle the feelings of pride, revenge, hatred and jealousy, which every now and then burst their bounds and deluge whole countries with blood; those feelings which nourish the poison of war and conquest."—RICHARD COBDEN

Trade, free: "the economic advantages of commerce are surpassed in importance by those of its effects, which are intellectual and moral. It is hardly possible to overrate the value, in the present low state of human improvement, of placing human beings in contact with persons dissimilar to themselves, and with modes of thought and action unlike those with which they are familiar. Commerce is now, what war once was, the principal source of this contact. There is no nation which does not need to borrow from others, not merely particular arts or practices, but essential points of character in which its own type is inferior."
—JOHN STUART MILL

Training, responsibility of ambassadors for: As the most senior member of his profession present in an embassy, an ambassador has a duty to tutor his juniors in the essentials of diplomatic tradecraft, to evaluate their potential successfully to pursue a diplomatic career, and to ensure that the most promising among them are assigned to places and positions where they can begin to develop into what they have the capacity to be.

Tranquility, respect: "No government could give us tranquility and happiness at home, which did not possess sufficient stability and strength to make us respectable abroad."
—ALEXANDER HAMILTON

Transactions, diplomatic: "Something-for-something is good business; it is equally good diplomacy."
—ELLIS BRIGGS, 1968

Translation, courtesy: Written communications with a foreign government should be provided both in one's own language and in the language of the host country. It is important to retain control over the way in which one's own government's positions are stated, even in languages other than its own. Providing a courtesy translation in the other side's language reduces misunderstanding, speeds consideration of the issues under discussion, and reduces problems in translating the text of a final agreement.

Translation reveals meaning: "The ultimate assay of the thought content and real meaning in any utterance is to put it through the acid test of interpretation. What is good honest metal rings true with meaning that remains in any words and any language. What is gilt and dross, mere verbiage, can be put into another language, but the process reveals how empty of significance it was in the first place, and the interpreter recoils from the degrading and cynical search for something equally meaningless in another tongue."
—ROBERT B. EKVALL

Transnational: Referring to activities carried out across national borders by the citizens, corporations, or subnational levels of government of two or more states. See also *International* and *Multinational*.

Treaties, duration of: "Treaties at best are but complied with so long as interest requires their fulfillment. Consequently, they are virtually binding on the weaker party only; or, in plain truth, they are not binding at all." —WASHINGTON IRVING, 1809

Treaty: A solemn, formal, and mutually binding contractual agreement between two states. See also *Agreements*.

Trends: "Statesmen stand or fall on their perception of trends." —HENRY A. KISSINGER, 1994

Tribe: A tribe is a political identity based on claims of kinship.

Tribes: "Great powers should never get involved in the politics of small tribes." —KAMAL SALIBI

Tripwire: A relatively modest force stationed where it would surely be overwhelmed by enemy attack, generating a compelling political case for military reprisal and counterattack. The deployment of a tripwire force on the territory of allies or protectorates is an earnest of resolve—a classic technique of deterrence.

Triumph: "Victory and defeat are the negation of diplomacy. The diplomat should never forget that the problem he is working on is of only relative importance in that it is one of of an unending series that must be discussed with the other party through the years, and therefore, while he must do as much as is expedient for his country, it must be within such limits and under such terms as will obviate resentment and a sense of injustice in future negotiations. It is important to have everybody satisfied, so that they bring to the next meeting a desire for further agreement and not a yearning for revenge—the inevitable result of defeat." —HUGH GIBSON, 1944

Trouble, sources of: "At any moment of the day or night, two thirds of the world's people are awake, and some of them are up to no good." —DEAN RUSK

Truce: "If without reason one begs for a truce it is assuredly because affairs in his country are in a dangerous state and he wishes to make a plan to gain a respite. Or otherwise, he knows that our situation is susceptible to his plots and he wants to forestall our suspicions by asking for a truce. Then he will take advantage of our unpreparedness." —CHEN HAO

Trust, bluffing and: "It is in the interest of the sharpest, most antagonistic negotiator to sincerely foster feelings of trust, since discovery of false deadlines and bad faith destroys

the element he needs to draw a sharp bargain. The more a negotiator wants to bluff, the more he needs to appear trustworthy in order to carry off his deception when its moment comes."
—I. WILLIAM ZARTMAN AND MAUREEN R. BERMAN, 1982

Trust, enhancing: "Trust is enhanced if a negotiator can demonstrate a genuine interest in trying to help the other side reach its objective while retaining his own objective and making the two appear compatible. . . . Trust is enhanced when a party can show or be shown that the action [it is being persuaded to take] is in its interest."
—I. WILLIAM ZARTMAN AND MAUREEN R. BERMAN, 1982

Trust, in agreements: "Trust is enhanced by step-by-step agreements with 'accounting points' along the way [and] when there is an early return on the agreement."
—I. WILLIAM ZARTMAN AND MAUREEN R. BERMAN, 1982

Truth: "True artifice is the truth, spoken sometimes with force and always with grace."
—CHOISEUL

Truth: "The highest diplomacy consists largely of plain and truthful statement."
—CHARLES G. DAWES, 1935

Truth: "In politics, what is believed becomes more important than what is true."
—TALLEYRAND

Truth: "Truth is such a precious article, let us all economize on its use."   —MARK TWAIN

Ultimata: Ultimata are dangerous tools in diplomacy. To be effective, ultimata must be credible to those to whom they are directed and must convey the prospect of intolerable losses to them, quite disproportionate to any conceivable gain from noncompliance. This means not only that those making the threat must clearly have the capacity to carry it out and that it must be believed that they will do so at the threatened moment, but also that the damage they propose to wreak must be such that the adversary will assess it to outweigh pride and the emotional gains to be had from continued defiance. Judging whether an adversary will reach this conclusion involves careful consideration of his mindset and of that of his domestic supporters and opponents. No ultimatum should be so final that an adversary lacks time to digest it and to choose his answer after the mature reflection born of internal consultation and debate.

Ultimatum: A threat, indicating a final position that, if not accepted within a time limit, will lead to action, often military in nature.

Understanding, mutual: It is not true that greater understanding between peoples leads inevitably to better relations. Sometimes the more one people knows of another, the less regard it has for them. Wars are caused as often by excessively accurate mutual understanding as by the lack of it.

Understandings: Unwritten understandings between friendly nations reflective of a community of interest tend to be more durable than written treaties between adversaries.

Undertakings: "Never agree to do something unless you know you can do it. If you give your word, you had better deliver. That way you develop trust. Trust is the coin of the realm." —Bryce Harlow, quoted by George P. Shultz, 1993

Undiplomatic: Part of diplomacy is knowing when to be undiplomatic.

United Nations: "The legislative process in the United Nations is not a substitute for diplomacy. It serves its purpose only when it helps diplomacy to arrive at agreements between the national states concerned. It is diplomacy, not speeches or votes, that continues to have the last word in the process of peace-making." —Dag Hammarskjöld, 1958

United Nations: "You can safely appeal to the United Nations in the comfortable certainty that it will let you down." —Conor Cruise O'Brien, 1985

United Nations: "The United Nations was not designed to be, nor is it adequate to serve as, either a law-making body for the world or a court to judge the nations of the world. It is a forum for diplomacy, and true diplomacy is the art of dialogue in pursuit of common goals and the avoidance of war."   —ANDREW YOUNG

United Nations, debate at: "Since the legislative processes of the United Nations do not lead to legislation, and the power of decision remains in the hands of the national governments, the value of public debate can be measured only by the degree to which it contributes to the winning of agreement by the processes of diplomacy. If public debate contributes to winning consent either immediately or in the long run, it serves the purpose of peace-making. If it does not so contribute, then it may be a useless, or even harmful exercise."   —DAG HAMMARSKJÖLD, 1958

United Nations, infirmities of: "The United Nations perfectly embodies in institutional form the tragic paradox of our age; it has become indispensable before it has become effective. To exist at all it cannot depart very far from its present structure; to develop at all it requires the focus and drive which only a permanent and potent leader can give it."
                                                                      —HERBERT NICHOLAS

United Nations, representation at the: The United Nations provides a convenient central point of contact with other governments for states that cannot afford to establish or do not have the personnel to staff many embassies internationally.

Unprecedented: "In foreign policy, the term 'unprecedented' is always somewhat suspect, because the actual range of innovation is so circumscribed by history, domestic institutions, and geography."   —HENRY A. KISSINGER, 1994

Useful: "There are few ironclad rules of diplomacy but to one there is no exception. When an official reports that talks were useful, it can safely be concluded that nothing was accomplished."   —JOHN KENNETH GALBRAITH, 1969

Uti pssidetis: What is currently held (possessed) by participants in a dispute or conflict.

Values, interests: Shared moral views can ease communication between peoples and unite nations in condemnation of those with contrasting values and standards of behavior, but they do not provide a basis for joint action. The resolve of states to exert themselves for a common purpose comes from their perception that they share political, economic, and security interests.

Values, national: Peoples assign the highest value to what is scarcest among them. Thus a nation that extols sincerity may reasonably be suspected to lack it. And one that emphasizes the virtue of plain dealing is likely to be uncommonly tricky.

Vanity: "Diplomatists, especially those who are appointed to, and liable to remain in, smaller posts, are apt to pass by slow gradations from ordinary human vanity to an inordinate sense of their own importance. The whole apparatus of diplomatic life—the ceremonial, the court functions, the large houses, the lackeys and the food—induces an increasing sclerosis of personality." —Harold Nicolson

Vanity: "The dangers of vanity in a negotiator can scarcely be exaggerated. It tempts him to disregard the advice or opinions of those who may have had longer experience of a country, or of a problem, than he possesses himself. It renders him vulnerable to the flattery or attacks of those with whom he is negotiating. It encourages him to take too personal a view of the nature and purposes of his functions and in extreme cases to prefer a brilliant but undesirable triumph to some unostentatious but more prudent compromise. It leads him to boast of victories and thereby to incur the hatred of those whom he has vanquished. It may prevent him, at some crucial moment, from confessing to his government that his predictions or his information were incorrect. It prompts him to incur or to provoke unnecessary friction over matters which are of purely social importance. It may cause him to offend by ostentation or ordinary vulgarity. It is at the root of all indiscretion and most tactlessness. It lures its addicts into displaying their own verbal brilliance, and into such fatal diplomatic indulgences as irony, epigrams, insinuations, and the barbed reply. And it may bring in its train those other vices of imprecision, excitability, impatience, emotionalism and even untruthfulness." —Harold Nicolson, 1939

Vengeance: Vengeance is gratifying but invites retaliation by survivors connected to those against which it is exacted.

Venue: The site of a meeting or conference.

Venue: It is often thought to be humiliating for a powerful state to send its negotiators to the capital of its weaker adversary, but there may be advantages in doing so. There are benefits to being on home ground, but liabilities as well. Those who are far from home can plausibly claim a lack of authority to respond on the spot to the positions of the other side. This excuse is not readily available to those who are in their own capital. The willingness of one side to visit the other's capital gives away nothing but can be portrayed as a significant gesture in itself, placing the burden for reciprocal gestures on the government receiving it. Obligations of hospitality to visitors may also come into play. Most importantly, the visiting delegation may be able to draw out the other side and to explore the flexibility of their negotiating position, while reserving its own on the grounds that it must refer to its leadership before answering.

Verification: The process of confirming the adherence of another party to its treaty or other obligations, usually related to arms control or redeployment of forces, with this party's cooperation through agreed inspection procedures, as well as without its cooperation through unilaterally obtained intelligence.

Vice consul: A consular official ranking below a consul but above a consular agent. See also *Consul*.

Vice consulate: A small consulate headed by a vice consul. See also *Consulate*.

Viciousness: The human animal is vicious. If attacked, it will defend itself.
—French aphorism

Victor, bargaining position of: "The bargaining position of the victor always diminishes with time. Whatever is not exacted during the shock of defeat becomes increasingly difficult to attain later."
—Henry A. Kissinger, 1994

Victor, vanquished: Wars are not over when the victor proclaims his triumph; they end only when the vanquished accepts defeat.

Victors, rights of: "War gives the right to the conquerors to impose any conditions they please upon the vanquished."
—Julius Caesar, c. 51 b.c.

Victory: "In victory, magnanimity; in peace, good will."
—Winston Churchill

Victory: "The only excuse for going to war is to be able to live in peace undisturbed. When victory is won we should spare those who have not been bloodthirsty or barbarous in their warfare."
—Cicero

Victory: "Victory is by nature insolent and haughty."
—Cicero, 46 b.c.

Victory: "Victory consists not solely of overcoming the enemy forces; it must include attainment of the objective for which the conflict was waged."
—Carl Maria von Clausewitz

Victory: "Victory in the true sense implies that the state of peace, and of one's people, is better after the war than before. Victory in this sense is only possible if a quick result can be gained or if a long effort can be economically proportioned to the national resources. The end must be adjusted to the means." —BASIL LIDDELL HART, 1974

Victory: "Certain peace is better and safer than anticipated victory." —LIVY, C. 29 B.C.

Victory: "To win without fighting is best." —SUNZI

Victory, best: "The most complete and happy victory is this: to compel one's enemy to give up his purpose, while suffering no harm oneself." —BELISARIUS

Victory, causes of war: Victory conveniently erases memories of what caused a war to happen in the first place.

Victory, dangers of: "Nothing is more dangerous to a nation than victory. Very few people know how to taste a victory without being swallowed up by it. Defeat is the supreme stimulus for a nation of spirit." —LÉON GAMBETTA

Victory, defeated rulers and: "A defeated ruler should never be spared." —STENDHAL (HENRI BEYLE), 1818

Victory, painless: "A victory gained before the situation has crystallized is one the common man does not comprehend. Thus its author gains no reputation for sagacity. Before he has bloodied his blade the enemy state has submitted." —DU MU

Victory, problems of: Victory is a more difficult art than war.

Victory, problems of: "The problems of victory are more agreeable than those of defeat, but they are no less difficult." —WINSTON CHURCHILL

Victory, problems of: "Next to a battle lost, the greatest misery is a battle gained." —WELLINGTON

Victory, strategy of: The wise are careful to establish the conditions for victory before beginning to fight. Fighting first and then trying to wring victory from the results is a recipe for strategic defeat.

Victory, tasks of diplomacy and: "A military victory always has two components, its physical reality and its psychological impact, and it is the task of diplomacy to translate the latter into political terms." —HENRY A. KISSINGER, 1964

Victory, use of: Victory counts for nothing if those who gain it don't know what to make of it.

Victory, use of: "It is no doubt a good thing to conquer on the field of battle, but it needs greater wisdom and greater skill to make use of victory." —POLYBIUS, C. 125 B.C.

Vienna Convention on Consular Relations: A convention, dated 1963, that codified international practice with regard to consular privileges and immunities.

Vienna Convention on Diplomatic Relations: A convention, dated 1961, that codified international practice with regard to the privileges and immunities of diplomatic missions, diplomats, and their functions.

Violence: Violence sires violence; atrocities beget atrocities. Revenge fathers revenge.

Virtues, in different societies: Generally, political cultures place the highest value on those traits that are rarest among their officials. Thus, a society that values sincerity is most likely to lack it; one that esteems straightforwardness is probably prone to sharp practices; and one that reserves its highest praise for probity may reliably be presumed to be wanting in it.

Visa: A recommendation by a consular officer that the immigration officials of his sending state admit a foreign national for temporary or permanent residence.

Vision: "Where there is no vision, the people perish." —PROVERBS XXIX, v. 18

Vituperation: "Strong and bitter words indicate a weak cause." —VICTOR HUGO

Voting in international organizations: "If we vote this way, what are the consequences? If we vote that way, what are the consequences? This is how I make my policy. The rights and wrongs of the matter will make interesting reading, but not to decide my policy." —S. RAJARATNAM, QUOTED BY MARTIN MAYER

Wallets, wits: Those who cannot live by their wallets must live by their wits.

War: War is the ultimate argument of the state.

War: War is what happens when politics fails.

War: "War must be regarded as only a means to peace; action as a means to leisure."
—ARISTOTLE

War: "War is too important to be left to the generals." —GEORGES CLEMENCEAU

War: "War is delightful for those who have had no experience of it." —ERASMUS

War: "It is simply not true that war never settles anything." —FELIX FRANKFURTER

War: "Against war it may be said that it makes the victor stupid and the vanquished revengeful."
—NIETZSCHE, 1878

War, abolition of: "The only way to abolish war [is] to make peace heroic."
—JOHN DEWEY

War, abolition of: "War can only be abolished through war, and in order to get rid of the gun it is necessary to take up the gun."
—MAO ZEDONG

War, alliances in: "Whenever you go to war, establish cordial relations with neighboring countries. Form alliances to draw them into helping you. If you attack your enemies from the front while your allies attack from behind, your enemies will surely be vanquished."
—LIU JI, FOURTEENTH CENTURY

War, causes of: "In the nature of man we find three principal causes of quarrel. First, competition; secondly, diffidence; thirdly, glory. The first maketh men invade for gain; the second, for safety; the third, for reputation."
—THOMAS HOBBES, 1651

War, civil: "A civil war is a violent conflict within a country, fought by organized groups that aim to take power at the center or in a region, or to change government policies."
—JAMES D. FEARON

War, cold: "Cold wars are covert and protracted wars." —ADDA BOZEMAN, 1992

War, conflict resolution: "The point of war as an instrument of policy, as a means of resolving a conflict of interests, is lost if the use of force does not issue in the establishment of new relations between the belligerents; that is, if the new relationship between them is not legitimized by agreement. No more than the mere decision to use force can guarantee a victorious outcome, can the successful use of force by itself ensure that the political effects of decisions reached in fighting will be long-lasting. To achieve these lasting effects, shifts in the relative positions of states which have been made manifest on the field of battle have to be translated into accepted settlements. This is the work of diplomacy."
—Adam Watson, 1982

War, conventional: War excluding the use of weapons of objectionably indiscriminate destructive power, such as nuclear, biological, or chemical weapons or other means of mass destruction.

War, costs and benefits: "There should be no action in the absence of benefit; there should be no effort in the absence of gain; there should be no fighting in the absence of a threat. A lord should not use armed forces because of anger, and a general should not fight because of anger. Act when a benefit can be achieved; stop when the course of action is harmful to achieving a benefit."
—Sunzi

War, defined: War is "a violent clash of interests between or among organized groups characterized by the use of military force."
—U.S. Army Field Manual

War, defined: "War is . . . an act of force to compel our enemy to do our will."
—Carl Maria von Clausewitz

War, delight in: "To delight in war is a merit in the soldier, a dangerous quality in the captain, and a positive crime in the statesman."
—George Santayana, 1906

War, democracies and: "Peoples (because they have no conception of what war means) are thoughtlessly ready sometimes to plunge into war, but Governments are usually reluctant."
—R.B. Mowat, 1936

War, diplomacy and: War refutes the fundamental assumption of diplomacy that states are rational actors rather than aggregations of temporarily deranged human beings.

War, diplomatic prelude to: "When the enemy's envoys speak in humble tones but he continues his preparations, he will advance."
—Sunzi

War, economics of: "The object of those who make war, either from choice or ambition, is to conquer and to maintain their conquests, and to do this in such a manner as to enrich themselves and not to impoverish the conquered country. To do this, then, the conqueror should take care not to spend too much, and in all things mainly to look to the public benefit."
—Niccolò Machiavelli

War, guerilla: Irregular warfare by forces not in uniform and intermingled with a populace, who lack a commitment to defend specific territory and frequently engage in acts of terrorism.

War, guerilla: "The guerilla wins if he does not lose; the conventional army loses if it does not win."
—HENRY A. KISSINGER, 1969

War, guerilla: "Guerilla wars are about winners and losers, not about compromise."
—HENRY A. KISSINGER, 1994

War, impact of: "Wars transform the future. They move boundaries, topple governments, expand or break up empires, and leave scars of death and destruction. The battles fought during a war, of course, contribute to its aftermath; but it is the way in which a war is brought to an end that has the most decisive long-term impact."   —FRED C. IKLÉ, 1991

War, instigators: "Monarchs ought to put to death the authors and instigators of war, as their sworn enemies and as dangers to their states."   —QUEEN ELIZABETH I

War, just: "A just war is in the long run far better for a nation's soul than the most prosperous peace obtained by acquiescence in wrong or injustice. Moreover, though it is criminal for a nation not to prepare for war, so that it may escape the dreadful consequences of being defeated in war, yet it must always be remembered that even to be defeated in war may be far better than not to have fought at all."
—THEODORE ROOSEVELT, 1906

War, justification for: War may rightly be undertaken to diminish the strength of a power whose growth implies a future danger to its neighbors.

War, justification for: "To enfeeble a prince of a state whose power increases day by day for fear that, if permitted to increase too much, it may upon occasion inflict injury is unjustifiable that one has a right to attack another because he has power to do harm, is contrary to all the rules of equity. Such is the constitution of human life that one never exists in perfect security. It is not by the employment of force, but in the protection of Providence and by innocent precautions that one should seek resources of defence against the fear of uncertain danger."   —HUGO GROTIUS, 1625

War, justification for: "War is not merely justifiable, but imperative, upon honorable men, upon an honorable nation, where peace can only be obtained by the sacrifice of conscientious conviction or of national welfare."   —THEODORE ROOSEVELT, 1906

War, liberty: "Of all the enemies to public liberty war is, perhaps, the most to be dreaded because it comprises and develops the germ of every other. War is the parent of armies; from these proceed debts and taxes . . . known instruments for bringing the many under

the domination of the few. . . . No nation could preserve its freedom in the midst of continual warfare."
—James Madison

War, limited: War for objectives declared by those conducting it to be narrow and limited rather than broad and open-ended. The purpose of such a declared limitation of objectives is to diminish the apparent challenge to the strategic interests of potential adversaries and thereby forestall the broadening of the war to include them. Limited war, in a self-defeating variant, is also occasionally taken to mean the pursuit of broad ends by strictly limited means, an approach more likely to produce frustration than victory.

War, limited: "There are three prerequisites for a strategy of limited war: (1) the limited war force must be able to prevent the potential aggressor from creating a fait accompli; (2) they must be of a nature to convince the aggressor that their use, while involving an increased risk of all-out war, is not an inevitable prelude to it; (3) they must be coupled with a diplomacy which succeeds in conveying that all-out war is not the sole response to aggression and that there exists a willingness to negotiate a settlement short of unconditional surrender."
—Henry A. Kissinger, 1960

War, location of: "A prince who has his people well armed and disciplined for war should always await a powerful and dangerous enemy at home, and should not go to meet him at a distance. But a prince whose subjects are unarmed, and the country unaccustomed to war, should always keep it as far away from home as possible; and thus both one and the other will best defend themselves, each in his own way."
—Niccolò Machiavelli

War, logic of: "For any war effort—offensive or defensive—that is supposed to serve long-term national objectives, the most essential question is how the enemy might be forced to surrender, or failing that, what sort of bargain might be struck with him to terminate the war."
—Fred C. Iklé, 1991

War, military vs. diplomatic influence during: "Changes in the internal structure of government furnish a further and particularly important reason why wars are easier to start than to stop. When a nation becomes engaged in a major war, a new set of men and new government agencies often move into the center of power. As 'diplomacy breaks down' at the beginning of hostilities, the role of foreign ministries in dealing with the enemy is much diminished. The influence that comes with day-to-day decisions is transferred to military staffs. At the very moment that diplomats are being expelled from the enemy capitals, the military leaders come to command a vastly increased segment of national resources. This shift in political influence means that the governments on both sides in a war will be concerned primarily with their current military efforts."
—Fred C. Iklé, 1991

War, moral position in: Before entering a war, a great state must secure not only its military but also its moral position.
—Attributed to Metternich

War, negotiation as path to: The object of a negotiation can be either agreement or rupture. If the desired outcome of the negotiations is rupture and the manufacture of a casus belli, it is best to phrase one's demands in terms of principles with wide appeal, the application of which would be ruinous for one's opponent in the matter at issue. One should insist on discussing these principles rather than practical solutions to the problems at hand in order to lay a basis for charging one's opponent with such unreasonable disregard for principle as to have made dealing with him impossible. On the other hand, if the object is to reach agreement, it is best to phrase one's demands in terms of the practical results they will produce and to stress the benefits or lack of concrete injury their acceptance will bring to the other side.

War, objectives of: "He who wishes to fight must first reckon the cost."　　—Cao Cao

War, objectives of: "The aim of war is to be able to live unhurt in peace."　—Cicero, 78 b.c.

War, objectives of: "When you strike at a king, you must kill him."
　　　　　　　　　　　　　　　　　　—Ralph Waldo Emerson

War, objectives of: "It is fatal to enter any war without the will to win it."
　　　　　　　　　　　　　　　　　　—Douglas MacArthur, 1952

War, objectives of: "Nations ought in time of peace to do to one another all the good they can, and in time of war as little harm as possible, without prejudicing their real interests."
　　　　　　　　　　　　　　　　　　—Montesquieu

War, objectives of: "Stay your hand or strike to kill; half measures leave walking enemies."
　　　　　　　　　　　　　　　　　　—Proverb

War, objectives of: The first question anyone planning to start a war, or to respond with force to an act of aggression, should ask is not whether his nation's forces can prevail in battle. That is indeed a vital question. In addition, he should ask what objectives, once achieved, would justify ending the war, and why anyone on the other side should regard these changes in the status quo as either temporarily or permanently acceptable. How will the fighting be ended? On what terms? Negotiated by and with whom? What happens after the conflict is over? Will the seeds of future military actions be planted in the terms of the peace? If there are no clear answers to these questions, the better course may well be to refrain from threatening or initiating military action.

War, offensive: "Time . . . is less likely to bring favor to the victor than to the vanquished . . . An offensive war requires above all a quick, irresistible decision. . . . Any kind of interruption, pause, or suspension of activity is inconsistent with the nature of offensive war."
　　　　　　　　　　　　　　　　　　—Carl Maria von Clausewitz

War, order: "War decides order."
　　　　　　　　　　　　　　　　　　—Chinese military aphorism

War, outcome of: "Governments tend to lose sight of the ending of wars and the nation's interests that lie beyond it, precisely because fighting a war is an effort of such vast magnitude. Thus it can happen that military men, while skillfully planning their intricate operations and coordinating complicated maneuvers, remain curiously blind in failing to perceive that it is the outcome of the war, not the outcome of the campaigns within it, that determines how well their plans serve the nation's interests. At the same time, the senior statesmen may hesitate to insist that these beautifully planned campaigns be linked to some clear ideas for ending the war, while expending their authority and energy to oversee some tactical details of the fighting. If generals act like constables and senior statesmen act like adjutants, who will be left to guard the nation's interests?"
—FRED C. IKLÉ, 1991

War, peace: In war, one fights one's enemies; in peace, one contends with one's friends.

War, peace: "Although every war is fought in the name of peace, there is a tendency to define victory as the absence of war and to confuse it with military victory. To discuss conditions of peace during wartime seems almost indecent, as if the admission that the war might end could cause a relaxation of the effort. This is no accident. The logic of war is power, and power has no inherent limit. The logic of peace is proportion, and proportion implies limitation. The success of war is victory; the success of peace is stability. The conditions of victory are commitment, the condition of stability is self-restraint. The motivation of war is extrinsic: the fear of an enemy. The motivation of peace is intrinsic: the balance of forces and the acceptance of its legitimacy. A war without an enemy is inconceivable; a peace built on the myth of an enemy is an armistice. It is the temptation of war to punish; it is the task of peace to construct. Power can sit in judgment, but statesmanship must look to the future."
—HENRY A. KISSINGER, 1964

War, peace: "The only thing you prevent by war is peace."
—HARRY S. TRUMAN

War, peace, success in: "The success of war is victory; the success of peace is stability."
—HENRY A. KISSINGER, 1964

War, policy: "War is nothing but the continuation of policy with other means."
—CARL MARIA VON CLAUSEWITZ

War, policy failure: Without clear and attainable objectives, war is the entrenchment of policy failure by other means.

War, policymakers and: "War hath no fury like a non-combatant." —C.E. MONTAGUE, 1922

War, preventive: "Preventive war is like committing suicide out of fear of death."
—ATTRIBUTED TO OTTO VON BISMARCK

War, starting: "No one starts a war—or rather, no one in his senses ought to do so—without first being clear in his mind what he intends to achieve by that war and how he intends to conduct it."
—CARL MARIA VON CLAUSEWITZ

War, weapons: "Weapons are an important factor in war, but not the decisive factor; it is people, not things, that are decisive. A contest of strength is not only a contest of military and economic power, but also a contest of human power and morale."   —MAO ZEDONG

Wars, popular: "There have been almost as many popular as royal wars."
—ALEXANDER HAMILTON, 1788

War, preventing: "The surest way to prevent war is not to fear it."   —JOHN RANDOLPH, 1806

War, punishment and: "War may be defined as punishment, which is one of the functions of government."
—DU MU

War, purpose of: "The legitimate object of war is a more perfect peace."
—WILLIAM TECUMSEH SHERMAN, 1882

War, purpose of: "The object of war is to obtain a better peace—even if only from your own point of view. It is essential to conduct war with constant regard to the peace you desire. If you concentrate exclusively on victory, with no thought for the aftereffect, you may be too exhausted to profit by the peace, while it is almost certain that the peace will be a bad one, containing the germs of another war."   —BASIL LIDDELL HART, 1974

War, purpose of: "War is a highly concentrated and specialized form of violence between states. It is usually on a much larger and deadlier scale than other forms of violence, and is also usually subject to certain rules and conventions, like the treatment of prisoners, which other forms of international violence do not respect. But like other forms of planned and organized violence it is a means to an end. Political entities do not resort to force for pleasure, though some individuals may enjoy the thrill and excitement of violence and war. They resort to force in order to attain a political goal: for instance, in order to correct what they consider an unjust or unfair situation, or to defend what they consider just and right against violence by others."   —ADAM WATSON, 1983

War, resort to: Never take by force what you can induce the other side to agree to give you, however reluctantly, by means short of unilateral or violent action.

War, risk of: See *Power, distribution of.*

War, rules of: "The laws of war, that restrain the exercise of rapine and murder, are founded on two principles of substantial interest: the knowledge of the permanent benefits which can be obtained by a moderate use of conquest, and a just apprehension lest

the desolation which we inflict on the enemy's country may be retaliated on our own."
—EDWARD GIBBON

War, rules of: "It is impossible for one belligerent to depart from rules and precedents and for the other to remain bound by them."
—LORD GREY OF FALLODON

War, starting point of: "Wars begin in the minds of men."
—UNITED NATIONS EDUCATIONAL, SCIENTIFIC AND CULTURAL ORGANIZATION CHARTER

War, state of: "Every city [state] is in a normal state of war with every other, not indeed proclaimed by heralds, but everlasting."
—PLATO

War, termination of: "Do not exact conditions which will compel your former adversary to await his time for revenge."
—ATTRIBUTED TO COUNT OTTO VON BISMARCK

War, termination of: "If it is difficult to start a war, it is almost impossible to end it until it has run its course—that is, until one side is completely ruined and the other side almost, if not quite, ruined."
—R.B. MOWAT, 1936

War, termination of: ". . . the timing of a war's end is determined more by the loser than by the winner; that is, it is probably more sensible to think of wars being lost than won."
—JOHN MUELLER, 1989

War, termination of: "A peace to be durable—though nothing in this world is durable or permanent—should, as far as human foresight can provide, be moderate and just."
—ARTHUR NICOLSON, QUOTED BY HIS SON, HAROLD NICOLSON

War, termination of: "The quickest way of ending a war is to lose it." —GEORGE ORWELL

War, termination of: "It is always easy to begin a war, but very difficult to stop one, since its beginning and end are not under the control of the same man. Anyone, even a coward, can commence a war, but it can be brought to an end only with the consent of the victors."
—SALLUST

War, termination of: "Diplomacy has an important part to play at the onset of a war. When no adjustment can be found which satisfies all the parties, and they are left with the decision to resort to force, the role of the diplomat is to look to the future, to the conditions in which after the clash of arms the effort to compel can once more give way to the dialogue of persuasion. . . . Wise statesmen . . . will . . . bear in mind the future settlement with the enemy, and will see the advantage of making their demands on him as palatable as possible, so that he will be more easily brought to accept them and easier to live with in international society afterwards."
—ADAM WATSON, 1983

War, total: "When men become locked in battle, there should be no artifice under the name of politics which should handicap your own men."　　—Douglas MacArthur

War, victory in: "War is not only destructive, it is sterile of positive result. The most that military victory can do is to provide opportunity to attempt anew the establishment of durable international peace."　　　　—Dwight D. Eisenhower, 1946

War, victory objective of: "In war there is no substitute for victory."
　　　　　　　　　　　　　　　　　—Dwight D. Eisenhower, 1944

War, victory objective of: "War's very object is victory, not prolonged indecision. In war there is no substitute for victory."　　　　—Douglas MacArthur, 1951

War, without victory: If there is no clear victor in war or combat fails to secure the terms set by the victor, the issues will become less, not more, tractable. The bitter memory of conflict will imbue these issues with an emotional fervor far beyond that which they originally possessed.

War and diplomats: "While war is merely hell for the soldiers, it is unemployment and degradation for the diplomats."　　　　　　　—Martin Mayer, 1983

War begets war: "What can war beget except war? But good will begets good will; equity, equity."　　　　　　　　　　　　　　　　—Erasmus

War crime: A wartime act or pattern of behavior by the vanquished that the victor judges to be worthy of punishment through a judicial process.

War criminal: Someone on the losing side of a war who is punished for committing atrocities. (Those who commit atrocities for the winning side are promoted and celebrated as heroes.)

War strategy, diplomacy and: "Politics uses war for the attainment of its ends; it operates decisively at the beginning and at the end [of the conflict], of course, in such a manner that it refrains from increasing its demands during the war's duration or from being satisfied with an inadequate success. . . . Strategy can only direct its efforts toward the highest goal which the means available make attainable. In this way, it aids politics best, working only for its objectives, but in its operations independent of it."
　　　　　　　—Helmuth von Moltke ("The Elder"), 1872

Warfare, political: Political warfare is an aspect of grand strategy that combines polemics, propaganda, public diplomacy, subversion, and psychological operations.

Warriors: "The soldier is the statesman's junior partner."　　—Matthew B. Ridgway, 1954

Warriors: "Men who excel in the organization of victory are often blind to the special demands of writing the peace." —KENNETH W. THOMPSON, 1962

Warriors, as peacemakers: "A man who is used to command finds it almost impossible to learn to negotiate, because negotiation is an admission of finite power." —HENRY A. KISSINGER, 1964

Warriors, civilians and: "Civilians, with the timidity of amateurs when confronted by experts, often give way before . . . plain-spoken military men with their crisp language and resolute countenances. They do not realize that the military men (if minds could only be read) are equally timid when confronted by resolute civilians with political arguments." —R.B. MOWAT

Warriors, diplomats and: "When soldiers deal with one another, all goes well; but, as soon as the diplomats step in, the result is unadulterated stupidity." —ALEXANDER II (OF RUSSIA), 1863

Warriors, diplomats and: "The diplomat is the servant, not the master of the soldier." —THEODORE ROOSEVELT, 1897

Warriors, diplomats and: "The military wants to do what the diplomats don't think is necessary, and the diplomats want the military to do what the military is too nervous to do." —GEORGE P. SHULTZ, 1982

Warriors, diplomats and: "Politics and arms seem unhappily to be the two professions most natural to man, who must always be either negotiating or fighting." —VOLTAIRE

Warriors, politics and: "There is no greater fatuity than a political judgment dressed in a military uniform." —DAVID LLOYD GEORGE

Wartime, diplomacy in: "If we accept the notion that the object of war is to induce a certain frame of mind in the consciousness of the adversary and not to destroy him or to render him helpless in the determination of the postwar settlement, it follows that diplomacy is never in suspense. It has a three-phased task: to prevent war when possible; to control its course once it has broken out; and to end it as soon as possible in conditions likely to prevent its renewal." —ABBA EBAN, 1983

Wartime, diplomacy in: "In the course of the campaign the balance between the military will and the considerations of diplomacy can only be held by the supreme authority." —HELMUTH VON MOLTKE ("THE ELDER"), 1890

Wartime, diplomatic contacts in: "War is the negation of diplomacy, which means contact without arms. In war there is no contact between belligerents except by shot, shell, and bayonet. If the diplomatists on both sides were allowed to keep contact with each

other throughout hostilities, every war would find its end far sooner than it does."
—R.B. Mowat, 1936

Weakness: An appearance of weakness invites assault. Therefore, even the weak should strive to seem strong.

Weakness, client state: The very fragility of a client state is often the greatest source of its ability to manipulate its patron. By arguing that it may collapse, be forced to compromise with a common enemy, or otherwise damage its patron's interests if it is denied support, a client state can gain broad immunity from both pressure to reform and the consequences of acting against its patron's views and interests. Thus weakness becomes the basis for a game of blackmail, enabling the client state not merely to frustrate the will but sometimes to command the policy of its patron.

Weapon, best: "The best weapon against an enemy is another enemy."
—Friedrich Nietzsche

Weapons: Weapons are tools for making your enemies change their minds.

Weapons: "Weapons are of little use on the field of battle if there is no wise counsel at home."
—Cicero

Wickedness: There are many more stupid people than there are wicked. Never attribute something to wickedness when stupidity can explain it.

Will: "There are no purely political solutions any more than purely military solutions and . . ., in the relation among states, will may play as great a role as power."
—Henry A. Kissinger, 1957

Winning, losing: You can't win unless you try to win, but you can lose by trying not to lose.

Wisdon: "Men and nations do behave wisely, once all other alternatives have been exhausted."
—Abba Eban, 1967

Wits, power: The more power, the dimmer the wits can be. Absolute power is the prerequisite for utter witlessness.

Words: "To jaw-jaw is always better than to war-war."
—Winston Churchill

Words: "Nothing is more important to diplomacy than care in choosing and reporting words. Whether the formulations are vague or precise, other nations must assume that they were selected deliberately and with thought. That is why such care must be given

to statements made during official visits and in official speeches. In foreign ministries around the world, what you say gets quoted back to you, and you are expected to stand behind your words."
—George P. Shultz, 1993

Words: "The word is older than the state. Words form and reform states. Those who run states know the power of words and attempt to control them."
—Richard Stern, quoted by George P. Schultz, 1993

Words: "Words are swords."
—Talleyrand

Words, actions and: "A diplomat's words must have no relation to actions—otherwise what kind of diplomacy is it? Words are one thing, actions another. Good words are a concealment of bad deeds. Sincere diplomacy is no more possible than dry water or iron wood."
—Attributed to J.V. Stalin

Wrath, deflection of: "A soft answer turneth away wrath."   —Proverbs XV, 1, c. 350 b.c.

Zeal: "Above all, not too much zeal!"

—Attributed to Talleyrand

Zealotry: Not everyone regards survival as an imperative. Some prefer the dignity of death to the ignominy of peace on an enemy's terms.

Zealots: In games of "chicken," best let zealots have the right of way. Step aside to try a rematch against better odds!

Persons

Acheson, Dean (1893–1971). American statesman; Secretary of State, 1949–53.

Acton, Lord: John Emerich Edward Dalberg–Acton, 1st Baron Acton (1834–1902). English historian.

Adams, Abigail (1744–1818). Wife of John Adams, second President of the United States.

Adams, Henry Brooks (1838–1918). American historian.

Adams, John (1735–1826). American revolutionary leader, diplomat, and statesman; President of the United States, 1797–1801.

Adams, John Quincy (1767–1848). American diplomat and statesman; Secretary of State, 1817–25; President of the United States, 1825–29.

Adenauer, Konrad (1876–1967). German statesman.

Aeschylus (c. 525–456 B.C.). Greek poet and dramatist.

Aesop (c. 620–560 B.C.). Greek writer.

Alexander II: Aleksandr Nikolaevich (1818–81). Czar of Russia, 1855–81.

Allen, George Venable (1903–70). American diplomat.

Almeida, Francisco de. Early-nineteenth-century Portuguese statesman; Foreign Minister.

Ambler, Eric Clifford (1909–98). British author.

Annan, Kofi (1938–). Ghanaian diplomat; Secretary General of the United Nations, 1997–2006.

Antisthenes (445–365 B.C.). Greek philosopher.

Aristophanes. Late-fifth-, early-fourth-century B.C. Greek comic playwright.

Aristotle (384–322 B.C.) Greek philosopher.

Aron, Raymond (1905–83). French scholar.

Assad, Bashar ibn Hafez Al- (1965–). President of Syria, 2000–.

Augustine, Saint: Aurelius Augustinus (354–430). Christian philosopher.

Austin, Warren (1877–1963). American politician and diplomat.

Azo (Gialamo Giganti) (d. 1560). Venetian jurist.

Bacon, Francis (1561–1626). English philosopher and statesman.

Bagehot, Walter (1826–77). English economist.

Bailey, Nathan (d. 1742). English lexicographer.

Bailey, Thomas A. (1902–83). American historian.

Bakunin, Mikhail A. (1814–1876). Russian anarchist.

Balfour, Arthur James, 1st Earl of Balfour (1848–1930). British politician and statesman; Prime Minister, 1902–05.

Balzac, Honoré de (1799–1850). French novelist.

Barbaro, Ermolao (1410–71). Italian (Venetian) prelate and diplomat.

Barnet, Richard J. (1929–2004). American writer.

Beaumarchais, Pierre Augustin Caron de (1732–99). French playwright.

Belisarius (c. 505–65). Eastern Roman general and statesman.

Berle, Adolf A. (1895–1971). American lawyer and diplomat.

Berman, Maureen R. (1948–). Coauthor (with I. William Zartman) of *The Practical Negotiator* (1982).

Beyle, Henri. See *Stendhal*.

Bierce, Ambrose (1842–1914). American journalist.

Bismarck, Otto von: Count Otto Eduard Leopold von Bismarck-Schönhausen (1815–98). Prussian diplomat and statesman; first Chancellor of the German Empire.

Black, Eugene (1898–1992). American economist and diplomat.

Blaker, Michael (1940–). American academic.

Boerne, Ludwig (1786–1837). German man of letters.

Bohlen, Charles E. (1904–74). American diplomat.

Bonham-Carter, Violet, Baroness Asquith of Yarnbury (1887–1969). English politician.

Boren, James H. Late-twentieth-century American humorist.

Boswell, James (1740–95). Scottish lawyer and man of letters.

Boyce, Richard Fyfe. Early-twentieth-century American diplomat.

Bozeman, Adda (1908–94). American scholar.

Bujold, Lois McMaster (1949–). American author.

Bragaccia, Gasparo. Early-seventeenth-century Italian diplomat.

Braun, Konrad (1491–1563). German jurist and theologian.

Briggs, Ellis O. (1899–1976). American diplomat.

Broglie, J. V. Albert, Duc de. Nineteenth-century French man of letters, diplomat, and statesman; Premier, 1873, 1877.

Bryan, William Jennings (1860–1925). American politician; Secretary of State, 1913–15.

Brzezinski, Zbigniew (1928–). American academic and official.

Bülow, Baron Heinrich von (1792–1846). Prussian diplomat.

Bülow, Prince Bernard Heinrich von (1849–1929). German statesman; Foreign Secretary, 1897; Chancellor, 1900–09.

Bundy, McGeorge (1919–96). American historian and official.

Burke, Edmund (1729–97). British philosopher.

Burton, Sir Richard Francis (1821–90). English explorer, writer, and diplomat.

Busk, Douglas (1906–90). British diplomat.

Caccia, Harold. Late-nineteenth-, early-twentieth-century British diplomat; Ambassador to the United States.

Caesar, Caius Julius (c. 102–44 B.C.). Roman general.

Caligula, Caius Caesar (12–41). Roman emperor, 37–41.

Callières, François de (1645–1717). French diplomat; author of *De la manière de négocier avec les Souverains* (1716).

Cambon, Jules (1845–1935). French official and diplomat.

Cambon, Paul (1843–1924). French diplomat.

Canning, George (1740–1827). English statesman; Prime Minister, 1827.

Cao Cao (Ts'ao Ts'ao) (155–220). Chinese general.

Castlereagh, Viscount: Robert Stewart, Viscount Castlereagh, 2nd Baron of Londonderry (1769–1822). British statesman; Foreign Minister.

Caitlin, Wynn (1930–). American writer.

Catherine II (1729–96). Empress of Russia, 1762–96.

Cavour, Count Camillo Benso di (1810–51). Italian statesman.

Cecil, Hugh (1869–1956). British statesman.

Chamberlain, Sir Austen (1863–1937). English statesman; Foreign Secretary, 1924–29; Nobel peace prize, 1925.

Chen Hao. Early-twelfth-century Chinese (Song [Sung]) military official.

Cheng Yi (1033–1107). Chinese (Northern Song [Sung]) philosopher.

Chesterfield, Lord: Philip Dormer Stanhope, 4th Earl of Chesterfield (1694–1773). English statesman and man of letters.

Childs, J. Rives (1893–1987). Diplomat and author.

Choiseul: Etienne François, Duc de Choiseul-Amboise (1719–85). French soldier, diplomat, statesman, and spymaster.

Churchill, Sir Winston (1874–1965). British politician, historian, and statesman; Prime Minister, 1940–45, 1951–55; Nobel prize for literature, 1953.

Cicero, Marcus Tullius (106–43 B.C.). Roman orator.

Clark, Eric (1937–). English writer.

Clausewitz, Carl Maria von (1780–1831). Prussian military officer, author of *On War*.

Clemenceau, Georges Eugène Benjamin (1841–1929). French statesman; Premier, 1906–09, 1917–20.

Cobden, Richard (1804–65). British merchant and statesman.

Colton, Charles Caleb (1780–1832). English clergyman.

Commines, Philippe de (1445–1511). French historian and statesman.

Cooper, James Fenimore (1789–1851). American novelist.

Cornford, F.M. (1874–1943). British academic and official.

Couve de Murville, Maurice-Jacques (1907–99). French diplomat and statesman; Foreign Minister, 1958–68; Prime Minister, 1968–69.

Craig, Gordon A. Late-twentieth-century American historian; coauthor of *Force and Statecraft* (1983).

Cramb, J.A. (1862–1913). British historian.

Crocker, Chester A. (1941–). American academic and statesman.

Cromwell, Oliver (1599–1658). English general and dictator; Lord Protector, 1653–58.

Culbertson, Ely (1893–1955). American author.

Curzon, Lord: George Nathaniel, 1st Baron and 1st Marquis Curzon of Kedelston (1859–1925). English statesman; Viceroy of India, 1899–1905.

Danès, Bishop Pierre (1497–1577). French classicist, diplomat, and prelate.

Dargent, Joseph. Late-twentieth-century French vintner.

Davies, John Paton (1908–99). American diplomat.

Dawes, Charles Gates (1865–1951). American financier and diplomat; Vice President of the United States, 1925–29.

De Gaulle, Charles André Joseph Marie (1890–1970). French general and statesman; President, 1959–69.

Debrah, Kojo (Ebenezer Moses) (1928–). Ghanaian diplomat.

Defoe, Daniel (1660–1731). English novelist, journalist, and political agent.

Demiashkevich, Michael (1891–1938). American scholar.

Demosthenes (c. 384–22 B.C.). Greek (Athenian) statesman.

Dewey, John (1859–1952). American philosopher.

Diodorus the Athenian. Second-century B.C. Greek philosopher.

Disraeli, Benjamin, 1st Earl of Beaconsfield (1804–81). English statesman and novelist.

Dobrynin, Anatoly (1919–). Soviet diplomat.

Douglas-Home, Alexander Frederick, Baron Home of the Hirsel (1903–96). British statesman; Prime Minister, 1963–64.

Drake, Sir Francis (c. 1540–96). English admiral and buccaneer.

Dryden, John (1631–1700). English poet.

Du Mu (803–c. 852). Chinese (Tang) scholar-official.

Dulles, Allen (1893–1969). American spymaster.

Dulles, John Foster (1888–1959). American diplomat and statesman; Secretary of State, 1953–59.

Dumreicher, Armand von. Nineteenth-century Austrian politician.

Durant, Will (1885–1981). American writer.

Earle, Edward Mead (1894–1954). American scholar.

Eayrs, James (1926–). Canadian journalist.

Eban, Abba (1915–2002). Israeli diplomat and statesman.

Eden, Anthony, Earl of Avon (1897–1977). English statesman; Prime Minister, 1955–57.

Egan, Maurice Francis (1852–1924). American writer and diplomat.

Einstein, Albert (1879–1955). German physicist; Nobel prize, 1921.

Eisenhower, Dwight D. (1890–1969). American general; President of the United States, 1953–61.

Ekvall, Robert B. Mid-twentieth-century American military officer and interpreter.

Elizabeth I (1533–1603). Queen of England, 1558–1603.

Ellings, Richard J. (1950–). American academic.

Emerson, Ralph Waldo (1803–82). American philosopher.

Erasmus, Desiderius (1466–1536). Dutch philosopher.

Farquhar, George (1678–1707). English playwright.

Faure, Guy-Oliver. Late-twentieth-century French academic.

Fearon, James D. (1952–). American academic.

Felice, Fortune Barthélemy de (1723–89). Swiss publicist.

Fénelon: François de Salignac de la Mothe-Fénelon (1651–1715). French prelate and writer.

Fingar, Charles Thomas American official.

Fisher, Roger (1922–). American lawyer and student of negotiations.

Fletcher, Henry Prather (1873–1959). American diplomat.

Ford, Gerald R. (1913–2006). American politician; President of the United States, 1974–77.

Frankfurter, Felix (1882–1965). American jurist.

Franklin, Benjamin (1706–90). American diplomat, statesman, writer, printer, inventor, and scientist.

Frederick the Great: Frederick William II (1744–97). Prussian general; King of Prussia, 1786–97.

Freedman, Lawrence British strategist.

Freeman, Chas. W., Jr. (1943–). American diplomat.

Friedrich, Carl J. (1901–84). German-American scholar.

Galbraith, John Kenneth (1908–2006). American economist, publicist, and ambassador.

Gallieni, Joseph (1849–1916). French general.

Gambetta, Léon (1838–82). French statesman.

Gandhi, Indira (1917–1984). Indian prime minister, 1966–77, 1980–84.

Gandi, Mohandas (1869–1948). Indian political and spiritual leader.

George, Alexander L. Late-twentieth-century American academic.

Germonius, Bishop (Anastasio). Late-sixteenth-, early-seventeenth-century Italian (Savoy) diplomat and prelate.

Gibbon, Edward (1737–94). English historian.

Gibran, Kahlil (Gibran Khalil Gibran bin Mikhael bin Sa`ad) (1883–1931). Lebanese-American poet.

Gibson, Hugh S. (1883–1954). American diplomat.

Giraud, Charles Joseph Barthélemy (1802–81). French historian.

Goethe, Johann Wolfgang von (1749–1832). German poet and playwright.

Goldberg, Arthur J. (1908–90). American jurist and diplomat.

Gracián, Baltasar (1601–58). Spanish priest and writer.

Grew, Joseph C. (1880–1965). American diplomat.

Grey of Fallodon, Lord: Edward Grey, Viscount Fallodon (1862–1933). British statesman; Foreign Minister, 1905–16.

Grotius, Hugo: Huig van Groot (1583–1645). Dutch jurist and statesman.

Griswold, A. Whitney (1906–63). American diplomatic historian; President of Yale University, 1950–63.

Gruber, Karl (1909–95). Austrian statesman and diplomat.

Guicciardini, Francesco (1483–1540). Italian historian and diplomat.

Guizot, François Pierre Guillaume (1787–1874). French historian and statesman.

Habib, Philip (1920–92). American diplomat.

Hamilton, Alexander (1757–1804). American statesman.

Hamilton, Sir Ian (1853–1947). British general.

Hamilton, Keith. Late-twentieth-century British foreign policy official.

Hammarskjöld, Dag (1905–61). Swedish statesman; Secretary-General of the United Nations, 1953–61.

Han Feizi (d. 233 B.C.). Chinese legalist philosopher.

Hankey, Lord: Maurice Pascal Alers Hankey (1877–1963). British diplomat.

Harlow, Bryce (1916–87). American businessman and official.

Harriman, W. Averell (1891–1986). American politician and diplomat.

Harrison, Benjamin (1833–1901). American politician; President of the United States, 1889–93.

Hart, Parker T. (1910–1997). American diplomat.

Hauser, Henri (1866–1946). French historian.

Hawthorne, Nathaniel (1804–1864). American author; Consul at Liverpool 1853–57.

Hay, John (1838–1905). American statesman; Secretary of State, 1898–1905.

Henderson, George Francis Robert (1854–1903). American military historian.

Herbert, George (1593–1633). English clergyman and poet.

Herodotus (c. 484–25 B.C.). Greek historian.

Herz, Martin F. (1917–83). American diplomat.

Hill, David J. (1850–1932). American historian and diplomat.

Hitler, Adolf (1889–1945). German politician and dictator; Führer of the "Third Reich," 1933–45.

Hobbes, Thomas (1588–1679). English philosopher.

Hochhuth, Rolf (1931–). German playwright.

Hotman de Villiers: Jean Hotman de Villiers-St. Paul. Late-sixteenth-century French diplomat.

Hübner, Count Joseph von (1811–92). Austrian diplomat.

Huddleston, Sisley (1883–1952). English journalist.

Hufbauer, Gary Clyde (1949–). American academic; coauthor, with **Jeffrey J. Schott** (1949–) and **Kimberly Ann Elliott** (1960–), of studies on economic sanctions.

Hughes, Charles Evans (1862–1948). American jurist and statesman; Secretary of State, 1921–25; Chief Justice of the United States, 1930–41.

Hull, Cordell (1871–1955). American politician; Secretary of State, 1933–44; Nobel peace prize, 1945.

Huxley, Aldous (1894–1963). English novelist.

Iklé, Fred C. Late-twentieth-century American academic and government official.

Inoue, Kaoru (1836–1915). Japanese (Meiji) statesman; Foreign Minister, 1879–87.

Irving, Washington (1783–1859). American essayist.

Ishii, Itaro (1889–1954). Japanese diplomat.

Jackson, Sir Geoffrey (1915–87). British diplomat.

Jefferson, Thomas (1743–1826). American diplomat and statesman; Secretary of State, 1789–93; President of the United States, 1801–09.

Jerome, Saint (Eusebius Sophronius Hieronymus) (C.A. 347–420). Christian theologian.

Johnson, Hugh S. (1882–1942). American general.

Johnson, Lyndon B. (1908–73). American politician; President of the United States, 1963–68.

Johnson, Samuel ("Dr. Johnson") (1709–84). English lexicographer.

Jomini, Antoine Henri, Baron (1779–1869). Swiss general and military writer, in service of France and Russia.

Jusserand, J.J. (1855–1932). French diplomat and writer; ambassador to the United States, 1902–25.

Kampelman, Max M. (1921–). American lawyer and diplomat.

Kautilya (Chanakya). Third-century B.C. Indian (Maurya) statesman; author of *Arthasastra*.

Kelly, Sir David V. (1891–1959). British diplomat.

Kennan, George F. (1904–2005). American diplomat and historian.

Kennedy, A. L. (Aubrey Leo). Early-twentieth-century British historian.

Kennedy, John F. (1917–63). American politician; President of the United States, 1961–63.

Kennedy, Paul. Late-twentieth-century historian.

Kertesz, Stephen D. (1904–). Hungarian-American academic.

Khrushchev, Nikita Sergeyevich (1894–1971). Soviet politician; Premier of the USSR, 1956–64.

Kirk, Alexander. Early-twentieth-century American businessman and diplomat.

Kirkpatrick, Ivone (1897–1964). British diplomat.

Kissinger, Henry A. (1923–). American academic, historian, and statesman; Secretary of State, 1973–77.

Kitahara, Hideo (1914–). Japanese diplomat.

Komura, Jutaro (1855–1911). Japanese diplomat; Foreign Minister, 1901–06, 1908–11.

Laberius, Decimus (c. 105–43 B.C.). Roman writer.

Langhorne, Richard T. B. (1940–). British academic and foreign policy official.

Lawrence, Thomas Edward (T. E.) (1888–1935). British soldier and author, known as "Lawrence of Arabia".

Lenin, V.I. (1870–1924). Russian revolutionary; Soviet Premier, 1918–24.

Lennox, Charles, 3rd Duke of Richmond and Lennox (1735–1806). British statesman.

Leo X, Pope: Giovanni di Medici (1475-1521). Pope, 1513–21.

Lescalopier de Nourar (1709–79). French man of letters.

Liddell Hart, Basil (1895–1970). English military journalist and historian.

Lie, Trygve Halvdan (1896–1968). Norwegian statesman; Secretary-General of the United Nations, 1946–53.

Lippmann, Walter (1889–1974). American journalist.

Liu Ji (1311–75). Chinese (Yuan and Ming) official, general, and strategist.

Livingston, Edward (1764–1836). American politician; Secretary of State, 1831–34.

Livy (Titus Livius) (59 B.C.–A.D. 17). Roman historian.

Lloyd George, David, 1st Earl of Dwyfor (1863–1945). British politician; Prime Minister, 1916–22.

Lodge, Henry Cabot (1850–1924). American politician.

Lodge, John D. (1903–85). American politician and diplomat.

Lomax, Sir John (1896–1987). British diplomat.

Louis XIV (1638–1715). King of France, 1643–1715.

Luard, Evan (1926–91). British academic.

Luce, Clare Booth (1903–87). American politician and diplomat.

Luke. Early Christian disciple and author of the third Gospel.

Luttwak, Edward N. Late-twentieth-century American academic, author of numerous works on strategy and military affairs.

Lyons, Lord (1790–1885). British admiral and diplomat.

Mably, Abbot Gariel Bonnot de (1709–1885). French historian.

MacArthur, Douglas (1880–1964). American general.

MacGregor, Douglas American soldier and author.

Machiavelli, Niccolò (1469–1527). Italian (Florentine) statesman and philosopher.

Mackinder, Sir Halford J. (1861–1947). British geographer.

MacLean, Fitzroy Hew Royle MacLean, First Baronet of Dunconnel (1911–1996). British diplomat, soldier, and author.

Macmillan, Harold (1894–1987). British politician; Prime Minister, 1957–63.

Macomber, William (1921–2003). American

official, ambassador.

Madariaga, Salvador de (1886–1978). Spanish historian and diplomat.

Madison, James (1751–1836). American statesman; Secretary of State, 1801–09; President of the United States, 1809–17.

Maggi, Ottaviano. Sixteenth-century Italian (Venetian) diplomat.

Malmesbury, Lord: James Harris, 1st Earl of Malmesbury (1746–1820). English diplomat.

Manu. In Hindu mythology, the progenitor and lawgiver of the human race.

Mao Zedong (Mao Tse-tung) (1893–1976). Chinese communist revolutionary and strategist; Chairman of the Chinese Communist Party, 1943–76.

Marshall, George C. (1880–1959). American general and statesman; Secretary of State, 1947–49; Nobel peace prize, 1953.

Martens, Charles de (1790–1863). Prussian diplomat and author.

Martens, G.F. de. Late-eighteenth-, early-nineteenth-century German jurist.

Matthew. Early Christian disciple and author of the first Gospel.

Mayer, Martin (1928–2008). American writer.

McClintock, Robert (1908–76). American diplomat.

Meir, Golda (1898–1978). Israeli prime minister, 1969–74.

Melville, Herman (1819–91). American novelist.

Mencius (Mengzi) (372–289 B.C.). Chinese philosopher.

Mencken, H.L. (1880–1956). American journalist.

Merchant, Livingston (1903–76). American diplomat.

Metternich, Prince Klemens Wenzel Nepomuk Lothar von (1773–1859). Austrian statesman.

Milton, John (1608–74). English poet.

Mohieddin, Zakaria (1918–). Egyptian military officer and politician.

Moltke, Helmuth, Graf von ("The Elder") (1800–91). German general.

Monat, Pawel (1921–). Polish military attaché.

Monnet, Jean (1888–1979). French economist and statesman.

Monroe, James (1758–1831). American diplomat and statesman; Secretary of State, 1811–15; President of the United States, 1817–25.

Montague, C.E. (1867–1928). English writer.

Montaigne, Michel de (1533–92). French essayist.

Montesquieu: Charles de Secondat, Baron de la Brède et de Montesquieu (1689–1755). French philosopher.

Moore, John Bassett (1860–1947). American jurist-official.

Moore, Robert J. (1931–). Guyanan academic and diplomat.

Morgenthau, Hans J. (1904–80). American academic.

Morris, William (1875–1946). American historian.

Morrow, Dwight (1873–1931). American banker and diplomat.

Mothe le Vayer, François de la (1588–1672). French historian.

Mowat, Robert Belmain (1883–1941). British academic.

Mowrer, Paul Scott (1887–1971). American journalist and poet.

Moynihan, Daniel Patrick (1927–2003). American politician.

Muaawiya. Founder of the Omayyad dynasty; caliph, 661–80.

Mueller, John. Late-twentieth-century American academic.

Murray, Grenville (1824–81). British diplomat.

Nabokov, Vladimir (1899–1977). Russian-American novelist.

Napoleon: Napoléon Bonaparte (1769–1821). French general and dictator; Emperor, 1804–15.

Nicholas II (1868–1918). Czar of Russia, 1894–1917.

Nicolson, Sir Arthur, 1st Baron Carnock (1849–1928). English diplomat.

Nicolson, Sir Harold (1886–1968). English diplomat, politician, and writer.

Niebuhr, Reinhold (1892–1971). American theologian.

Nixon, Richard M. (1913–94). American politician, statesman, and author; President of the United States, 1969–74.

Norstad, Lauris (1907–88). American general.

Nyerere, Julius (1922–99). Tanzanian politician; President of Tanganyika, 1962–64; President of Tanzania, 1964–85.

O'Brien, Conor Cruise (1917–). Irish historian, journalist, and diplomat.

Odom, William E. (1932–2008). American soldier and educator.

O'Neill, Robert J. (1936–). Australian soldier and historian.

Orwell, George (pseud. of Eric Blair) (1903–50). British author.

Ovid (43 B.C.–c. A.D. 17). Roman poet.

Page, Walter Hines (1855–1918). American journalist and diplomat.

Palmerston, Lord: Henry John Temple, 3rd Viscount Palmerston (1784–1865). British statesman; Foreign Minister, 1830–41, 1846–51; Prime Minister, 1855–58, 1859–65.

Parkinson, C. Northcote (1909–1993). British historian.

Pascal, Blaise (1623–62). French philosopher and mathematician.

Pearson, Lester B. (1897–1972). Canadian politician and diplomat; Prime Minister, 1863–68.

Pecquet, Antoine (1662–1725). French military engineer, diplomat, and statesman.

Pehar, Drazen. Early 21st century Bosnian diplomat and scholar.

Plamandon, Benoît. Late-twentieth-century Canadian diplomat.

Plantey, Alain. Late-twentieth-century French official.

Plato (428–347 B.C.). Greek philosopher.

Plischke, Elmer (1914–). American academic.

Polk, William R. American historian.

Polybius (c. 205–123 B.C.). Greek historian.

Puzo, Mario Gianluigi (1920–1999). American author.

Quaroni, Pietro (1898–1971). Italian diplomat.

Rajaratnam, S. (1915–2006). Singaporean journalist and diplomat; Foreign Minister.

Randolph, John (1773–1883). American politician, envoy.

Raper, John Wolfe (1870–1950). American journalist.

Reagan, Ronald W. (1911–2004). American politician; President of the United States, 1981–89.

Reed, Thomas B. (1839–1902). American politician.

Renan, Ernest (1823–92). French writer.

Repplier, Agnes (1855–1950). American essayist.

Reston, James (1909–95). American journalist.

Richardson, Elliot L. (1920–99). American lawyer, politician, statesman, and diplomat.

Richelieu, Cardinal: Armand-Jean du Plessis, Duc de Richelieu (1585–1642). French statesman and prelate.

Ridgway, Matthew B. (1895–1993). American general.

Rochefoucauld, François, Duc de la (1613–80). French writer.

Roetter, Charles. Mid-twentieth-century British journalist.

Rogers, Will (1879–1935). American humorist.

Rommel, Erwin (1891–1944). German general.

Roosevelt, Franklin Delano (1882–1945). American politician; President of the United States, 1933–45.

Roosevelt, Theodore (1858–1919). American politician; President of the United States, 1901–09.

Rosebery, Lord: Archibald Philip Primrose, 5th Earl of Rosebery. Late-nineteenth-century British statesman; Foreign Minister, 1886, 1892–94; Prime Minister, 1894–95.

Rosier, Bernard du (d. 1711). French diplomat and prelate.

Rousseau de Chamoy. Late-seventeenth-century French diplomat.

Rowan, Carl (1925–2000). American journalist and official.

Rusk, Dean (1909–94). American statesman; Secretary of State, 1961–69.

Salibi, Kamal Suleiman (1929–). Lebanese historian.

Salisbury, Lord: Marquis Robert Arthur Talbot Gacoyne Cecil, 3rd Marquis of Salisbury (1830–1903). British statesman; Foreign Minister; Prime Minister, 1885–86. 1886–92, 1895–1902.

Sallust, Caius Valerius Sallustius Crispus (86–35 B.C.). Roman historian.

Santayana, George (1863–1952). American philosopher.

Sarpi, Paolo. Seventeenth-century Venetian friar.

Satow, Sir Ernest M. (1843–1929). British diplomat and author.

Sa`ud, `Abdullah bin `Abd Al-Aziz Al- (c. 1923–). Saudi Arabian Crown Prince.

Saunders, Harold H. (1930–). American official.

Schelling, Thomas C. (1921–). American academic.

Schofield, John MacAllister (1830–1906). American general.

Seneca: Lucius Annaeus Seneca (c. 4 B.C.–65 A.D.). Roman philosopher.

Serres, Jean (1893–1968). French diplomat.

Seton-Watson, G. Hugh N. (1916–84). British historian.

Seward, William Henry (1801–72). American politician; Secretary of State, 1861–69.

Shakespeare, William (1564–1616). English playwright and poet.

Sherman, William Tecumseh (1820–91). American general.

Shultz, George P. (1920–). American economist and statesman; Secretary of State, 1982–89.

Silvercruys, Robert, Baron (1893–1975). Belgian diplomat.

Smith, Paul A., Jr. (1925–). American official.

Smith, Walter Bedell (1895–1961). American general.

Solzhenitsin, Aleksandr (1918–2008). Russian novelist.

Sophocles (496–406 B.C.) Greek dramatist.

Spaulding, E. Wilder (1899–?). American journalist.

Spring, Howard (1889–1965). British novelist.

Staël, Germaine de (1766–1817). French writer.

Stalin, Joseph V. (1879–1953). Soviet dictator; Secretary General of the Communist Party, 1922–53.

Steed, H. Wickham (1871–1956). English journalist.

Steiner, George (1929–). British academic.

Stendhal (Henri Beyle) (1783–1842). French novelist.

Stern, Richard (1928–). American author.

Stevenson, Adlai E., Jr. (1900–65). American politician and diplomat.

Stinnett, Caskie (1911–). American writer.

Sumner, William Graham (1840–1910). American economist.

Sunzi (Sun Tzu): Sun Wu. Late-sixth-century B.C. Chinese warrior-philosopher.

Swift, Jonathan (1667–1745). English satirist.

Sylvester, Arthur (1901–79). American journalist and official.

Szilassy, Gyula, Baron of Szilas and Pilis (1870–1935). Austrian-Hungarian diplomat, author of *Traité pratique de Diplomatie moderne.*

Tacitus, Cornelius (c. 55–117). Roman historian.

Talbott, Strobe (1946–). American journalist and government official.

Talleyrand: Charles-Maurice de Talleyrand-Périgord (1754–1838). French diplomat and statesman.

Tarle, Evgenii Viktorovich (1875–1955). Soviet historian.

Tasso, Torquato (1544–95). Italian poet.

Tauscher, Ellen (1951–). American politician and diplomat.

Thayer, Charles W. (1910–69). American diplomat and writer.

Thompson, Kenneth W. (1912–). American academic.

Thucydides (c. 460–400 B.C.). Greek historian.

Timur (Tamerlane) (1336–1405). Central Asian conqueror.

Tocqueville, Alexis de: Count Alexis Charles Henri Maurice Clérel de Tocqueville (1805–59). French historian and writer.

Togo, Shigenori (1882–1950). Japanese diplomat; Foreign Minister, 1945–46.

Torcy, Marquis de: Jean-Baptiste Colbert (1665–1736). French diplomat and statesman.

Trevelyan, Humphrey, Lord (1905–85). British diplomat.

Trône, Guillaume François le (1728–80). French jurist.

Truman, Harry S. (1884–1972). American politician; President of the United States, 1945–53.

Tusi, Nizam al-Mulk. Twelfth-century Prime Minister of the Seljuq Turks; author of *Siyasat-Namah.*

Twain, Mark: Samuel Langhorne Clemens (1835–1910). American writer and humorist.

Ugaki, Kazushige (1868–1922). Japanese soldier; Foreign Minister, 1938.

Urquhart, Sir Brian (1919–). British UN official; UN Under-Secretary-General for Special Political Affairs, 1974–86.

Valéry, Paul (1871–1945). French poet.

Vansittart, Robert: Robert Gilbert, 1st Baron Vansittart of Denham (1881–1957). British diplomat and statesman.

Vauvenargues, Marquis de: Luc de Clapiers (1715–47). French moralist.

Vegetius Renatus, Flavius. Fourth-century Roman military writer.

Vera y Çuniga, Juan Antonio de (1588–1658). Spanish historian and diplomat.

Voltaire: François Marie Arouet (1694–1771). French philosopher.

Walsingham, Sir Francis (c. 1530–90). English diplomat, statesman, and spymaster; Secretary of State, 1573–90.

Walters, Vernon A. (1917–). American military officer, official, and diplomat.

Washington, George (1732–99). American general and statesman; President of the United States, 1789–97.

Watson, J. H. Adam (1914–2007). British diplomat and academic.

Weinreich, Max (1894–1969). American linguist.

Wellesley, Sir Victor Alexander Augustus Henry (1876–1954). British diplomat.

Wellington, Duke of: Arthur Wellesley, 1st Duke of Wellington (1769–1852). British general and statesman; Prime Minister, 1828–30.

White, E.B. (1899–1985). American writer.

Wicquefort, Abram de (1598–1682). Dutch diplomat and spy; author of *L'Ambassadeur et ses Fonctions* (1680).

Wight, R. J. Martin (1913–72). British historian.

Wilson, Woodrow (1856–1924). American academic, politician, and statesman; President of the United States, 1913–21; Nobel peace prize, 1919.

Windsor, Duke of (1894–1972). Reigned as Edward VIII, King of Great Britain, from January 1936 until his abdication in December 1936.

Wood, John R. Early-twentieth-century American diplomat.

Wotton, Sir Henry. Early-seventeenth-century diplomat; ambassador of James I of England to Venice.

Wright, Quincy (1890–1970). American academic.

Wrong, Hume (1894–1954). Canadian diplomat.

Yamagata, Aritomo (1838–1922). Japanese soldier-statesman; Prime Minister, 1889–91; Chief of General Staff, 1904–05.

Young, Andrew (1932–). American clergyman and politician.

Zakaria, Fareed (1964–). American political commentator.

Zartman, I. William (1932–). American academic.

Zhou Enlai (1898–1976). Chinese politician and statesman; Premier, 1949–72.

Zhuangzi (Chuang Tzu) (c. 369–286 B.C.) Chinese philosopher.

Zhuge Liang (c. 180–234). Chinese (Three Kingdoms–Shu) general.

❧ Bibliography ❧

Acheson, Dean. *Grapes from Thorns*. 1972.

_____. *Present at the Creation*. 1969.

Adcock, Frank E. *Diplomacy in Ancient Greece*. 1975.

Adler, Mortimer J., and Charles Van Doren. *Great Treasury of Western Thought*. 1977.

Anonymous. *La embajada espa–ola*. [A late-seventeenth-century Spanish guide to diplomatic procedure.] Reprinted and translated in *Camden Miscellany*, vol. 14. London, 1926.

Aristotle. *Politics*. c. 325 B.C.

Aron, Raymond. *Guèrre et paix entre les nations*. Paris, 1964.

Bacon, Francis. *Essays*. 1597.

Bailey, Thomas A. *The Art of Diplomacy*. 1968.

Barbaro. Ermolao. *De officio legatio*. c. 1940.

Bartlett, John, et al. *Familiar Quotations*. 1955.

Blaker, Michael. *Japanese International Negotiating Style*. 1977.

Bonham-Carter, Violet. *Winston Churchill as I Knew Him*. 1965.

Boyce, Richard Fyfe. *The Diplomat's Wife*. 1956.

Bozeman, Adda B. *Strategic Intelligence and Statecraft*. 1922.

Bragaccia, Gasparo. *L'Ambasciatore*. 1626.

Briggs, Ellis. *Anatomy of Diplomacy*. 1968.

Busk, Douglas. *The Craft of Diplomacy*. 1967.

Callières, François de. *De la manière de négocier avec les Souverains*. 1716.

Cambon, Jules. *Le diplomate*. 1926.

Campbell, John C., ed. *Successful Negotiation: Trieste 1954*. 1976.

Carruth, Gorton, and Eugene Ehrlich, eds. *American Quotations*. 1988.

Clark, Eric. *Corps Diplomatique*. 1973.

Clausewitz, Carl Maria von. *On War*. 1832.

Cohen, Ira S. *Realpolitik: Theory and Practice*. 1975.

Cooper, Duff. *Talleyrand*. 1932.

Craig, Gordon A., and Alexander L. George. *Force and Statecraft*. 1983.

Creaghe, John St. G. "Personal Qualities and Effective Diplomatic Negotiation." Ph.D. diss. University of Maryland, 1965.

Crocker, Chester A. *High Noon in Southern Africa*. 1992.

Dobrynin, Anatoly. *In Confidence*. 1995.

Dulles, Allen. *The Craft of Intelligence*. 1963.

Dyne, Frederick van. *Our Foreign Service*. 1909.

Eban, Abba. *Interest and Conscience in Modern Diplomacy*. 1985.

_____. *The New Diplomacy: International Affairs in the Modern Age*. 1983.

Ellings, Richard J. *Embargoes and World Power*. 1985.

Faure, Guy Olivier. *The Mediator as a Third Negotiator* in Frances Mautner-Markhof: Processes of International Negotiation. 1989.

Feltham, R.G. *Diplomatic Handbook*. 1988.

Fisher, Roger. *Getting to Yes: Negotiating Agreement without Giving In*. 1991.

_____. *Improving Compliance with International Law*. 1981.

_____. *International Conflict for Beginners*. 1969.

Foster, John W. *The Practice of Diplomacy*. 1900.

Frankel, Joseph. *The Making of Foreign Policy*. 1963.

Freeman, Chas. W. "The Angola/Namibia Accords," *Foreign Affairs* 68, no. 3 (1989).

George, Alexander L. *Bridging the Gap: Theory and Practice in Foreign Policy*. 1993.

Graciàn, Baltasar. *The Art of Worldly Wisdom*. 1647. Translated by Christopher Maurer. 1992.

Guicciardini, Francesco. *Storia d'Italia*. 1564.

Guizot, F. *Memoirs to Illustrate the History of My Time*. Translated by J. W. Cole. 1859.

Hamilton, Keith, and Richard T. B. Langhorne. *The Practice of Diplomacy: Its Evolution, Theory, and Administration*. 1995.

Han Feizi (Han Fei Tzu). *Essays*. c. 250 B.C.

Harmon, Robert B. *The Art and Practice of Diplomacy*. 1971.

Hart, Parker T. *Two Nato Allies at the Threshold of War: Cyprus, A Firsthand Account of Crisis Management, 1965–1968*.1990.

Herz, Martin F., ed. *The Modern Ambassador*. 1983.

Hindmarsh, Albert E. *Force in Peace*. 1933.

Huainanzi (Huainan Masters). *Essays*. Translated by Thomas Cleary as *The Book of Leadership and Strategy*. 1992.

Hufbauer, Gary Clyde, Jeffrey J. Schott, and Kimberley Ann Elliot. *Economic Sanctions in Support of Foreign Policy Goals*. 1983.

_____. *Economic Sanctions Reconsidered: History and Current Policy*. 1990.

Hume, David. *Essay on the Balance of Power*. 1651.

Iklé, Fred Charles. *Every War Must End*. 1991.

_____. *How Nations Negotiate*. 1991.

Jiang, Tai Gong. *Six Secret Teachings*. Chinese political manual originally thought to date from the Zhou dynasty in the 11th century B.C., now dated 4th century B.C.

Johnson, E.A.J., ed. *The Dimensions of Diplomacy*. 1964.

Jusserand, J.J. *L'école des ambassadeurs*. 1924.

Kampelman, Max. M. *Entering New Worlds*. 1991.

Kennan, George F. *American Diplomacy 1900–1950*. 1953.

_____. *Measures Short of War: Lectures at the National War College 1946–47*. 1990.

_____. *Memoirs*. 1967.

_____. *Realities of American Foreign Policy*. 1954.

Kennedy, A. L. *Old Diplomacy and New*. 1922.

Kissinger, Henry A. *Diplomacy*. 1994.

_____. *The Necessity for Choice*. 1960.

_____. *Nuclear Weapons and Foreign Policy*. 1957.

_____. *White House Years*. 1979.

_____. *A World Restored*. 1964.

_____. *Years of Upheaval*. 1982.

Liang, Congjie. *The Great Thoughts of China: 3000 Years of Wisdom that Shaped a Civilization*. 1996.

Lippmann, Walter. *The Public Philosophy*. 1955.

Liu Ji. *Lessons of War*. c. 1370. Translated by Thomas Cleary in *Mastering the Art of War*, 1989.

Luttwak, Edward N. *Strategy*. 1989.

Machiavelli, Niccolò. *Discourses*.

_____. *The Art of War*. 1521

_____. *The Prince*.

Macomber, William. *The Angels' Game*. 1975.

Magalhães, José Calvet de. *The Pure Concept of Diplomacy*. Translated by Bernardo Futscher Pereira. 1988.

Marsden, C. R. S. *The Dictionary of Outrageous Quotations*. 1988.

Martens, Charles de. *Guide Diplomatique*. 1866.

Mattingly, Garrett. *Renaissance Diplomacy*. 1955.

Mautner-Markhof, Frances, ed. *Processes of International Negotiations*. 1989.

Mayer, Martin. *The Diplomats*. 1983.

Mencken, H.L. *A New Dictionary of Quotations*. 1942.

Morgenthau, Hans J. *Politics Among Nations*. 1948.

Mowat, R.B. *Diplomacy and Peace*. 1936.

Nicolson, Harold. *The Congress of Vienna*. 1946.

_____. *Diplomacy*. 1960.

_____. *The Evolution of the Diplomatic Method*. 1954.

_____. *Portrait of a Diplomatist*. 1930.

Nierenberg, Gerard I. *The Art of Negotiating*. 1968.

_____. *Fundamentals of Negotiating*. 1973.

Nixon, Richard. *The Real War*. 1980.

_____. *Seize the Moment*. 1992.

Orieux, Jean. *Talleyrand*. Translated by Patricia Wolf. 1974.

Padover, Saul K. *Foreign Affairs*. 1964.

Pecquet, Antoine. *Discours sur l'Art de Négocier*. 1964.

Phillips, Brig. Gen. Thomas R. (U.S. Army), ed. *Roots of Strategy*. 1964.

Pisani, Edgar."La pratique de la négotiation européenne." *Pouvoirs* 15 (1980).

Plischke, Elmer. *Foreign Relations: Analysis of Its Anatomy*. 1988.

_____. In *Instruction in Diplomacy: The Liberal Arts Approach*. American Academy of Political and Social Science. 1972.

Regala, Roberto. *The Trends in Modern Diplomatic Practice*. 1959.

Richelieu, Cardinal. *Testament Politique*. 1638.

Ridley, Jasper. *Lord Palmerston*. 1970.

Roetter, Charles. *The Diplomatic Art*. 1963.

Rule, Gordon Wade. *The Art of Negotiation*.

Sabbagh, Isa Khalil. *As the Arabs Say . . .* vol. 1, 1983; vol. 2, 1985.

Satow, Ernest. *A Guide to Diplomatic Practice*. 1917.

Schelling, Thomas C. *The Strategy of Conflict*. 1960.

Schultz, George P. *Turmoil and Triumph*. 1993.

Smith, Paul A., Jr. *On Political War*. 1989.

Spaulding, E. Wilder. *Ambassadors Ordinary and Extraordinary*. 1961.

Sunzi. *The Art of War*. c. 500 B.C.

Swift, Jonathan. *A Treatise on Good Manners and Good Breeding*. c. 1720.

Thayer, Charles W. *Diplomat*. 1959.

Thompson, James Westfall, and Saul K. Padover. *Secret Diplomacy: Espionage and Cryptography, 1500–1815.* 1963.

Thompson, Kenneth W. *American Diplomacy and Emergent Patterns.* 1962.

Trevelyan, Humphrey. *Diplomatic Channels.* 1973.

Tripp, Rhoda Thomas. *The International Thesaurus of Quotations.* 1970.

Trône, Guillaume François le. *De l'Ordre Social.* 1777.

Tusi, Nizam al-Mulk. *Siyasat-Namah* [Book of Politics]. Twelfth century.

Walker, Richard Louis. *The Multi State System of Ancient China.* 1953.

Watson, Adam. *Diplomacy: The Dialogue between States.* 1983.

Wellesley, Victor. *Diplomacy in Fetters.* 1925.

Weng Liang and Yang Shixi. *A Complete Dictionary of English Phrases with Bilingual Explanations.* 1925.

Winokur, Jon. *Friendly Advice.* 1990.

Wood, John R., and Jean Serres. *Diplomatic Ceremonial and Protocol.* 1970.

Wright, Quincy. *Problems of Stability and Progress in International Relations.* 1955.

_____. *A Study of War.* Vol. 1, 1942.

Zartman, I. William. *The 50 Percent Solution.* 1976.

_____. *Ripe for Resolution.* 1985.

Zartman, I. William, and Maureen R. Berman. *The Practical Negotiator.* 1982.

Zhuangzi (Chuang Tzu). *Essays.* c. 300 B.C.

Zhuge Liang. *The Way of the General.* c. 225. Translated by Thomas Cleary in *Mastering the Art of War,* 1989.

✿ Index ✿

273

Canning, George
 allies in balance of power defined by
  enemies, 8

Cao Cao
 who wishes to fight must first reckon the cost,
  244

Capabilities
 national purposes must be proportional to, 189

Capabilities and intentions
 foreign policy must plan on basis of both, 27
 reporting on, influencing, 27

Capitals
 great capitals foster great delusions, 27

Capitulation
 defined, 27

Cartel
 defined, 27

Castlereagh, Viscount
 right of interference in internal affairs, 111

Casus
 belli, defined, 28
 foederis, defined, 28

Catherine II (of Russia)
 power without nation's confidence is
  nothing, 175

Catlin, Wynn
 diplomacy saying 'nice doggie' till you
  find a rock, 54

Censorship
 defined, 28

Ceremonies
 get the formalities right, never mind
  moralities, 28

Chamberlain, Austen
 conferences inhibit compromise and
  agreement, 38

Champagne
 no government could survive without, 28

Chancery
 defined, 28
 head of, defined, 28

Change
 balance of power uncertain during, 174
 difficulties of initiating new order, 156
 nations are changed by time, 28
 nations wax and wane, 28
 perils of reform by evil governments, 195

Change of government
 criteria for recognition, 28

Character
 indicated by company a man keeps, 28

Character, judging
 to understand a person, look at aspirations, 29

Chargé d'affaires
 ad interim, defined, 29
 defined, 29

Charity
 beware its recipients, 29
 donor shouldn't publicize, 29
 donor values more than recipient, 29
 generosity captures the decent, antagonizes
  the mean, 29

Charm
 getting the answer without asking the
  question, 29

Charter
 defined, 29

Chen Hao
 truce proposal may be a plot, 230

Chesterfield, Lord
 never seem wiser than others, 100

Childs, J. Rives
 policy is substance, diplomacy is process, 169

Choices, bad
 when all bad, worst not so dreadful, 29

Choiseul
 truth is artifice, 231

Churchill, Winston
 allies develop opinions of their own, 8
 appeasement, 17
 diplomatic relations a convenience, not a
  compliment, 197
 doctrine helps deal with surprises, 69

management of ambassadors' residences, 200
money opens the most secret cabinets, 75
moral duties of ambassadors to sovereigns, 137
probity essential in ambassadors, 182
prudence and learning avail little without eloquence, 71
reporting must conceal nothing, 198
standards for recruiting apprentice diplomats, 66
style of speech appropriate to ambassadors, 156
training of diplomats in discretion, 66
welfare of nations in hands of ambassadors, 15

Justice
America goes not abroad in search of monsters to destroy, 117
better served by diplomatic adjustment than force, 116
charity not substitute for justice withheld, 118
enters human affairs only when backed by power, 118
may be slighted in peace, 162
vengeance imposed by judge, 117
when decision is in your favor, 117
without force is impotent, 118

Kampelman, Max M.
conduct of negotiations, 145

Kautilya
See *Arthasastra* of Kautilya, 182

Kelly, David
open diplomacy a contradiction in terms, 57
qualifications of good diplomats, 64

Kennan, George F.
breaking relations, 196
conditions favoring international law, 209
control personnel and control policy, 165
diplomats suffer from domestic political distractions, 70
diplomats view propaganda with distaste and scepticism, 185
domestic political imperatives no excuse for failure, 70
economic protectionism ignominious, 186
every government a problem for others, 191
leadership requires self-mastery, 123
methodology of foreign policy, 87
personal diplomacy risks ephemeral results, 57
purposes of foreign policy, 87
subject matter, scope of diplomacy, 59

Kennedy, A. L.
conferences only succeed when results arranged beforehand, 38
qualities of the perfect diplomat enumerated, 65

Kennedy, John F.
domestic mistakes not fatal, foreign policy can be, 86
every nation determines policies in terms of interests, 110
mere absence of war is not peace, 160
purpose of foreign policy not sentiment, 87

Kennedy, Paul
vital role of diplomacy in grand strategy, 217

Kertesz, Stephen D.
skill of negotiators influences history, 87

Khrushchev, Nikita S.
war, not conference, alters borders, 25

Kirk, Alexander
never do anything abrupt. It never pays, 1

Kirkpatrick, Ivone
defeatism makes a bad diplomat, 47

Kissinger, Henry A.
absolute security for one, absolute insecurity for others, 207
achieve war aims while at war, 163
acid test of foreign policy domestic support, 86
advantages and disadvantages of summit meetings, 220
bargaining power depends on perceived options, 24
circumstance imprisons statesmen, 29
coalitions at the mercy of most determined members, 31
conditions for balance of power, 174
creation of moral consensus to preserve status quo, 216
criteria for effective strategy, 217
dangers of coalitions between status quo and acquisitive powers, 32
dedication to peace empowers the ruthless, 161
defeat and occupation, 47
deterrence dependent on combination of factors, 51
dilemmas of negotiation by democracies, 144
eagerness a liability in negotiations, 71
foreign policy needs domestic support to succeed, 87

About the Author

Chas. W. Freeman, Jr., has led a distinguished diplomatic career, including service overseas in India, Taiwan, the China mainland, Thailand, and Saudi Arabia. He was assistant secretary of defense for international security affairs from 1993 to 1994 and U.S. ambassador to the Kingdom of Saudi Arabia from 1989 to 1992 (during the Gulf War). Before serving in Riyadh, he had been the principal deputy assistant secretary of state for African affairs; deputy chief of mission at the U.S. embassies at Beijing and Bangkok; director of three offices in the Department of State and one in the United States Information Agency; and deputy United States coordinator for refugee affairs. He was the principal American interpreter during President Richard Nixon's historic visit to the People's Republic of China in February 1972.

Freeman attended the Universidad Nacional Autónoma de México, Yale University, and the Harvard Law School. He was a Jennings Randolph fellow at the United States Institute of Peace from 1994 to 1995, following his decision to retire from the United States Foreign Service. He was elected to the American Academy of Diplomacy in 1995.

Freeman is currently chairman of Projects International, Inc., a Washington-based business development firm specializing in the arrangement of joint ventures for its American and foreign clientele.

United States Institute of Peace

The United States Institute of Peace is an independent, nonpartisan, national institution established and funded by Congress. Its goals are to help prevent and resolve violent conflicts, promote post-conflict stability and development, and increase peacebuilding capacity, tools, and intellectual capital worldwide. The Institute does this by empowering others with knowledge, skills, and resources, as well as by directly engaging in peacebuilding efforts around the globe.

Board of Directors